BURNED

ALSO BY EDWARD HUMES

Buried Secrets
Murderer with a Badge
Mean Justice
Baby ER
School of Dreams
Over Here
No Matter How Loud I Shout
Mississippi Mud
Monkey Girl
Eco Barons
Force of Nature
A Man and His Mountain
Garbology
Door to Door

BURNED

A STORY OF MURDER AND THE CRIME THAT WASN'T

EDWARD HUMES

DUTTON

DUTTON

An imprint of Penguin Random House LLC
penguinrandomhouse.com

Floor plan on page ix by Daniel Lagin.

LIBRARY OF CONGRESS CATALOGING-IN-PUBLICATION DATA
has been applied for.

ISBN 978-1-524-74213-3

Printed in the United States of America
1 3 5 7 9 10 8 6 4 2

Book design by Nancy Resnick

"I am afraid," said I, "that the facts are so obvious that you will find little credit to be gained out of this case."

"There is nothing more deceptive than an obvious fact," he answered, laughing.

—Dr. John Watson and Sherlock Holmes,
The Adventures of Sherlock Holmes,
Arthur Conan Doyle, 1892

Contents

PART ONE: A LONG FUSE LIT

1. April 9, 1989 — 3
2. 1,100 Degrees — 7
3. Firefighting — 13
4. Statements — 27
5. Victims — 35
6. Arson Expert — 43
7. Three Days in October 1991 — 51

PART TWO: STIRRING THE ASHES

8. The Pit — 65
9. Growing Up Jo Ann — 77
10. They Told Me I Couldn't — 87
11. It's All Gonna Come Out in the End — 107
12. Everything Which Is Not Law — 125
13. "If I Am Wrong, Then Everything I Have Ever Been Taught . . . Would All Be Wrong." — 153

PART THREE: FIRE ON TRIAL

14. Sherlock Was Wrong 183

15. The Monster Speaks 205

16. The Bias Man 213

17. Unhinged 229

18. What Revolution? 251

Epilogue: The Curse of Uncertainty 265

Sources 275

Acknowledgments 295

Index 297

PARKS HOME

6928 ½ Sherman Way, Bell, California

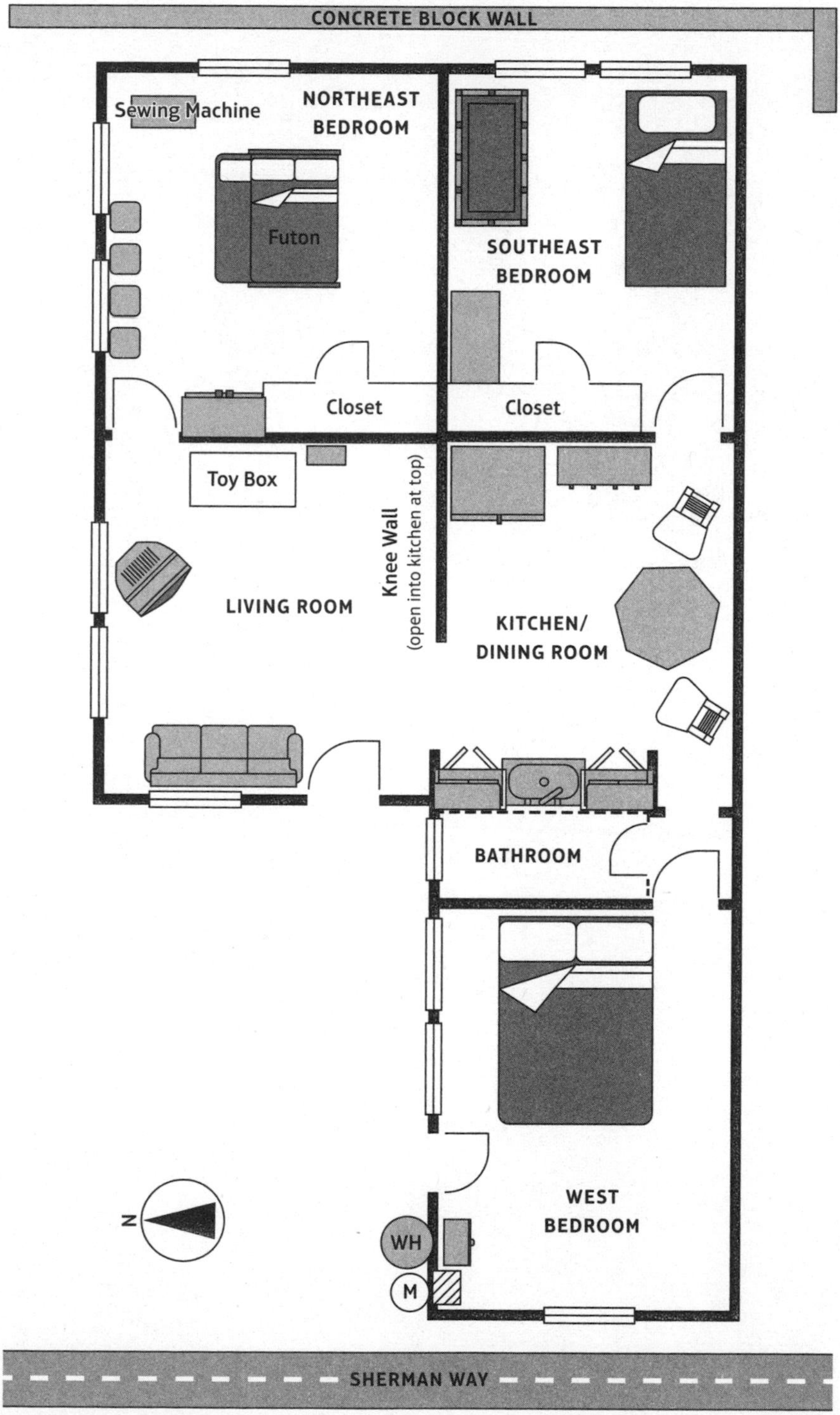

PART ONE

A LONG FUSE LIT

1

April 9, 1989

The banging and screaming began shortly after midnight, fists rattling the front door, a woman's voice crying and moaning for help.

Shirley and Bob Robison, ready for bed and relieved that the heat wave plaguing Los Angeles that week had abated at last, stumbled through the dark house and threw open the door.

On the welcome mat stood their young neighbor—disheveled in her nightgown and housecoat, shaking and wailing. "My babies," Jo Ann Parks gasped. "Help them, please, please. They're still in there!"

The Robisons needed no explanation for what "there" meant. A garish orange light had painted their white stucco house the color of glowing coals. The weedy driveway normally obscured by darkness at this hour was lit up, and the Robisons could feel the furnace-hot air pumping up its length like a chimney stack. At the back end of the driveway, the converted garage apartment blazed.

The twenty-three-year-old Parks, her husband, and their three small children had moved into this dingy rental in the cramped Los Angeles suburb of Bell less than a week before, clothes and knickknacks and photo albums still piled in half-unpacked boxes, the place a mess. Now the apartment crackled and hissed, flames flaring as bright as camera flashes in the darkness, revealing gouts of black smoke pouring up into a leaden, starless sky.

"My children!" Parks shrieked. "They're in back!"

Bob hesitated. He was too old for this, he thought. At fifty-seven, his health wasn't the greatest. He was bone tired, his job wearing him down day by day. But . . . three little kids. Three little kids trapped in a burning house. *Somebody* had to do something. Staring at the doorway Parks had left open, he could see inside to the front room of the apartment, the master bedroom, flames and smoke roiling inside. He told his wife to call 911. Then Bob Robison took a deep breath, held it, and screwed up his eyes as if he were jumping off the high dive platform. He walked to the door and disappeared inside.

Shirley and Parks gawked at the doorway, then ran back into the front house to phone for help. Then they raced back to the driveway, waiting for the fire engines, waiting for Bob, waiting for the children to emerge. Parks started moving toward the doorway into the burning house, too, but Shirley grabbed her from behind, shouting, "No, Jo Ann, don't!" She wrapped her arm around Parks's shoulders and would not let go, certain a distraught woman could not survive long in that house in her flimsy summer nightclothes. "You can't go in there."

Parks seemed to be bordering on hysteria to Shirley, but the younger woman heeded the command and didn't fight to free herself. After that, she made no more moves toward entering the house.

"Oh, God," Parks moaned a few seconds later. She spoke so softly, Shirley had trouble hearing what she said next. But it sounded something like "I hope Ronnie wasn't playing with matches again."

"What was that?" Shirley asked. Ronnie Jr. was the Parkses' oldest child and only boy, four years old, clever, occasionally mischievous. Was Jo Ann really revealing that the fire could be Ronnie's fault? Or was she just gibbering her fears and guesses in a moment of hysteria? Shirley couldn't tell. Nearly three decades would go by, her husband long passed, and still she would wonder just what Jo Ann Parks had said in that moment, and what, if anything, it meant.

Shirley pulled her eyes away from the fire, which seemed to be growing more intense with each passing second. She asked, "Jo Ann? What did you say Ronnie did?"

Parks shook her head, though whether that gesture came in negation, regret at her words, or simply to clear her head, Shirley once again could not tell. Jo Ann had seemed a bit odd to Shirley, no doubt about that. But this did not seem like the time to press the point, not with the apartment aflame and three little children in jeopardy. So Shirley just hugged the younger woman again around the shoulders, stayed close, and murmured words of comfort.

"My babies," Parks said. "Will he find them? Will they be okay?" She kept repeating variations of this. It sounded almost like a chant.

Shirley didn't know what to say. The apartment, with its 528 square feet of living space, had become an inferno. The heat was growing painful just standing in the driveway. She could not see her husband through the open door and feared he might not be able to save himself, much less three kids. And where were the police? Where were the fire trucks? Had it been only seconds since she called 911? It seemed like many minutes to her. It seemed like forever.

"Yes," Shirley finally said. "Yes. Help is on the way. They're going to be all right." But she didn't really believe it, not for a second.

2

1,100 Degrees

There are three basic truths about house fires: Most fires begin small. Most spread fast. Most start stupid.

An untended frying pan and a few tablespoons of overheated cooking oil are all it takes to destroy a home in minutes. An ember dropped in the wrong spot by a sleepy smoker can, with a bit of time, be as devastating as a blowtorch. Poorly maintained furnaces can start fires while unsuspecting homeowners sleep. So can overused and overloaded extension cords, of which the Parks family had many. Daily life and the modern home contain pervasive fire hazards, though these potentially lethal objects are so familiar, ubiquitous, and habitual they might as well be invisible. A common match, after all, can be snuffed with a pinch of the fingers with no ill effect, yet this seemingly innocuous everyday item burns at 1,100 to 1,500 degrees Fahrenheit. That's more than enough to set aflame upholstery, newspapers, a bag of chips, or most anything hanging in your closet. The flame of a cheap pocket cigarette lighter is more than three times as hot as a match. And the gas burners of a typical stove run five times hotter, providing virtually unlimited capacity for havoc—which helps explain why nearly half of all accidental house fires start in the kitchen. This was as true in 1989 as it is today: The deadliest fire in New York City in a quarter century, killing twelve in 2017, started in a first-floor apartment with a boy Ronnie Jr.'s age playing with the knobs on a stove.

And then there are the minority of fires, about one in twelve, that are not accidental. The combination of flame and mischievous child—or ill-intentioned adult—has reduced many buildings to smoldering scenes of loss and grief. An entire industry, body of law, and branch of forensic science have evolved over generations to try to ferret out that one in twelve.

But the ease with which fires start belies the difficulties in figuring out their causes from the debris and ashes left behind. Distinguishing accidental fires from intentional blazes remains one of the toughest challenges of forensic investigation, as arson is the one criminal act that consumes rather than creates vital trace evidence. The DNA, fingerprints, footprints, hair, and fiber that investigators use to try to solve other sorts of crimes all can vanish in the flames, and what isn't destroyed by the fire is often wiped away by the firefighting. At the same time, an accidental fire is the one blameless catastrophe that can disguise itself as a crime. Fires that burn hot enough and long enough can create false signs and suspicious artifacts that mimic arson, particularly in modern homes filled with petroleum-based plastic products that can burn similarly to petroleum-based fuels. This dual nature of fire poses one of the great, if rarely acknowledged, paradoxes of the criminal justice system.

Just after midnight on April 9, 1989, Jo Ann Parks would find herself caught in this paradox—one that, three decades later, science and the law are still struggling to resolve.

This struggle is waged daily: On average, a building burns in the United States once every sixty-three seconds. Every two and a half hours, someone dies in those flames. These fires strike with astonishing speed, with a typical house fire evolving from minuscule to massive in mere minutes.

The physics of fire follows a relentless ticktock of destruction. It can take only thirty seconds for an errant spark or flame to spread from a small starting place in the living room, kitchen, or bedroom. In that short half minute, a fire can take root in nearby napkins or newspapers, pillows or dishtowels, slipcovers or blankets, or, as investigators would later conclude after studying the Parks apartment, curtains and drapes.

Once this spread occurs, there may be only seconds remaining in which a quick-witted person can easily extinguish a fire with simple materials at hand: by smothering the flames with a blanket, towel, or water, or, ideally, a household fire extinguisher. If there's no one in the room during those first moments of flame, if everyone's asleep—as Jo Ann Parks would later recall she and her children were—then the threshold between smoky nuisance and deadly threat can be crossed quickly. After that, the flames can easily take charge.

By the end of the first minute, if no one intervenes, the flames in a typical house fire can grow higher and hotter, allowing them to spread from the initial foothold to adjacent furniture, window coverings, paneling, moving boxes—whatever is close by and flammable, which is to say, most of the objects we own and live with. To fire, our possessions are nothing more nor less than fuel. If some of them happen to be plastic, vinyl, or other synthetic materials, their burning doesn't just produce heat and more flame. They can release compounds of cyanide and other toxins into the air. Then there are the suffocating plumes of carbon monoxide that black, sooty fires pour into the atmosphere, the same deadly stuff emitted by car exhaust pipes.

These gases and particles combine to form a cloud of hot, acrid smoke that collects beneath the ceiling, a wispy, barely visible layer at first that soon darkens and thickens. Once this searingly hot gaseous mixture grows sufficiently concentrated, as little as two inhalations can render a person unconscious. Long before that, the depletion of oxygen and addition of toxins causes mental confusion and disorientation in the room. Occupants of a burning house at this stage can literally forget what to do or where to go. This is not a matter of individual susceptibility or strength. This is chemistry and biology. It's one reason why self-contained breathing apparatus are as essential for firefighters as they are for scuba divers.

By the two-minute mark the air in the room where the fire originated—a house fire's ground zero—can reach the temperature of boiling water. The lighter-than-air smoke cloud, blocked from rising any higher than the ceiling, grows downward instead, its bottom eventually dipping below the tops of doorways and hallway entrances. Then this toxic cloud can flow into adjoining rooms on a current of very hot gas—hot enough to burn respiratory tracts if inhaled.

After three minutes, the flames typically begin to spread by direct contact into adjacent areas of the house, a monster extending tentacles of flame, drawn not just by fuel but also by open doors or windows that offer ready sources of oxygen, the essential partner to sustain any fire. A fire initially governed by the availability of fuel is now governed by the availability of oxygen, burning most fiercely not at the actual point of origin, but where there are openings—ventilation, as the firefighters call it—to the outside. The exchange of cold air rushing in and hot gases venting out can cause a swirl of air, smoke, and heat currents—leaving behind a confusion of burn patterns on walls and floors for investigators to puzzle out, or be puzzled by. The atmosphere surrounding the fire origin might still be 100 degrees near the floor but can reach 400 degrees at eye level by this time, the descending gas hot enough to kill. Once it tops 600 degrees, clothing can melt to your skin and the fire can move outward into the house not only by direct contact with spreading flame, but also by the smoke and gases now radiating enough heat to ignite nearby objects on their own.

Between the three-and-a-half- and four-minute marks, temperatures can reach up to 1,100 degrees. At that point, a phenomenon known as flashover can occur, in which every flammable surface in the room not already burning will ignite in rapid succession—even gases and partially burned particles of ash in the air. Flashover can kill instantly, and poses a threat even to firefighters wearing protective suits and breathing apparatus. Oxygen in the space is rapidly consumed during flashover. If there are intact windows, they often shatter, which allows more oxygen to rush in, further feeding the flames. Or this can unfold in reverse order: Windows can fail from growing heat, allowing an influx of oxygen that pushes a burning room into flashover.

Once flashover occurs, ground zero has morphed from a fire in a room into a room on fire. Just about everything that can burn is burning, although some materials will burn faster than others, another way in which investigators can be fooled about the nature of house fires. After flashover, a room is said by firefighters to be "fully involved," which sounds like jargon but is, in fact, a literal description.

Flashover in one room can propel superheated smoke, gas, burning debris, and jets of flame into other rooms, out windows, up staircases, or through the ceiling and into the spaces above. Between the fourth and fifth minutes, the spreading flames and hot gases can begin building toward flashover in other areas of the house. The smaller the home or apartment, the faster a fire can reach this point. Within five to six minutes of a fire's origin, every room in a house can be fully involved, with no place to hide, no safe air to breathe, no way to see a path to safety, and many ways to take a fatal wrong turn.

Long before this point, people sleeping in such a house can be overcome by carbon monoxide fumes, lapsing into coma and death, never knowing what killed them. More fire victims die of asphyxiation than burns—a very small mercy, perhaps, but also a cautionary lesson. This is why household smoke alarms and carbon monoxide detectors are so vital, and why homeowners and landlords today—as well as in the 1980s in California—are required to install such lifesaving devices in apartments and homes for rent and sale.

The owners of 6928 ½ Sherman Way had been accused over the years of being slumlords. Firefighters could find no evidence in the Parks apartment, with its dry, old wooden walls, flammable ceiling tiles, and plastic-lined drapes, that smoke alarms were ever installed.

3

Firefighting

The city of Bell began life as a pastoral slice of the California Dream, rising from a prosperous Spanish land grant known as Rancho San Antonio, a lush and green oasis populated mostly by fat grazing cattle. In the late 1870s, two rutted roads served all the rancho's needs, one way leading south to the wild coast and a fledgling port that is now America's busiest, the other ambling northward to what was then a mean and insignificant little town called Los Angeles.

Once enough settlers were lured by its charming and fertile grasslands, the rancho evolved into a town in its own right. They rechristened the rancho "Bell," named for the richest among them, James Bell, who donated land for the town's first church and first school. Explosive growth arrived in the prewar era, putting Bell on the map as a desirable suburb instead of a scattering of homes in the countryside. The community's economy boomed even as it denuded itself of the pastures and groves that were once its residents' pride and joy. Then came the era of relentless and unchecked building in the empty spaces between Southern California's towns—the creation of modern Los Angeles's infamous sprawl. This "in-fill" reached the borders of Bell in the sixties, then enveloped the town like a concrete tide, until only the illusion of a separate place existed in the form of marks on a map. Bell became one of a slew of decaying municipal islands embedded in the asphalt archipelago that is Greater Los Angeles.

By 1989, the city of Bell had become a griddle-flat two-and-a-half square miles of potholed, oven-baked concrete, chronically clogged freeway interchanges, half-vacant strip malls, and dilapidated rental homes. It was well on its way to becoming what it is today: one of the poorest communities in the Los Angeles Basin, its treasury looted by the corrupt denizens of city hall, who enriched themselves with tax dollars even as one out of every six residents slipped below the poverty line. This was the Bell that greeted the Parks family in April 1989—the Bell where a converted garage apartment, poorly maintained on its weedy back lot, with three tiny bedrooms, a living room, kitchen, and bathroom somehow crammed into 528 square feet, would soon burn to the ground.

As Bob Robison rushed into the burning building, another neighbor raced to help, climbing over the wall in back, then running along the flaming north side of the apartment, garden hose in hand. This first responder was neither police officer nor firefighter. He was a determined teenager from the neighborhood—in a tuxedo.

They called him Tuxedo Man after this night. Nineteen-year-old David Haney had just returned from a formal, still wearing his classic black tux, when he spotted the garish aura of the fire from a friend's house several blocks away. Fearing an elderly friend of the family might be the victim of the fire—the friend, it turned out, lived next door to the Parks apartment—Haney had cut through multiple neighbors' backyards, hopping wall after wall. As he approached the Parkses' place, Haney snatched a hose from next door, dragged it over, and began pouring water through the living room windows, which had already shattered by the time he arrived. He noticed that smoke and flames were coming through the north-facing windows of a back bedroom, too: little Ronnie's room. Haney, a lifelong resident of Sherman Way who lived five houses up the street, knew the Parks apartment well; the previous tenants had been his friends. As he scaled the block wall and dropped into the Parkses' tiny backyard, he saw no sign of flames in the other back bedroom that the two Parks girls shared. Haney would later recall arriving at the burning apartment just as the 911 operator was finishing with Shirley Robison's call.

Haney found the heat so intense he couldn't stand closer than ten feet from the house. The puny garden hose spray seemed to do nothing. The house, he'd later recall, was already an inferno by the time he got there. He used the word *engulfed.*

From inside the house, Haney heard what sounded like screams—the faint sound of children crying out for help. Despite the waves of heat radiating from the house, those small voices made him shiver. For weeks after that night, just thinking about it could make him weep, so determined had he been to save those kids.

Haney forced himself to stand closer to the house, trying to get more water in through the windows. But there was no way he could knock down the flames with a garden hose's feeble flow, much less do what he longed to do: wet things down enough to allow him to climb inside a shattered window. Then he could track down the source of those screams and carry the kids to safety.

It was not to be. Nothing Haney tried had any effect on the mounting ferocity of the flames. His tuxedo began to smolder, suddenly painful on his skin, and he had to douse himself with the hose in order to continue trying to fight the fire. Steam rose from his outfit, the black cloth drying almost immediately. This forced him to spray himself again, then again. Through the smoke and steam enveloping him, he could hear a woman's voice crying and calling out repeatedly from the driveway: "My kids are in there."

When a house burns, the ravaged rooms and furniture do not come with handy time stamps. Reconstructing the sequence of events, the start and progress of a fire, can be difficult, even impossible, for investigators poking through the ruins. Tuxedo Man's recollections could have helped, suggesting, among other things, that the girls' bedroom became engulfed later than other parts of the building, and that at least one and possibly all three children were still alive at the time of the 911 call. Yet, as investigators pondered what happened that night, Haney's information began to undermine the official version. Eventually one of the first people to arrive on the scene would be dropped as a witness.

Despite the hour, a crowd began gathering at the curb, drawn by the overpowering smell of smoke and by what appeared from a distance to be a gigantic torch lighting the darkness. This night also brought the first cool weather after a weeklong April heat wave in which temperatures had topped 100 degrees. Now they had mercifully dipped to the low sixties, though across the street from the burning apartment it felt as if the heat wave had never ended. As neighbors drew close enough and became spectators, the giant "torch" they had seen shining into their windows resolved into the towering old orange tree that rose between the Robisons' house and the garage apartment in back. The massive tree bore thousands of pieces of fruit. Now those oranges were turning black and dropping from branches wreathed in fire.

Bob Robison, meanwhile, had reappeared on the apartment

patio, doubled over with deep, hoarse coughs. Parks and his wife rushed to him, helping him stagger away from the heat. He had barely escaped the flame and smoke by crawling to the door. The fire had spread quickly into the master bedroom after Parks fled, he said, and he couldn't get farther into the house. Just before he got out, he thought he saw the air and smoke begin to spark and flash around him. Parks peppered him with questions about her children, but he only shook his head.

"I didn't see the kids," he gasped between coughs. "I couldn't get very far. Too hot. Too much smoke." Then he stooped, groaned, and picked up his own garden hose.

Moments later, the wail of sirens turned all heads toward the street. The wait for emergency vehicles to arrive had seemed agonizingly long, but in truth the first three police cars arrived within three minutes of the 911 call at 12:25 A.M. The city of Bell's tiny proportions became an asset then. Its quaint redbrick police headquarters and fire station were just a few blocks from the burning apartment.

Parks ran to the curb to wave in the police cruisers, crying out to the officers what their dispatcher had already told them: Her three children were still trapped in the back rooms. They ran up the driveway to look for a way into the house to attempt a rescue.

One officer commandeered the garden hose Robison had just picked up and told him to go to safety. Another did the same with Tuxedo Man. Parks and Shirley Robison, who again had her arm around the younger woman, were ordered to the sidewalk across the street. After that, nearly every time she saw someone in a uniform pass close or rush by, Parks would call out and ask if her children would be okay. If they heard her and took the time to respond, the answer was usually on the order of, "I don't know," though sometimes, "Yes." One officer, Pete Cacheiro, later testified that he told Parks in no uncertain terms, "Everything will be okay. Your kids are okay."

He told her that multiple times. Not just that they would be okay. But that the children *were* okay, and that she shouldn't worry.

Everyone, it seemed, wanted to calm her rather than crush a mother's hopes, though they all knew, with each passing minute, that the likelihood of a tragic outcome was rapidly approaching certainty.

Shirley Robison would later say Parks wept silently most of this time. She kept an arm around Parks constantly, frequently hugging and consoling her. She and her husband hardly knew her, but they perceived what seemed to them a grieving, worried parent, and they wanted to comfort and help.

Others who saw Parks in passing or from a greater distance that night, however, would recall thinking she looked strangely unemotional, perhaps dazed or in shock or, less charitably, as if she were putting on a pretense of grief. Tuxedo Man was among these latter, recalling he felt far more hysterical than the mother at the curb appeared to be. "It didn't seem right," he'd say, though he also admitted never getting closer to her than fifty feet. None of these accusatory observations surfaced at first—not until the police had gone public with allegations that they believed the fire had been intentional. Yet the authorities gave more credence to these views than to Shirley Robison, who had been with Parks that whole dreadful night.

Several of the newly arrived officers tried to bull their way through the front of the house to reach the children, just as Robison had tried earlier. They did this by entering the door to the master bedroom, which was the closest to the street, due to the fact that it had been added on to the front of the former garage during the apartment conversion decades before. This unusual floor plan led to confusion later, as many assumed this frontmost door opened into the living room.

One officer who entered the house in that first rescue attempt would later describe how he felt driven forward by the sound of the children's screams. But within moments of entering the apartment the officers found themselves on their knees, blinded and overcome by heat and smoke. They crawled back toward the open door, barely reaching the outside. They could no longer hear the screams.

Meanwhile, Reserve Officer Timothy McGee, whose volunteer work put him on patrol once a week and paid him a symbolic one dollar a year, took in the sight of what he described as an apartment completely engulfed in flames, with smoke streaming out of virtually every crack and joint, flames burning through walls and windows and roof. He paused a moment to think how best to reach those trapped children. Why run *through* a burning house to get to the kids, he thought, when there might be a way to run *around* the building to reach the outer walls of their rooms? There would be windows in back, he reasoned, maybe even a back door.

McGee dashed down the narrow space between the Parks apartment and the next house to the south. But before he got halfway to the rear of the house, dense smoke and heat pouring off the apartment enveloped him, leaving him unable to see or breathe. He had to turn around, barely making it back up the driveway on his hands and knees, patches of his uniform smoldering as he choked and gagged upon finally reaching fresher air.

Around the same time Officer McGee sought to quell his coughs and catch his breath before making a second attempt to crawl to the back, another Bell patrol officer would later report having the same idea of trying to enter through the rear. But Officer Jeff Bruce recalls running along the north side of the apartment, where there was more open space along the property line, offering a buffer from the intense heat and smoke streaming from the building. He made it on the first try, finding a tiny backyard illuminated by the wavering light of flames and some spillover light from a back porch fixture next door. Squinting through the smoky haze, Bruce saw that the apartment's rear wall lacked a back door but had three windows large enough to climb through. He recalls that all were intact. He peered into one with no screen on it. Inside, Bruce could see nothing but thick black smoke and, perhaps, the flicker of flames, though he was not positive about that. Much later this would become a crucial and disputed detail, as would everything Bruce had to say, although he would be one of the few first responders to write a detailed report about the fire within a day, rather than relying on years-old memories alone.

Bruce tried to open the window. Hot to the touch, it wouldn't budge. Was it locked? Painted shut? According to Ron and Jo Ann Parks, they recalled the room with stuck windows belonged to Ronnie Jr. Bruce, however, would later report that he was peering into the room shared by one-year-old Jessica Parks and her sister, RoAnn, one month shy of her third birthday.

To avoid wasting precious seconds trying to wrestle the window open, Bruce raised his heavy-duty department-issue flashlight and swung it like a hammer hard into the large windowpane. He expected the brittle music of breaking glass and the feel of his flashlight punching through into the room. Instead, he felt his blow rebound with a dull thud. Some kind of plastic! His blow had caused no damage. He cursed the cheap windows and pounded furiously until the plastic finally cracked and gave way. He knocked away some of the soot-coated shards with his flashlight handle, then started to hoist himself into the room. Inside, billowing smoke obscured everything. For a heartbeat, he saw no children. No furniture. Just blackness. And then, after the briefest of pauses, light—the light of a rapidly expanding fire blooming inside.

Air rushed in from outside and, very quickly, the room exploded in flame. Before he could drop into the room, which likely would have left him badly burned or killed him outright, Bruce realized breaking the window had made matters worse. Much worse. The room had plenty of fuel to burn, but until he broke the window, too little ventilation had kept the fire starved even as the room filled with very hot air and smoke from other areas of the apartment.

As Bruce half leapt, half fell back from the windowsill, a gout of smoke and fire shot through the window. Both Bruce and a next-door neighbor, Lloyd Richard Powell, who had been watching the police officer's rescue attempt from his own backyard, were overcome by the explosive plume of smoke and heat pouring through the window. The neighbor was already frail with heart disease—Powell was the friend who Tuxedo Man had been worried about. Now he retreated into his house to lie down and calm his coughing fit.

When he filed his police report the next day, Bruce seemed to overstate his heroics, claiming he entered and searched the bedroom for kids to scoop up and rescue, only to be driven back outside empty-handed by flames that nearly consumed him. This version of events, which Bruce later recanted, would have a major impact on the investigation and trial to come. It would be used to cast doubt on everything he had to say, including his recollection of little or no visible flames inside the girls' bedroom before he broke the window. The fact that a neighbor corroborated most of

Bruce's story would be ignored. None of his observations would be used by police fire investigators in constructing their official story of how the fire progressed from room to room—a theory that assumed the girls' bedroom had been aflame long before the 911 call was placed. Prosecutors would insist for decades that Bruce was discredited completely as a witness and should not be believed.

After breaking the window, Bruce made his way back to the front of the apartment for fresh air and to see if the other officers had better luck in their rescue efforts. With the burning house serving as the primary illumination and no one yet in command, none of the first responders who flocked to the fire scene knew what anyone out of their line of sight was doing. Individual officers tried whatever came to mind, knowing that the fire trucks were mere minutes away but that the children inside the apartment might not have those minutes to spare.

Reserve Officer McGee had recovered sufficiently by then to make another race along the south side of the house to the backyard. This time he made it, unaware of Bruce's aborted attempt just as Bruce had been unaware of McGee's. Once at the rear of the apartment, McGee began struggling to pry loose a stubborn window screen on one of the other windows, cutting and burning his hands, but never managing to gain access. McGee recalled two years after the fire—the first time investigators asked him to describe what he saw and did that night—that all the windows in back of the house were still intact, contrary to Bruce's report and the neighbor's account. Because very few witnesses and first responders wrote reports or were interviewed about the fire until years had passed, there are many inconsistencies and differing versions of what happened that night.

As McGee struggled unsuccessfully with a window screen, the

fire trucks arrived in front. A young firefighter, one who had never experienced a fatal fire before and who was determined to keep it that way, charged into the house first. Even from the street, Dirk Wegner had seen that the apartment appeared to be what he called "ripping"—a fully involved structure, with deadly temperatures as high as 1,200 degrees ripping through the place. At that stage, flashover could suddenly envelop firefighters in flames so intense that they could be burned to death even inside their fire-resistant garb, face masks, and breathing apparatus.

Foremost in Wegner's mind, however, was what he heard while pounding up the driveway: a mother pleading for help for her trapped children. He concluded their only hope lay in his racing directly to the back rooms as quickly as possible, no matter the danger. Taking the "nozzleman" position—the firefighter who directs the hose spray—he used his high-pressure line to blitz the flames as he advanced into the living room, cutting a path toward the rear. Several times the fire almost closed back around him as he dashed through. Years later, testifying without benefit of notes or other memory refreshers, Wegner recalled this harrowing journey took several minutes or possibly as little as forty-five seconds, his passage eerily lit by walls of flame yet obscured by toxic smoke.

With the advantage of hindsight, fire experts would later describe Wegner's action as a brave but high-risk tactic. An alternative approach would have been to do what Bruce and McGee had tried: run to the backyard. Then fire hoses could have been sprayed directly through the windows and safely into the rear rooms from the outside—as would eventually be done by other firefighters. The problem with first launching a driving frontal attack was that, while knocking down the flames in the front of the house, the high-pressure hose stream could push hot gases, smoke, and flames toward the rear of a building, literally chasing hot gases and burning material into the very part of a building rescuers hoped to reach and evacuate. It's an unavoidable effect of firefighting and, given the chaos and intensity of the fire, most firefighters would likely do the same as Wegner and attack the flames head-on.

It was around this time that Reserve Officer McGee, still struggling with a window in back, heard Bruce shouting from the front, "Where's McGee?" Then, louder and closer, he heard Bruce calling directly to him, "McGee, get out of there, it's gonna blow!"

Reluctant to give up on his rescue attempts, McGee didn't really believe there was imminent, explosive danger. He knew nothing of fire dynamics and firefighting techniques; he didn't know yet that the firefighters had arrived and that they were converging on the rear bedrooms from inside. But he heard what sounded like fear or panic in Bruce's voice. So he grudgingly heeded the warning, taking cover by jumping over the same cinder-block wall on the property line that Tuxedo Man had scaled ten minutes before. A moment later the apartment's remaining rear windows blew out in a rush of scorching flames and smoke.

Inside the apartment, Wegner finished his dash to the back and found himself in a small bedroom in the southeast corner. He could see nothing in the burning, smoke-filled space, so after he knocked down the flames in the bedroom he recalled that he directed his hose spray through the blown-out windows, chasing the smoke and steam outside. The atmosphere cleared enough for the firefighter to see where he was: the girls' bedroom. He saw walls, floor, and ceiling blistered by fire, smoldering debris on the floor nearly tripping him as he turned on the spot to survey the scene.

The room had been devastated, the walls blackened and charred in places all the way through. He saw a badly burned bed under one window, and beneath a second window, he saw what looked like a crib or playpen that had been consumed entirely but for its sooty metal frame. Both beds were covered with charred bedclothes, along with other burning debris and blackened ceiling tiles that had fallen from above.

On each bed there appeared to be a severely burned doll, also partially covered with debris. Except Wegner knew those blackened figures were not dolls at all. RoAnn, the older girl, lay facedown, sprawled diagonally across the foot of the bed, one leg dangling over the edge as if she fell or dove there. Jessie lay faceup amid rubble that had fallen from the burning ceiling. Wegner's stomach roiled. There would be no rescuing anyone from this hellish room. By the extent of the damage to the walls, to the furniture, and to those little girls, it seemed they had died before he even entered the building. His effort had neither helped nor hurt. It simply came too late.

Wegner wanted to search the other back bedroom next, but there was no direct access from the girls' room. He would have to circle back through the kitchen and into the living room where the door to Ronnie's room opened. But before he could make that move his air-supply alarm went off, signaling only five minutes of breathing left. Standing orders required Wegner to leave immediately for a fresh tank. Other firefighters would search for the boy as they extinguished the fire, Wegner knew. So he worked his way back outside to switch tanks and to report his grim discovery.

4

Statements

A voice in the darkness finally tore Jo Ann Parks's gaze from the burning apartment and its surrounding chaos. A uniformed police officer had materialized at her side, leaving her struggling to make sense of his words: "I've been ordered to drive you to the department to take your statement."

After a few moments, she nodded woodenly, murmuring assent. Parks had been standing where she had been told to stand, at the curb across the street. Word had not yet spread about the discovery of her daughters' bodies. Not even Frank Espejo, the Bell police officer now standing before her, had been told.

"What about my children?" she asked once again as he ushered her to his police cruiser. "Are they going to be okay?"

Espejo told the truth: He did not know. He had taken the original 911 call at the police station, then had broadcast the "all units" emergency over the radio, called the fire department, and raced over to the apartment to see if he could help. Now he would complete the circle by questioning Parks about what happened. He would get her statement on the record, and then wait with her in the quiet of the station for word about her children.

Shirley Robison, who had stayed by Parks's side since the first bang and scream at the front door, rode in the back of the police car with the younger woman, clinging to her new neighbor's side out of an instinctual kindness she never really fathomed. She even accompanied her into the station house, where she bore witness to everything that followed. Parks continued seeking assurances about her children's fate and asked one of the officers if her husband, Ron, could be called to the station from the graveyard shift at the Darigold ice cream packing plant in Los Angeles. Then she gave the police her first—and most concise—account of what happened.

Any first statement to the police—whether it is by a witness, a suspect, a victim, or a police officer—automatically becomes part of the gospel of an investigation. For better or worse, no matter the circumstances or stress under which a first statement is made, it will become the standard against which all future recollections will be compared. Any deviation in the future can be ignored or written off as normal vagary of memory. Or divergences from the gospel can be used to savage even the most saintly person's credibility. Changing the story can be viewed as an act of increased honesty, bravery, virtue, or understanding, or as a lie that proves dishonesty, lack of credibility, and guilt. Jo Ann Parks had just entered perilous, life-changing territory, where each word, each nuance, each fact uttered, withheld, or forgotten could determine her fate. If she had done something wrong, she already would know she was in danger before saying a word. If she was innocent of any wrongdoing, she had walked into a trap unwarned and unaware of the stakes.

According to Espejo's report on this conversation, Parks said she put her three children to bed quite early in the evening. Espejo wrote down six P.M. as their bedtime—an hour and a half before dark that time of year in LA. As soon as Parks was sure the kids were sound asleep, Espejo reported, she went to her bedroom and shut the door, falling asleep early as well.

The next thing she knew, the sound of her children screaming jolted her awake. Parks told Espejo she opened her bedroom door to go to them, but a blast of heat and smoke met her immediately, driving her back. Unable to move farther into the house toward her children, unable even to see anything through the smoke and flames, she had run in a panic outside to the patio and onward to the Robisons' house to get help. Investigators would later deduce that she left both the interior and exterior doors from her bedroom open when she fled, providing fresh ventilation for the fire, which quickly advanced into the master bedroom. This provided one possible explanation for why Bob Robison encountered more severe heat, smoke, and flame conditions entering the house than Parks had faced leaving a minute or two earlier.

In that first statement to police Parks also volunteered that one of the Parkses' previous homes had burned down a year earlier in the nearby suburb of Lynwood. The fire had been caused by an air conditioner with faulty wiring, she told Espejo. No one had been home at the time and so there were no injuries in that fire, but the family had lost most of their clothes and possessions. They had no insurance. They had moved to another place after that, but then Ron was laid off, forcing them to lodge at a homeless shelter. They had only just gotten back on their feet because the ice cream plant had rehired Ron, allowing them to move into the Sherman Way apartment a week earlier.

Parks said nothing about Ronnie playing with matches, and Espejo's report provides no indication he even questioned her about any possible cause of the fire. Yet the same report quotes the Robisons' recollection that Parks arrived on their doorstep voicing fears that her son might have started the fire.

This first statement was not tape-recorded, and Espejo's questioning was nothing like an interrogation. His written report was a bare-bones distillation of their conversation, not a stenographic word-for-word account. There was a reason for this casual approach, which also helps explain why few of the other officers and firefighters took notes or wrote reports about their observations and actions during the fire: No one imagined a crime had been committed. The fire was treated as a tragedy, an accident. They were there to rescue, not investigate, and they acted accordingly. Parks and her attorneys would later say she was in a state of shock at the time and could not clearly recall events. Yet this truncated version of events inevitably became her credibility baseline, against which all future statements by the only survivor of the Sherman Way fire would be compared.

All the officers and civilians who entered or stayed near the burning apartment came away smelling strongly of smoke, with some showing soot or burns on their clothing and skin. Five police officers, including Jeff Bruce, had to get hospital treatment for smoke inhalation. Several had to throw away their burned and stinking uniforms that were beyond cleaning or repair. But Parks showed no such signs of exposure to fire or smoke. Much later this, too, would be deemed highly suspicious. But at the time of the fire, no one expressed suspicion or doubt because, as Parks had told Espejo in that first account, she fled the flames almost immediately, without trying to fight her way through the burning house to the back bedrooms where the children slept. A mother had escaped a fire, tried to get help for her kids, but help arrived too late. Nothing about her behavior, appearance, or the fire scene itself led them to suspect otherwise at that time. Not even the voluntary revelation of a prior fire (which records quickly revealed had been ruled accidental) turned their compassion to suspicion. At first.

Back at the apartment, the firefighters had wrestled the inferno down to scattered smoldering hot spots by the time Parks completed her statement. But a mystery had emerged, along with a new hope: The oldest Parks child, Ronnie Jr., could not be found in the ruined apartment. Firefighter Wegner had swapped out his oxygen tank and gone back inside, moving room to room with particular attention to the two most common places children hide during fires: under beds and inside closets. Firefighters call this a "primary search," performed more with quickness in mind than thoroughness. In Ronnie's burned-out bedroom he found the boy's futon sleeper had been reduced to a pile of ashes and melted plastic. It was obvious he had not hidden under there. Wegner then looked in the small closet. Whether the door stood open or closed when he got there would become a seminal point of contention in the fire investigation. In his first full account, at a preliminary hearing two years after the fire, he didn't make clear whether it was open or closed when he got there. Later he would insist that it was closed. Either way, he saw nothing of interest inside the closet—only a large pile of burned debris and clothing, which seemed to have fallen down from hangers at some time during the fire or the firefighting.

Had one child somehow survived? Had the four-year-old escaped the flames and ended up wandering the streets? Was he hurt? Was he hiding? Did he flee because he knew he'd be in trouble for playing with matches? A search party quickly formed to walk the area, officers and neighbors moving up and down the streets, calling for Ronnie, looking for a small form walking or hiding in the shadows. Young Haney—Tuxedo Man—ranged many blocks looking for the boy, still desperate to answer those voices he heard crying out when he first arrived at the scene.

At this point word was sent to police headquarters about the possibility of Ronnie's survival and the neighborhood search under way, as well as Wegner's discovery of the girls' bodies in their beds. No one told Parks any of this. Instead, the small contingent of officers manning the station in the early morning hours asked her if the Parks family had a minister they might call to provide support. She gave the number of the family's Christian Science pastor, who was called in to comfort Parks and to break the news to her and, once he arrived, her husband.

The neighborhood search and its horde of eager volunteers found no trace of the boy after forty-five minutes of looking behind hedges, fences, and parked cars. When the Los Angeles County Fire Department's on-call fire investigator, William Franklin, arrived around one thirty A.M., a more intensive examination of the still-smoldering apartment began. One of the firefighters assisting Franklin, Dirk Wegner, realizing his original search had been quick and cursory, zeroed in on Ronnie's closet for a more careful examination. With the closet door open, he saw some partially burnt debris—clothes, papers, toys, a tangle of hangers—had tumbled out and lay at the closet threshold, a ragged mound topped by a snatch of bright red material, an unburned piece of a boy's shirt. Protected by other objects during the blaze, this fragment of cloth provided an incongruously cheery splash of color atop the grays and blacks of ash and char.

This moment, investigators and experts later realized, needed to be perfectly documented on the night of the fire, from the second that this final search began to its conclusion. It was not perfectly documented, however.

Wegner and Franklin would later recall that the closet door had been shut when they entered the room, with debris piled in front of it that had to be moved before the door could be opened. Yet Wegner would also recall that he previously looked inside this closet during the hasty primary search for a child hiding or burned—which means Ronnie's closet had to have been opened and the debris moved away from in front before this more thorough search took place. Both recollections cannot be true.

County fire investigator Franklin had brought his camera and intended to begin photographing the scene in Ronnie's bedroom before the closet search began. His first picture shows the closet open, with debris in front of the threshold and severe burning on the inside surfaces of the closet, suggesting the door could have been open during the fire. Later Franklin would say no, he had inexplicably failed to take a picture of the closed door before the closet search began. No one at the time understood that evidence had been lost forever in this moment—evidence that could have helped determine whether this fire had been accidental or deliberate.

As the county fire expert looked on, snapping what would turn out to be a frustratingly grainy and incomplete series of photographs, Wegner reached into the debris pile inside the closet. After probing around a moment, his hand brushed an object that felt to him like a grapefruit. Then he realized he was touching Ronnie's bowed head. The little boy had been there all along, hunkered down out of sight beneath the ashes and fallen clothes, crouched behind a metal milk crate from the dairy that his dad had brought home for storage.

Ronnie's body showed severe burns and charring, though not as extreme as his sisters', as he had been partially protected by the contents of the closet. Ronnie's brown hair had not been burned away. The firefighter noted that the closet door had a knob on the inside, but that the outer knob was missing. Both sides of the door were badly and apparently equally charred. Whether the door was closed before firefighters arrived seemed of little importance at the time. Later that would change and become the subject of intense debate and accusations, complicated by the poor documentation, ambiguous photography, and contradictory recollections.

The coroner would later determine that the burns of all three children were potentially fatal, but that a primary cause of their deaths also was inhaling poisonous amounts of carbon monoxide. No closet door, open or shut, could have protected Ronnie from that invisible killer.

5

Victims

Back at the police station, a bleary Paul Garman arrived around two A.M. The Christian Scientist had been close to the Parks family for years, providing guidance about everything from California real estate to childcare tips to church strictures about healing with prayer rather than medicine. He had been close to Ronnie Jr. as well, counseling the four-year-old on his behavior from time to time, which included getting out of bed and wandering around the house at night to watch TV while everyone else slept, and at least one instance of his playing with matches. Now Garman went to Parks in the small break room at the Bell Police Department. He saw her sitting in a plastic chair, her short dark hair disheveled, her round face pale beneath the bluish lights buzzing overhead.

He hugged her, sat down with her, then took her hands. "Jo Ann, your babies are in heaven now," he said.

Her eyes teared up. Yet her face remained a little blank. Initially, Garman told her what had been explained to him earlier: The girls were dead, but there was still hope that Ronnie had survived. Then word came in about the body found huddled in the closet just a few minutes later, and Garman had to crush that brief hope as well.

His own eyes wet, he had to repeat everything several times, expressing his sorrow, his condolences, his support. Each time she just shook her head. Garman began to worry that she wasn't processing his words. It was so hard to tell with Jo Ann, he thought. In some ways she was childlike—the soft voice that sounded ten years younger than its owner, the round, unlined face framed by tousled dark hair. Yet Garman also found she had a somewhat flat emotional effect much of the time, making her hard to read. That's just the way she was, something he attributed to the numerous childhood traumas she had confided in him over time. Her husband had the same emotionless demeanor, but more so. Still, Garman wished Ron Parks would get there already to add his support and comfort, thinking his friend should have arrived by then.

Ron, it turned out, had taken a detour, ignoring the police request to come directly to the station house. He had been told only that there had been a fire, that it was under control, and that he should come quickly, with the police offering no information on the welfare of his children. That sort of news had to be delivered in person, they believed, with his wife and pastor at his side. But Ron had never been overly fond of the police. He wanted to see for himself. First he drove to a phone booth in that pre-cellphone era and called Paul Garman to tell him what happened and to ask for his prayers. Then he called the apartment and got a busy signal. Then he drove on toward Sherman Way to determine what had happened to his home and to his family.

When he reached his block, he couldn't get close to the apartment, with ready access obstructed by a welter of emergency vehicles and yellow police tape. But he chatted with gawkers on the sidewalk and, he would later say, eventually heard about how three children had been trapped inside a burning house and died before rescuers could reach them. The rumor going around the neighborhood was that the fire started because the parents had left the children home alone. The spectators didn't know who Ron was, and he said nothing in response to the gossip making the rounds. Instead, he drove to a phone booth at a nearby strip center and called Garman again, only to learn that his Christian Science mentor had already left the house, heading to the Bell Police Department. Only then did Ron head back to his car and drive to meet his wife at the police department.

When Ron Parks Sr. finally strode in and stood before Jo Ann, the first thing he said in his Missouri twang was, "You killed my kids."

Sitting a few feet away, close enough to hear and see everything, Shirley Robison gasped. She stared at the short, slight man with sandy hair, at the face Robison thought might have been pleasant, even pleasing, except that its default state seemed to her to be stripped of emotion and empathy. Even now, when uttering what she heard as breathtaking cruelty, Ron's expression remained flat. She saw no anger, hysteria, pity, or sadness on that face. He just wants to know what happened, she thought, and he wants to lay blame.

Robison took his meaning at the time not as a literal accusation of murder, but as recrimination for Jo Ann's failure to save the kids, for not acting more heroically in trying to reach them. Indeed, in subsequent retellings and testimony years later, Shirley would recall that moment differently and more in line with what she believed Ron meant, asserting that he said, "You let my kids die."

Whatever was said, Jo Ann appeared stricken by her husband's words. Her eyes welled with fresh tears. "No, I didn't," she pleaded. "No, I didn't. I did everything I could."

It was a pitiful moment of shaming, Garman thought, when a husband and a wife who should have been comforting each other did anything but.

In subsequent retellings to police, friends, and family, Parks would describe making a greater effort to save her kids before running for help, starting with small additions that, over time, grew more heroic and then improbable. Her second story to police had her crawling toward the kitchen through fire and smoke, then trying to telephone for help from inside the house before fleeing. Later she told a friend she had run around back and tried to break through a window. Much later this would profoundly affect Parks's own fate, as others would put wildly different interpretations on why she might change her story and exaggerate her actions that night. Was it because she felt ashamed at not appearing braver to people she cared about? Or was she lying to cover her crimes and sound more appealing to cops, prosecutors, and jurors? Was the lying understandable human frailty laid bare, or did it render her untrustworthy about everything?

Although she wouldn't know about it for years, Ron Parks quietly offered the police a very different version of what passed between them in the station house. He claimed that it was his wife who spoke when he first walked in, and that it was she who muttered, "I killed the children. I killed the children."

No one else present supported this version of events. Ron softened his statement a bit by saying he understood his wife's supposed mumbled words not as a literal confession to murder, but as an expression of shame at failing to save the kids. And he professed to have no idea that the police might put a more suspicious and literal interpretation on it.

Ron Parks provided one other perspective to the police that

night, though this one came unintentionally. Officer Espejo overheard him telephoning his manager on the graveyard shift at the ice cream plant. He called to explain that he would be missing work on his next shift. In what Espejo could only describe as a "cold and callous" manner, Ron told his boss flatly, almost offhandedly, "Yeah, the kids are dead. I'll call back later."

Such is the stuff of criminal cases every day and everywhere, assembled not with brilliant detective work and Perry Mason courtroom moments, but one little brick at a time, built of shifting memories, shifting stories, shifting theories, shifting details. Seemingly innocuous, insignificant, or ambiguous moments, disregarded in real time, can be reinterpreted months or years later, weaponized and made consequential by suspicion, then woven into something that seems sinister and damning. Mistakes by investigators can be magnified or buried or ignored, the loss of evidence transformed from handicap to advantage. Lives and justice and public safety depend upon how these building blocks are interpreted and pieced together.

And so it would be with the fire and death that swept through 6928 ½ Sherman Way on April 9, 1989. Each word, each nuance, each contradiction would be filed away, waiting to be reassembled into an official narrative, though no one yet knew if that would be a story of a deadly accident, a slumlord's neglect, or a monstrous and intentional crime.

In the hours and days after the fire, with the official story as yet unwritten, Jo Ann and Ron Parks remained victims, not suspects. They shuffled out of the police station into the predawn darkness, not holding hands, not touching, not looking at each other. Garman arranged a motel room for Jo Ann and Ron, then drove them over and saw them settled in. He left them there appearing stunned and exhausted, a family of five reduced to two, their future stripped bare, unable to comfort each other, barely able to speak to each other.

Back at the gutted apartment, the LA County Fire Department investigators went to work on determining the origin and cause of the fire. Because of the late hour and poor lighting, most of that work was put off until the following afternoon—a leisurely pace for the investigation that reflected no heightened sense of urgency, no suspicions that this was anything more than an accident, though by nature multiple fatalities always draw a greater level of scrutiny than fires with no loss of life. The investigators examined burn patterns, degrees of charring in walls and doors, and looked for the presence of gasoline, lighter fluid, or any other liquid accelerant an arsonist would use. They found none. Then they traced the likely path of the flames to determine where the fire started, which appeared to them to be beneath the living room windows. There they found a large V shape burned into the wall at floor level—the traditional cone-like burn pattern that reflects the shape of a heat and smoke plume as it expands upward, and that indicates a possible point of origin.

In that same area they found a tangle of overtaxed extension cords and appliance plugs connecting an old TV, box fan, and VCR to the same outlet, with the cords winding around and possibly beneath the burned remains of boxes of unpacked clothes and other household items. The county fire investigators found no evidence of a short circuit, but thought that a process known as "resistance heating" could have started the blaze—too much current passing through a single cord, especially with objects piled on top of it, can create enough heat through electrical resistance to cause a fire. It's rare, but it can happen—it had been singled out as a likely cause in the Parkses' first, nonfatal fire a year earlier.

From this same process on Sherman Way, flames could have spread to the new drapes the Parkses had just bought for the living room windows, then to the boxes and piles of clothes and toys yet to be unpacked. It wouldn't have taken long for the living room to become engulfed in flames while mother and children slept unawares, and the absence of smoke alarms would have sealed their fate. That, at least, was the initial theory when the two county fire department investigators reported to the Bell Police Department the evening after the fire with a tentative opinion that the cause could have been accidental and electrical.

The next few days brought an outpouring of support for the Parks family from neighbors, coworkers, places of worship, local charities, firefighters, and strangers who read about the fire in the newspaper or learned of it on the evening TV news. Checks came in the mail, along with offers of places to live, offers of jobs, offers of prayers and sympathy. Soon there were thousands of dollars sent care of Paul Garman's church, and more coming in every day.

The Parkses sat for a television interview in which Jo Ann seemed barely able to hold it together as she spoke haltingly of her children's transformation into "little angels up there."

"It's just realizing that and letting go that's so hard," she said, her features screwed up as if to hold back tears. "I miss 'em."

Ron's expressionless demeanor and words were in sharp contrast as he remarked that his children were now God's responsibility. He looked directly into the camera and said, "I know from my past experience I need to get it out of my thoughts and try to think about it as little as possible."

This coolly expressed notion of putting your three dead children out of mind two days after they perished caught the attention of many observers at the time, though no one seemed to know just what to make of it. Only much later would the other part of his statement draw notice: In the singularly dreadful, life-crushing context of a parent losing his children, just what comparable "past experience" was Ron Parks talking about?

Then the Bell Police Department received a phone call on the morning of April 12, three days after the fire and one day after the TV broadcast of Jo Ann and Ron. And everything changed.

"That fire was no accident," said the woman on the telephone. "Those children were murdered."

6

Arson Expert

Five days later, the big guns arrived.

A pair of investigators from the Los Angeles County Sheriff's Department's elite Arson/Explosives Detail drove to Bell to walk the Parks apartment and to take over the origin and cause investigation.

Detective Ronald R. Ablott, a senior arson investigator and former homicide detective with the imposing physique of an NFL lineman, took the lead. He had been briefed on the allegations made by the caller, Kathy Dodge, who described herself as a close friend and former neighbor of Jo Ann Parks. Over time, Dodge said, she had grown concerned about Jo Ann's behavior as a parent, and news of the fire had confirmed her worst fears. Dodge told the police Jo Ann didn't really like having children, that her house and her kids were always filthy, that she couldn't bear it when they cried, and that she boasted of dosing her youngest with cough syrup so she would fall asleep early and not wake in the night.

"You should try it with your baby," she recalled Jo Ann suggesting. And if that wasn't enough to let her sleep in peace, Dodge added, "She always wears earplugs at night."

The most damning recollection Dodge offered, however, concerned the fire that had destroyed the Parkses' previous home a year earlier. According to Dodge, Jo Ann once mused aloud, "If Ron had come home five minutes later, Jessica would be dead and we'd be rich."

The Bell police had been horrified. They went out to interview Dodge in person and found her convincing. The tenor of the case immediately transformed from accident review to homicide investigation, and the small department called the far larger, more experienced, and better-funded Los Angeles County Sheriff's Department for help. The department's arson unit had a long and storied history and reputation. While the county fire department operation was fine for routine investigations, the sheriff's arson unit handled major fatalities. Detective Ablott drew the case.

Coincidentally, Ablott had investigated that first fire a year earlier and concluded that it was accidental and electrical in origin—the same tentative finding reached in the Sherman Way fire by the fire department investigator. Now, in the wake of Dodge's information about neglect, drugging, and pining for profit from the death of a child, the possibility arose that Ablott could have been duped in the first case and was actually looking at serial arson. Or if not, could an accidental first fire have inspired the Parkses to stage a similar event a year later, one that would allow them to cash in on the deaths that were avoided the first time around?

With all this background information in mind, Ablott and his partner entered the charred apartment on Sherman Way for the first time on April 17, 1989, a week after the fire, accompanied by county fire investigator Franklin. The place had been completely overhauled—the term for what firefighters do after extinguishing the flames. They use axes and shovels to overturn ash, to break through walls, and to throw furniture and other possessions through windows into piles outside the house. Overhauling's goal is to eliminate any smoldering embers beneath the debris or hidden in furniture, closets, or roofing. Otherwise, home fires can reignite hours later, threatening neighboring homes long after the fire engines and police cruisers leave the scene. But overhaul also destroys evidence and makes reconstruction and investigation infinitely harder. Floors are shoveled, raked, and swept; doors and walls and ceilings are broken down or cut open; nothing remains in place. Overhaul has become an inevitable part of firefighting, but when foul play is later suspected, it's as if the crime scene had been struck by a tornado. Evidence is misplaced, destroyed, moved, and lost during overhaul—not just sometimes, but all the time.

And yet, years later, Ablott could still recall the visceral reaction he and his partner experienced as they walked through the shell of an apartment, looking everywhere, each of them repeatedly saying aloud, "This isn't right. Something's not right here. This isn't right."

They immediately had a gut feeling they were dealing with foul play, Ablott would later recall. Sometimes you just know. It's a sort of gestalt many cops talk about when they first walk a crime scene or interview a suspect. But then the real work starts. The arson investigators next began to search the Parks home for evidence to support this impression—or, in theory, to disprove it.

There would be no disproving this day, or in the days to come. Sure enough, in multiple rooms of the tiny apartment, they found evidence not of an accident, but of a crime.

That extension cord and other wires in the living room, first thought to have accidentally overheated, appeared to Ablott to have been deliberately sabotaged. He concluded that the insulation on one part of an extension cord had been cut intentionally in order to create a short circuit, while other parts of the cords were wrapped in small portions of the living room draperies. He deemed these "modifications" to be capable of starting a fire—with other investigators and prosecutors eventually characterizing his discovery as a homemade incendiary device. When a background investigation later revealed that Ron Parks had been trained as an electrician while serving in the army and in Vietnam, it seemed the know-how to create a deliberate electrical fire had been in the home all along.

Next Ablott found what he believed might be a second "point of origin" on the floor in the girls' bedroom—signs of a separate fire that might have been ignited purposely by a human hand, rather than initiated by flames spreading from the living room. Multiple points of origin have long been considered a sure indication of arson. Accidental fires almost always start in one place. If true, this meant the girls' bedroom must have been one of the first areas of the apartment to burn. Contradictory information from Officer Bruce and Tuxedo Man was dismissed or ignored; in the hierarchy of arson investigation, Ablott's long years of expertise would trump the fallible memories of mere eyewitnesses.

Then came the most disturbing discovery yet: Ablott spotted faint burn patterns in Ronnie Jr.'s room that were not noted in the initial walk-through by the county fire investigator. There appeared to be protected areas in the carpet in front of the closet where Ronnie's body was found—patterns Ablott felt showed that an object had been placed in front of the closet door. He later decided this had been a clothes hamper placed in front of the closet to barricade the child inside the burning apartment. This chilling evidence didn't prove how the fire started, Ablott knew, but it did provide strong evidence of murder.

He would later profess a reluctance to believe any parent could be so monstrous as to trap a child in order to burn him to death, causing him to delay making an official finding in the case. "But in the end, the evidence left me no choice."

Neither Ablott nor any other investigator seriously considered Ronnie Jr. as the cause of the blaze. After all, Jo Ann had angrily denied that her son Ronnie had anything to do with it, despite blurting a contrary sentiment immediately after running to the Robisons.

Ron Parks was the prime suspect from the outset, even though his time card and coworkers seemed to provide a solid alibi for him at the time of the fire. Everything about him put investigators on edge. He kept asking for police reports to give to his lawyer. He gave that awful TV interview. Coworkers who attended the children's funeral said he acted inappropriately and without displaying any signs of grief. Ablott later claimed that Ron and Jo Ann came to the gutted apartment on April 17 and acted guiltily, ignoring investigators assembled there, walking by without a word instead of questioning them about the cause of the fire. (Ron and Jo Ann denied this ever happened.) The Parkses had received about thirty thousand dollars in donations after the spate of publicity on TV and in the papers, and Ron's reaction to the windfall also seemed revealing to investigators: He used part of the donations to buy a used convertible and tooled around town to show it off to his friends. Then he and his wife left town on a road trip to visit his family in St. Louis. Along the way, Ron mailed a postcard to the dairy stating that he and his wife were vacationing, followed by the message, "We're having a great time, wish you were here." His coworkers were shocked.

More to the point, Ron had not only been trained in electrical wiring in the army, he had also held several jobs afterward in related fields. Kathy Dodge raved about his ability to fix any wiring or appliance—she told the police he was an electronics "wizard." Right before he left for work, just hours before the fire, he had connected a new VCR to their old swap-meet television set, fiddling with the very electrical cords Ablott believed had been sabotaged. He could have been creating a rough-and-ready timed device that would ignite a fire hours after he punched in at work.

It's conceivable Ron had acted on his own, the investigators theorized. But if little Ronnie had been trapped in the closet, and if a second blaze had been set in the girls' bedroom by hand, the culprit had to have been present in the apartment at the time of the fire. That meant Jo Ann Parks had to be involved as well. A murder charge against either or both parents appeared imminent.

But then it did not materialize. Instead, the case inexplicably went cold in the summer of 1989.

Detectives and prosecutors decided they needed more evidence than burn patterns and wires with little cuts on them. They knew a defense attorney could and would find other experts to dispute Ablott's findings, raising doubts. They wanted to construct a portrait of a murderous mom or killer dad or both, and to build a case too compelling for a jury to reject. So a pair of sheriff's homicide detectives joined the investigation and for the next two years—as time allowed, for there were long gaps of inactivity—they tried to bolster the case by seeking evidence of motive, conspiracy, or past crimes by Ron or Jo Ann Parks. But they found none. Rumors about Ron Parks's previous marriage and other house fires in his past tantalized but couldn't be verified. Then the detectives learned Jo Ann had been the single teenage mom of a son who died in infancy, raising suspicions that they might have a serial child killer on their hands. They spent months chasing that down before they realized they were pursuing a red herring.

The homicide detectives also failed to uncover any hard evidence to support Kathy Dodge, whose story started to change and become increasingly incoherent each time she retold it. The coroner had analyzed the children's bodies for any of the array of compounds used in cough medicine that could have kept the kids unconscious while they burned to death. None were found. There was no evidence of any narcotics or drugging.

The same autopsy of the three Parks children found no signs of child abuse—no recent injuries or old ones, no malnourishment, no vestiges of neglect. While several of Dodge's friends confirmed parts of her account (though no one else heard the comment about getting rich from Jessica's death), the family's Christian Science pastor, Paul Garman, told the police that the kids were well cared for, healthy, and happy. He had never seen them dirty and poorly dressed, as Kathy Dodge had claimed. He saw them regularly, he said, and would have taken action if he had any inkling of abuse in the home.

There was no insurance policy taken out on the children or even to cover fire losses, which is almost always step one in homeowner arson cases. The Parkses had lost everything in an earlier fire for which they had no insurance. If they were planning a second fire, getting insurance ought to have been the first order of business. Having been burned once—literally—by being uninsured, their failure to purchase coverage perplexed and frustrated the detectives.

Certain there had to be some sort of financial motive, the detectives next seized on the fact that Ron and Jo Ann pursued a lawsuit against their landlords in the first fire, and almost immediately hired an attorney to sue for wrongful death after the second. Jo Ann would later say Ron was the litigious one in the family, that he was the driving force behind both lawsuits—something he would later confirm in court testimony. But she was still a party to the lawsuits, she had signed the papers, and in August 1990 she had sat for a sworn deposition about the first fire.

This struck detectives as unseemly and suspicious. They felt the possibility of cashing in on a lawsuit could provide a possible motive for murder, though even they had to admit that virtually any parent who suffered such a loss and had a reputed slumlord for a landlord could be expected to sue.

And there the investigation stood. Two and a half years would pass with no charges and no arrests in the deaths of Ronnie, RoAnn, and Jessica Parks.

Eventually Ron and Jo Ann moved to St. Louis, initially staying with Ron's mother, then drifting through a series of shabby rental homes. Jo Ann finally found work managing a Christian Science–run retirement home, which provided housing for the couple on the premises. Ron worked as an aide at a nearby nursing facility, and the couple even started saving and planning to purchase a home. They remained unaware that a criminal investigation still brewed slowly in the background, waiting to kindle into a very different sort of inferno that would turn their lives upside down once again.

Meanwhile, the detectives on the Parks arson case also remained in the dark about events that would turn their own business of fire investigation upside down. A fire in Northern California was about to show the world that many of the forensic beliefs and practices in use at the time of the fatal fire in Bell—and thousands of others like it—were fatally flawed.

7

Three Days in October 1991

The worst fire to scorch the California Bay Area in 140 years began with just a few acres of blackened grass.

Initially, this seemed nothing more than an inconsequential accident on private land. Fire crews snuffed out the little blaze before it could reach the winding residential streets overlooking the steely arc of San Francisco Bay. Five years of drought had left the Oakland Hills area vulnerable to the merest spark, the desiccated grass crunching underfoot with the sound of broken glass. Yet it seemed luck prevailed and disaster had been averted on October 19, 1991.

And that would have been the end of it, but for an unlucky change in the weather: The Diablo winds kicked in on the morning of October 20. Blistering, dry, and moving at more than forty miles an hour, the Bay Area's analog to Los Angeles's legendary Santa Ana winds fanned to life small embers hidden beneath that patch of burnt grass. Then the gusts drove the renewed flames up into the maze of hillside homes with their lovely wood siding and oh-so-flammable shake rooftops.

One by one, hillsides, houses, parks, and apartment buildings succumbed to the spreading flames, until the Bay Area had a full-blown wildfire on its hands.

There weren't enough firefighters, hoses, or hydrants to stop what had become a wall of fire and choking smoke, even as an army of fire engines raced to the scene from dozens of communities, some as far away as Las Vegas. For every house where a fire crew knocked down the flames, five others on the same street would be gone by the time the firefighters were ready to move on. The fire grew so fierce that the resinous pine trees that covered the hillsides didn't just burn. They exploded.

The Oakland firestorm, as the wildfire came to be known, destroyed more than three thousand homes before the Diablo winds abruptly shifted and died around nine that night. Hundreds of people were injured. Twenty-five burned to death. Ashes rained down on Candlestick Park, packed with football fans twenty miles away. A sooty, greasy stench reminiscent of rancid burnt popcorn blanketed the landscape. Whole neighborhoods had been reduced to rubble, houses burned down to their foundations, leaving only brick chimneys standing. Sagging metal plumbing rose from the wreckage like charred dinosaur fossils. The twisted plumage of piano wire bristled from the black stumps of Baldwins, Steinways, and Yamahas. Gray powder coated everything.

In the aftermath, a crew of arson investigators and fire scientists descended on those spectral flame-scoured neighborhoods. Their mission was unique. They came not to do their usual thing, which is to figure out why a fire happened, and what—or who—was responsible. For once, the investigators already knew the fire's origin and how it spread: an accident of drought and complacency, and a seemingly extinguished brush fire resurrected by the devil winds. Instead, the team came to this disaster scene to learn about *other* fires.

It's not hard to see what attracted them. Here stood home after devastated home, many reduced to what firefighters call "black holes." Most had burned completely, until there was nothing left to burn, all without human intervention, without any arsonists splashing gasoline or kids playing with matches or, for a majority of homes, firefighters interrupting the process and destroying the evidence with their hoses, axes, foam, and shovels. The team of experts came to see and learn what a known accidental fire looks like when allowed to burn itself out, so they could find ways to distinguish these black holes from true arson fires.

Black holes are among the most difficult fires to investigate. The flames not only destroy buildings, they also scour away almost every bit of evidence of a crime. Investigators had long relied on a few tricks of the trade to find signs of arson in a black hole. Now the disaster in the Oakland Hills provided a real-world laboratory to test, refine, and add to those tricks. The team was drawn by the promise of finding some small silver lining beneath all those tons of soot, ash, and loss.

They found something, all right. Just not what they expected.

They found, to their amazement, signs of arson. Everywhere.

Their response as they walked through the blackened hills provided a curious mirror to Ron Ablott's reaction to the scene at the Parks apartment. They kept saying to one another, "This isn't right. Something's not right here."

They found crazed glass—windows fractured by webs of tiny cracks. They had been taught, like most arson investigators had been taught for decades, that crazing indicated the sort of fast-moving, very hot fires caused by the use of gasoline or some other flammable accelerant. Crazing was supposed to be a sure sign of arson. Yet they were finding it in one out of every four houses they visited—houses where they knew no arson had occurred. Subsequent experiments showed that crazing occurs not from rapid heating but rapid *cooling*—such as occurs when fire hoses douse a flaming building.

Even more common were twisted, melted bedsprings in the remains of bedrooms, another one of the tricks of the trade that, for decades, had been used as a sign of arson in a black-hole ruin. Melted copper plumbing and fixtures, and melted metal doorway thresholds turned up everywhere, too, which were only supposed to happen in the rapid, extreme fires caused by an arsonist with a gas can. Spalling of concrete, a surface chipping that was supposed to indicate the use of accelerants, also turned up.

John Lentini, a former police forensics expert working for a private fire investigation consultancy, was on the team of scientists digging around in the Oakland firestorm ruins. He would go on to the role of lead author of the report on the group's findings, which could be summarized very simply: Indicators of arson that had been passed on across generations of fire investigators, and that had been used to send people to prison for decades, were wrong. The same supposedly suspicious indicators occurred in accidental fires, too.

The Oakland firestorm investigation was undertaken to expand and refine scientific theories about fire and arson. Instead, it had become a real-world laboratory for disproving them. Those theories had never really been tested before in a scientific way. They merely had been the received wisdom in the fire investigation business, their admissibility in court becoming a legal precedent and never questioned after that—the way doctors had been taught for centuries that bloodletting of patients sick with fevers or infections was an effective treatment.

This became a pivotal moment for Lentini. He had been hired just months before to help convict a Jacksonville, Florida, man accused of setting a 1990 fire that killed his pregnant wife, his sister, and his four nieces and nephews. The man claimed his son had accidentally set fire to the living room couch while playing with a cigarette lighter. But the police arson investigators had found V-patterns that suggested a fire had been set elsewhere in the house, and "pour patterns" on the floor that suggested gasoline had been splashed there and set aflame. Dubbed the "Lime Street fire" in subsequent news accounts, the case had seemed an obvious multiple murder by arson, the arrest a foregone conclusion. But there was no seeming motive for the crime, and the prosecutor wanted an airtight case. So Lentini and a colleague were hired to see if there was any possibility that the fire could have started accidentally as the defendant claimed, or if the evidence proved this fire could not possibly have begun with a child, a couch, and a lighter.

It turned out there was an identical house nearby that was slated to be torn down. Lentini and his colleague decided to carpet and furnish this home in the same way as the Lime Street house where the fatal fire occurred, install video cameras, and set fire to the couch just as the suspect had claimed. Firefighters would stand by to extinguish the flames at the same stage at which the original fire was put out. Lentini expected the results would reveal the accident story as an impossible lie, and the prosecutor could proceed with putting the man away—possibly on death row—with righteous confidence.

Instead, the same suspicious burn patterns were found in the test house after the fire was put out. The indicators of arson had appeared where they should not have appeared.

The culprit: flashover, the transformation of a fire in a room into a room on fire. Flashover had occurred in both the fatal fire and in the Lime Street re-creation, and it was this then-poorly understood phenomenon that revealed serious problems with the traditional arson investigation playbook. Normally, the largest V-patterns and the area of greatest damage in a burning structure can reliably indicate where a fire started. The logic of this is obvious: The most damage generally occurs where the fire burns the longest, and that would be the starting point in many simple structure fires. But this rule of thumb doesn't work so reliably after flashover, when large V-patterns can form in areas away from the fire's starting point, and burn marks that mimic flammable-liquid pour patterns can emerge as well. When Lentini reported his findings, the prosecutor, instead of shoring up his case, ended up dismissing it. And an innocent man was saved.

Had the prosecutor not requested that test, the man who lost his wife, sister, and nieces and nephews almost certainly would have ended up convicted of a crime that never happened.

"I had come within twenty-four hours of giving testimony that could well have sent an innocent person to Florida's electric chair," Lentini would later say. "Needless to say, I was chastened by the experience."

He was more than chastened. The combination of the Lime Street fire and the Oakland firestorm changed the course of John Lentini's life. He realized that key elements of fire science as practiced in 1991, and for decades before, were wrong. Fatally wrong. There was no science to back up those beliefs. And hardly anyone even knew there was a problem.

But Lentini knew lives had been ruined because of this. Insurance payoffs had been denied, leaving families bankrupt and homeless. People had been sent to prison. *He* had sent people to prison—for crimes that might never have happened. Not every case, he knew. Probably not even a majority of arson cases, most of which were so simple or so obvious that such glaring injustices were all but impossible. But there would be enough that were wrong, that were infected by flawed science. Too many. Thousands of criminal and civil actions had been taken against people based on what amounted to fire mythology.

Lentini walked away from Oakland a shaken man, but a man with a mission: to put the science into "fire science" where it should have been all along. He would volunteer to review for free cases in which bad arson theories might have led to wrongful convictions. And he would lobby for national guidelines for how a proper fire investigation should be conducted.

A year later a committee of leading fire experts, Lentini among them, was organized by the National Fire Protection Association. This group published a landmark report with the bland title of *NFPA 921.* It set guidelines for a proper fire investigation intended for use nationwide by every fire department and in the investigation of every fire.

One of the key recommendations: Fire experts, including field investigators for police and fire departments, should follow the scientific method when rendering an opinion on the origin and cause of a fire. If, for instance, window crazing was present and introduced as evidence, an expert should have to prove with real science and real-world data that only an arson fire could cause crazing. That had never been done before and, after Oakland, never could be done, at least for crazing. All the other long-held beliefs about the indicators of arson would have to be backed up with clear scientific evidence from now on to comply with these new guidelines.

The *NFPA 921* recommendation—which basically requires testing, data, and proof before a scientific finding can be accepted as grounds for sending a person to prison—sounds innocuous and commonsensical. But it created, appropriately enough, a firestorm.

Firefighters, law-enforcement organizations, and the National District Attorneys Association fiercely opposed the new guidelines, which are influential but entirely voluntary. Expert opinions long considered rock solid, backed by legal precedent, and used to put away accused arsonists for years would be undermined. Old cases would be opened. New prosecutions made more complex and difficult. Worst of all, accomplished investigators who were just doing what they had been taught to do, who were acting in good faith even as they practiced bad science, would have to admit in an unknown number of cases that they had screwed up—and that those screwups had come at a terrible price.

Most, at least at first, found it easier to dispute rather than embrace the new guidelines, calling them misguided and mistaken. Some argued that they were the handiwork of the defense bar trying to get guilty people off the hook and out of jail. Others saw in the new guidelines the well-meaning naiveté of eggheads in spotless lab coats who practiced science in clean laboratories, but who lacked practical experience with the dirty business of crawling through ravaged, ash-filled fire scenes in search of truth.

One of the leading law-enforcement arson investigators in Los Angeles testified in April 1992 about his colleagues' unfavorable attitude toward the then-new *NFPA 921.* He dismissed the National Fire Protection Association, which produced the guidelines, as a group primarily interested in promoting better sprinkler and fire-door designs. And he opined that the group's investigation guidelines conflicted with techniques embraced by most arson investigators "worth their salt."

That leading investigator was Ron Ablott of the Los Angeles County Sheriff's Department Arson/Explosives Detail—the principal fire investigator in the Jo Ann Parks case.

Two days after the Oakland firestorm, a pair of Los Angeles County Sheriff's homicide detectives flew to St. Louis. There had been no major breakthrough in the Parks case, just a slow accumulation of information and one surprising twist: It was conclusively shown that the wires in the living room said to have been sabotaged and turned into a time-delayed incendiary device had not started the fire. Ron Parks, it seemed, was off the hook. If it was arson, then the fire had to have been set by whoever was home at the time. The prime suspect shifted then from husband to wife. The gung-ho prosecutor assigned to the case filed charges two and a half years after the fire. He would later describe Jo Ann Parks as one of the most evil defendants in Los Angeles history.

She was, the prosecutor proclaimed, a monster unlike any he had ever pursued before.

The two detectives drove in a rental car from the airport and, with local police backup, walked into the Lake St. Charles Retirement Community. Jo Ann Parks had worked there for several months as patient coordinator for this small assisted-living facility for elderly Christian Scientists. She had been hired away from a local nursing home where she and Ron had worked together. The new job required her to be on call at all times, so one of the benefits was a furnished, rent-free apartment on the retirement community's parklike grounds.

Jo Ann would later recall this apartment was one of the most pleasant dwellings she and Ron had ever shared. Not only was it comfortable, it also allowed the couple to bank their rent money toward purchasing their first house. Just the day before, they had made an offer on a ranch-style house with plenty of land and room for all the many pets Jo Ann craved. The years of rootlessness and constant moves from one hovel to another seemed finally to be behind them.

On the job, the woman police believed to have been a slovenly, neglectful, and ultimately murderous mother appeared to show a different personality at the retirement home, seemingly patient and gentle with the aged residents there. She helped the residents dress and bathe, she walked them to church services, and she escorted them to beautician and haircut appointments so they would look their best when family came to visit, her supervisor would recall.

Jo Ann Parks seemed to have no idea that the fire investigation in Bell remained open, that she and her husband remained murder suspects, or that this apartment she so loved could end up being her last home without bars.

The homicide detectives did not call ahead. There was no warning. When they approached Jo Ann Parks in the retirement home lobby holding an arrest warrant and handcuffs, she stared at them for one frozen moment, then collapsed and began to wail.

The warrant—naming only her, not her husband—accused her of arson and three counts of first-degree murder. The charging language included the term *special circumstances*—the phrase required under California law when prosecutors seek the death penalty.

One year later a tale of sabotage, arson, and a child locked screaming in a burning closet persuaded twelve jurors to convict Jo Ann

Parks of capital murder. She never spoke to police after her arrest, nor did she testify in her own defense at her trial. And so the jurors gave prosecutors everything they asked for but one thing: They voted no to the death penalty.

In a somewhat contradictory resolution, the jurors concluded a monstrous crime indeed had been committed, but that Parks was not so monstrous herself.

This compromise left the judge only one option for sentencing under California law: life in prison without possibility of parole. Times three.

For twenty-six years, more than half her lifetime, Parks remained behind bars, consigned to an institutionalized life, stripped of family and hope, branded a child killer by other inmates who were not interested in her protestations of innocence. Eventually she stopped offering them, resigned to a life behind walls, expecting she'd age and die there.

Then, as she began her twenty-seventh year in prison, a letter arrived from something called the California Innocence Project, offering both a chance at redemption and a prod to resurrect the most painful memories of her life, buried by then for more than a quarter century. She barely dared to believe it was possible: Somebody out there not only wanted to get her out of prison. They wanted to prove she had been convicted of a crime that never happened.

PART TWO

STIRRING THE ASHES

8

The Pit

There is a room on the ground floor of the California Western School of Law in downtown San Diego sometimes known as "the Pit." The size of the average apartment living room, the Pit can feel cramped, hot, crowded, and loud. The walls are lined with computer stations and desks covered with stacks of legal papers and correspondence, everything in a constant state of churn. On the floor in the room's center sit six laundry-basket-sized US Postal Service mail cartons spilling over with envelopes of every shape and thickness. The Pit more closely resembles a direct-mail boiler room than what it actually is: a critical part of a most unusual law office.

Somewhere in those boxes of mail, buried inside layers of legalese or handwritten rants, there is the story of an innocent woman or man languishing in prison, a cold closed case waiting to be teased into the light and reopened. The Pit is one of the few places in the country where this has an actual chance of happening. It is the gateway to representation by the California Innocence Project, part of a nationwide web of similarly minded nonprofit operations, neither the largest nor the smallest, dedicated to freeing people from unjust imprisonment. And as it prepared to take on Jo Ann Parks's case, the California Innocence Project had been on a roll, having freed twenty-eight men and women from wrongful convictions for murder, rape, and other serious cases across the past decade.

Project interns and volunteers find many of those cases by digging through the six postal boxes, which hold the weekly mail from defense lawyers, mothers, fathers, spouses, friends, and convicts begging for a champion to prove someone's innocence. As fast as they can be emptied, a new batch arrives to fill the mailboxes anew.

A cursory review by the volunteers in the Pit weeds out the cases that have no chance of success, which means most of this sad, mad influx—two to three thousand a year—never gets past the boiler room stage. These are the letters that reveal cases with exhausted appeals, or convictions supported by overwhelming evidence of guilt, or that are merely angry diatribes about the real, perceived, and fanciful corruption within the legal system. Many letter writers fume about some legitimate but minute contradiction in the evidence against them in an otherwise solid prosecution, not understanding that the flaw or lie or inconsistency they have spotted has to be so huge that, if corrected, it likely would change a jury's decision from guilty to not guilty. This is a hurdle only a very few can clear. Other convict correspondents will actually admit they are guilty but that they'd appreciate the change of scenery and relief from routine a court hearing would provide. Desperation, loneliness, and boredom, rather than sincere pleas of innocence, motivate many of these letter writers. While such qualities may be grounds for sympathy, they do not make for successful appeals.

The hardest entries in the slush pile are the anguish-laden letters from parents attacking the evidence against their children, the facts no parent can bear to accept about a son or daughter, the witnesses that surely must be lying, the DNA evidence that can't possibly be correct. These letters often consist of painstakingly long handwritten recitations of the perfidy of the authorities and their twisting of the facts of the case, all highly colored by the blindness only love and grief can sustain. These are the most heartbreaking letters to reject. But sorrow, no matter how profound, will not open a prison cell door, either.

The mail that remains after this basic weeding of the pile moves on to progressively more detailed layers of review until the tidal wave is reduced to a slim stack of possible clients worthy of being more deeply researched.

"She trusted the legal system," read one typical letter that survived this stage. "She had always respected authority . . . But once the local authorities began looking for a crime, all objectivity was lost—that their theories were adjusted to suit their mind-set was immaterial, as long as they 'had their man.' "

The letter was fairly typical in its claim of an innocent person betrayed by an official rush to judgment. But it was highly unusual in another respect: It came not from a convict or a family member, but from a forensics expert who had testified for the defense in a murder case. He had been devastated when a guilty verdict was returned, and he had devoted his own time and money to try to help. His analysis of the case and the proof of innocence he had offered at trial should have been enough to win the case, he complained, but he had been undermined by what he felt certain had been poor lawyering by the defense and overzealousness by the prosecution. Instead of providing decisive testimony, he wrote, he became "nothing more than window dressing going through the motions."

This was interesting—as much for the source of the correspondence as for the information it contained. The letter writer was a twenty-five-year veteran of the Los Angeles Fire Department who had spent his career *catching* arsonists, not setting them free, which gave him a level of credibility that was quite rare among the stacks of letters that flood the Pit. And so it was, way back in 2001, that a letter about the *People of the State of California v. Jo Ann Parks* survived the initial cut at the California Innocence Project.

At this stage, law students and interns gather background information for each remaining letter. Those that aren't winnowed out after that level of scrutiny are then presented at a roundtable meeting with the staff attorneys—there are seven at the California Innocence Project—where the merits and flaws in each case are discussed. And out of those, a rare few, twenty to twenty-five cases a year, survive to be assigned for a full legal and investigative review. The review determines which of the remaining cases, if any, are suitable candidates for filing the innocence project's primary legal tool, the habeas corpus petition, based on an ancient legal principle that has shielded individuals from government overreach since the days of William Penn. Each habeas petition absorbs a significant chunk of the project's finite resources, so choosing well is critical.

These final calls can be agonizing because it's just not enough to find evidence that a potential client is innocent. Contrary to public perception, the courts do not generally recognize even overwhelming evidence of innocence as a valid reason to open the cell door for someone after a guilty verdict has been rendered. There also must be legal proof that the accused did not get a fair trial leading up to a guilty verdict. The two ideas—*Are they innocent?* and *Did they get a fair trial?*—can overlap, but they are not one and the same. As the late Supreme Court Justice Antonin

Scalia repeatedly pointed out—approvingly—the US Constitution does not forbid the execution of an innocent man so long as he received a fair trial first.

Jo Ann Parks ran this review gauntlet not once but three times.

The project rejected the case that first time in 2001: The legal and scientific hurdles and prevailing beliefs about fire behavior appeared to make a successful outcome unlikely, the reviewers decided.

A decade passed before the project attorneys decided to take a fresh look. Several high-profile arson convictions had been overturned around the country because fire experts in those cases had used outdated and unproven methods, finding evidence of arson where none existed. John Lentini was involved in several of those exonerations. Working with other fire experts, he had started an arson review committee to examine cases for free. The first such report maintained that the State of Texas executed an innocent man, Cameron Todd Willingham, in 2004, due to flawed science and arson myths. A state commission agreed that the arson case against Willingham could not be supported, sparking reforms by the state fire marshal's office, though too late to stave off the execution. In 2012, Lentini's committee reached a similar conclusion about the Parks case and provided a free report to the innocence project that stated, "The evidence was tainted by the fire investigators' failure to understand the behavior of fire, and on unfounded beliefs about their ability to interpret post-fire artifacts. . . . But once the state's investigators committed to an incendiary classification, even the changing of the most important details did not persuade them to change their determination."

This time the Parks case made it to the final stage of review, but once again was rejected—based on a matter of law, not fact. For Jo Ann Parks to win her freedom, she would have to prove the evidence against her was false. But California at that time had one of the toughest legal standards in the country when it came to challenging the veracity of expert witnesses. In other states, Parks might have had a good case, the project lawyers decided. But in California, she had no chance. The law stated that expert opinions—about how a fire started, whether a footprint or a bite mark matched a murderer, or anything else—could not be considered false evidence, because opinions can be neither right nor wrong. Only facts could be true or false. And so Parks was out of luck.

But then in 2015, the Parks case came up for review once more, likely for the last time. Changes in the law, sparked by a provably innocent man who had no legal recourse under California's strict rules on challenging expert testimony, had opened a door for Jo Ann Parks to challenge her imprisonment at last. The state legislature decided expert opinions could be false evidence after all. Suddenly Parks had facts and the law to work with. The innocence project staff voted to take on her case.

The file landed in the tiny office shared by attorneys Raquel Cohen and Alissa Bjerkhoel. The young lawyers were ebullient from just winning the freedom of a man who had spent sixteen years in prison because of a mistaken eyewitness—a case that had taken years to resolve, even after it was clear to everyone their client had been blamed for someone else's crimes. Now it was time to find the next case.

Bjerkhoel was already diving into the conviction of a San Diego day-care center owner convicted of shaking a baby to death—with the government relying on scientific evidence against the woman that had since been rejected by the medical community as unreliable.

So the Parks case came to Raquel Cohen. She cracked open the file and leaned forward in her chair, trying and failing to get comfortable. At thirty-two, she was almost three months pregnant with her second baby, just far enough along to make getting her compact form settled at her desk more awkward than effortless. Normally this would be her cue to joke and complain about "the bump," as she referred to her unborn daughter. But this time the case file absorbed her attention and rendered her discomfort forgotten in mid-punchline.

There is a right way and a wrong way to read a case file, Cohen knows. She is practiced at this: You never read it cover to cover like a book, at least not at first, because legal files are never organized in narrative fashion. They are organized by the date on which pleadings were filed, which means the story is out of order, the snore-inducing minutiae mixed up with the momentous. Instead, you look for and begin with the highlights. She saw there had been an appeal right after the conviction—standard procedure in a capital case—and although it had been summarily denied without a hearing, the appellate document had an excellent summary of the facts and disputes in the case. Good ones read like a movie plot treatment, and this one was a good one. Perfect, Cohen thought.

Unsurprisingly, the trial defense had been in part that the fire was accidental, with the likeliest starting point identified as an old television set with a frayed and patched cord that Ron Parks had bought at a swap meet. It had been gathering dust in storage for months before the move to Sherman Way, and had been set up in the area where the prosecution claims the fire started: in front of the windows and inches from the drapes. The defense argued that law enforcement had destroyed the TV without properly examining it, justifying this by claiming—apparently incorrectly—that it was of no value because it had stood too far from where they believed the fire started. To the police, the TV was a distraction, unworthy of consideration as a fire cause. To Cohen, it was potential ammunition.

Other evidence had been destroyed, too, Cohen saw, even the closet door in Ronnie's room, making it difficult if not impossible to determine conclusively if it was open, closed, or barricaded during the fire. The authorities also repeatedly changed their theory about how the fire started, it seemed. Opposing lawyers *love* missing evidence and inconsistency on key points. Such issues can make their opponents' case seem weak, opportunistic, and untrustworthy.

But the trial jurors who heard the evidence for and against Jo Ann Parks in the end believed the state's case, not the defense's. Whatever doubts the defense mustered about televisions and closet doors, they hadn't been enough. Cohen scratched out notes as she read through the brief, knowing she'd have to find something more, something bigger.

Certainly there were questions about the choices made by the defense lawyer at trial. In his very first question to Ronald Parks, the lawyer accused him of starting the fire and trying to pin it on his wife. Cohen thought, How melodramatic! And possibly a mistake. If the defense wanted to sell the jury on the fire starting accidentally with an old TV, why undercut that theory by suggesting the fire had been sparked deliberately by someone else? The husband had a solid alibi, with no way of setting the fire without his wife knowing or helping. The defense fire investigator who first contacted the innocence project about the Parks case had been particularly incensed by this move by the original attorney.

The former fire captain turned expert witness felt certain this insinuating question had confused the jury by undermining his own testimony about the fire being caused by a dusty, old, fire-prone television. Cohen was not so sure; the trial lawyer, worried not just about a guilty verdict but also about a possible death sentence, undoubtedly felt compelled to raise reasonable doubt about the charges in any and every way he could.

In a trial, when a defendant is presumed innocent, doubt is all that's needed to win. After a conviction, however, the burden of proof shifts. To reopen the case, Cohen would have to do far more than raise doubt. She would have to find clear proof of an unfair trial, false evidence that had been instrumental in the verdict, or newly discovered evidence that was both unavailable at the original trial and pointed strongly to Parks's innocence. The time had passed for "reasonable doubt," the courtroom equivalent of a ground ball single. Cohen needed a home run now. So as interesting as it might be to second-guess judgment calls and lawyerly trial tactics from a quarter century ago, such issues would never get a habeas corpus hearing for Parks, much less a new trial or actual exoneration. The husband was a dead end for Cohen's purposes, as was the way the trial attorney questioned him. Cohen moved on in the file.

Next she turned to the potential gold mine: the analysis of the case written in 2012 by John Lentini and the Arson Review Committee. The group's report noted that the sheriff's arson investigator in charge of the case, Ron Ablott, had insisted the fire had been brought under control before flashover occurred in the house. To Lentini, that provided the key to reopening the case and to overturning Parks's conviction. He opined that photographs from the fire scene clearly showed the original investigator got it wrong: Flashover *had* occurred. Failure to take that into account undermined the entire scientific case against Parks, in Lentini's opinion. The science of fire had advanced since 1989, he wrote, arguing that it was now clear that many of the old ideas about fire behavior and traditional indicators of arson don't work once flashover enters the picture—particularly when an arson investigator fails to acknowledge that flashover occurred. This was the lesson of Lime Street and the Oakland wildfires and of many other inquiries since then, Lentini wrote.

Now Cohen was hooked, unable to stop reading.

"Simply stated, the rules for interpreting fire damage change once flashover occurs and a compartment becomes fully involved," Lentini wrote. "None of the evidence presented by the state against Mrs. Parks is valid. Mrs. Parks's conviction was the result of the miserable state of the art in fire investigation at that time. By today's standards, none of the allegedly inculpatory evidence would withstand scrutiny. The investigators and ultimately the jury were misled by bad science, or no science at all."

Fresh to the case and the subject of arson, Cohen wasn't quite sure what flashover was. Not yet. But if Lentini was correct, a pivotal piece of false information lay at the heart of the case against Jo Ann Parks—falsehood that could win a new trial for her.

Cohen closed the report. What had really happened in this case? How could flashover have been discounted by the original investigation when other experts deemed it both obvious and vital to understanding what happened inside that wretched two-car garage turned three-bedroom apartment? Was this a case of a murder conviction where no murder existed? Could it be that simple? That terrible?

For the third time across three decades, her muttered reaction to her friend and office-mate mirrored that of others involved in the case, though for very different reasons:

"Something's not right here. . . . Something isn't right."

Cohen next turned to the background material on Jo Ann Parks. The prosecutor had spent considerable effort portraying her as a poor parent, heartless, selfish, untruthful, and, most of all, *unmotherly*. A big part of the government's case boiled down to a claim that Parks hadn't "acted right" during the fire and in its aftermath—as if there is any correct response to fire, trauma, death, and loss. The allegations varied: She wasn't emotional enough. Or her emotions were an act. She didn't try very hard to run back into the house and allowed herself to be restrained too easily.

This sort of attack is uniquely deployed against women in criminal trials, Cohen thought with disgust. In her opinion, it suggested a case that relied on innuendo and personal smear tactics rather than hard evidence. She had seen it before. Such subjective and ambiguous testimony can be devastatingly effective with juries. Prosecutors can't come out and say: An innocent mother would have died trying to save her kids. But they can certainly get jurors to start thinking in those terms. After the trial, the jurors admitted as much.

Cohen wasn't too worried about this "bad mother" evidence, however. It might have had a potent effect on jurors, but such issues simply wouldn't matter for the purpose of the habeas corpus petition she envisioned for Parks. A judge, not a jury, would handle that, and he would not care about subjective opinions on whether she was sad enough or cried enough or seemed self-sacrificing enough. Cohen's case would depend on the science. On the experts. On hard evidence. Judges love a good narrative as much as anyone—engaging his or her interest with a good story line embedded in the legal briefs was an innocence project specialty. But Jo Ann Parks's tears quota would be irrelevant to whether the original fire investigator did a stellar job or screwed up. That was the tale Cohen wanted to spin, and one she needed the judge to focus upon.

Still, she kept reading. Cohen needed to know her new client. She needed to establish a rapport. She needed to persuade her closed-off, shy, traumatized new client to open up—the client who, for their first tense, difficult interview, could not talk about her kids or the fire or anything more emotionally challenging than her work as a clerk and bookkeeper for the prison.

Cohen needed to know, most of all: Who, really, was Jo Ann Parks?

9

Growing Up Jo Ann

I was born in Springfield, Illinois. My mom brought me to California when I was four years old. She divorced my dad. She had a daughter a year older and a year younger than me that she said passed away of crib death. She picked my stepfather up off the street. He was nothing but a bum. He was a drunk. We lived in Silver Lake in a back house.

My mom had a baby boy when I was six years old. My brother got everyone's attention but me. He would cry all the time. I used to wake him up and pick on him, break his toys.

I started to go to church with the family that lived in front of us. They were Mormons. My stepfather worked at a bar across from the Greyhound bus station in downtown LA. He was mugged coming home one night. He came in all bloody, had to have stitches and a cast on his arm. My mom started getting curious of why I was going to church. Next thing I knew we were all becoming Mormons.

Jo Ann Parks was born February 26, 1966, to an Illinois family strained by lack of money, lack of parenting skills, the death of Jo Ann's two infant siblings, and too much alcohol.

Her young mother, Lorraine, left her father when Jo Ann was still a toddler. They headed west with Lorraine's best friend, another single mom with child in tow looking for a fresh start. Once in California, Lorraine started a new family with a man she barely knew, and Jo Ann soon had a little brother and two sisters vying for attention from two parents ill-equipped for the job.

Strict, self-absorbed, and dominating as a parent, even Lorraine conceded she did not always put her kids first in those years. During the birth of one of her younger children, when both she and her baby were in distress, Lorraine heard her husband call out to the medical staff, "Save the baby!"

She immediately shouted a countermanding order: "Save *me!*"

This was a story Lorraine told about herself.

Jo Ann's biological father provided even less attention: He had no contact at all with her after the move, something Lorraine refused to explain. He eventually signed away parental rights so Jo Ann's new stepdad could adopt her.

Lorraine saw her husband as her sweeter, gentler counterpoint, certain that he treated his adopted daughter no differently than the other children. Jo Ann, however, did not see it that way. She recalls an abusive bully of a stepfather, who would pull her pants down and beat her with a belt well into adolescence. Her younger brother later told an investigator that while none of the kids had a good childhood, "Jo Ann received the worst of it because she was not his real child." The stepfather was careful, however, to hide his behavior from Lorraine, as Jo Ann recalls, and warned her never to tell what he did to her.

"If you do tell, no one would believe you," she recalls him whispering to her one day. "Because nobody in this family loves you. No one ever has."

Nothing else he said could have been more cruelly effective.

Young Jo Ann's deepest fear was that she really was the unloved and unlovable family outcast, the only one with a different father who never wanted to see her. She started to avoid her stepfather whenever possible, spending time roaming the streets rather than coming home when expected. She would tell herself constantly that when she grew up and got married, she'd find a husband who was the complete opposite of her stepdad, a good partner and a great father.

Jo Ann ended up turning to other adults for help in her early teen years when she felt she couldn't confide in her own mother. Carey Corrigan, a schoolteacher and member of the Mormon church Jo Ann's family attended, became something of a surrogate mom to the teenager. Whenever Jo Ann was down or in trouble or feeling lonely, she would call and ask to talk. Corrigan would pick her up, then drive her to the neighborhood Thrifty Drug Store for ice cream cones. Then they'd sit in the parking lot and chat about Jo Ann's life and fears, sometimes for hours, with Corrigan providing a sympathetic ear and some occasional kindly advice. Jo Ann imposed one condition on these conversations: Corrigan had to swear never to divulge anything to Lorraine.

This initially made Corrigan uneasy, but she soon found this was not a very difficult vow of silence to maintain. Corrigan recalls Jo Ann offered no major revelations during these conversations, no intimations of abuse, no alarming thoughts, and no behavior the young teacher would feel compelled to report in order to protect Jo Ann or anyone else. "Just normal teenager angst and self-esteem issues," Corrigan recalls. "She was sweet and insecure. Like many young women her age."

She and her husband, David Corrigan, then a police officer in the Los Angeles suburb of Monterey Park, lost touch with Jo Ann after she married Ron. When the news broke of the fire and her subsequent arrest, they were shocked. Neither of them believed she had killed her children, as they had seen no propensity for violence or rage in the girl they knew. They perceived her as a basically sweet girl who seemed a little lost at times, extremely dependent, and fearful of being alone, with a tendency to attach herself to kindly friends and neighbors, and even acquaintances. This attachment and dependence sometimes reached the point of imposition. To others, the Corrigans included, this seemed obvious. But Jo Ann seemed oblivious.

This tendency continued into adulthood. Years later, just a day after moving into the Sherman Way apartment that was destined to burn down within the week, Jo Ann had asked Shirley Robison to babysit her three children for her while she and her husband ran some errands. They had only just met the Robisons, had only a single, brief conversation, yet Jo Ann seemed perplexed when Robison expressed discomfort and demurred. Hadn't Robison said if there was anything she or her husband could do to make the move easier, to just let them know? That polite welcome, as the Robisons saw it, meant letting them use their phone or answering questions about the property or the neighborhood. It certainly did not include taking charge of three little kids they didn't know. Yet Jo Ann seemed surprised and disappointed by the rebuff.

While still in elementary school, Jo Ann—once she was tall enough to operate the stove—was ordered to handle the care and feeding of her siblings. This did not always go well. Jealous at the attention lavished on her colicky little brother, she would pinch and pull his hair at times, take or break his toys, and generally be the prototypically rotten older sister. Eventually, though, they bonded. Decades later, long after her family had written her off and cut her off, Jo Ann still fondly recalls how he tried to cover for her when her stepdad berated or threatened to punish her. "My brother," she says, "was a savior in a lot of ways."

Jo Ann's home life improved after the whole family followed her lead and joined a nearby Church of Jesus Christ of Latter-day Saints congregation she had started attending with a friend. Jo Ann recalls that after converting to Mormonism, her stepfather's drinking slowed, then stopped. He got a better job. Lorraine returned to school in order to improve her own work prospects. Soon the family was able to purchase a nicer house in the LA neighborhood of Highland Park.

But after a period of stability, the stepfather began drinking to excess again and behaving bizarrely, and the marriage deteriorated. After Lorraine awoke one morning and found him trying to tie up and blindfold her in her sleep, she threw him out, asked him to seek counseling, and threatened divorce if he failed to get it.

Later, when it appeared the couple might reconcile, Jo Ann finally told her mother that she had been physically abused by her stepdad for years. She described to Lorraine one occasion when her stepdad grabbed her from behind while she washed the dishes and roughly shoved her head under the faucet. Then she claimed he told the sputtering, coughing girl that he'd kill her if she told anyone. Another time, she said, he dragged her across the room by her hair.

"She's just saying that to stop us from getting back together," he said when Lorraine asked about it. "It makes me sad."

Her husband really did sound more sad than angry to her, and Lorraine did not trust her daughter's motives. So not only did marital reconciliation remain on the table, but Lorraine insisted Jo Ann have regular visits with her stepfather, too, so they could repair their own relationship.

Jo Ann dreaded those visits. Her grades began to plummet. The excellent student in elementary school became a poor performer in middle school, then a disaster in high school. She failed to do homework. She dodged tests. She skipped classes, making up stories about going to school even as she missed more than two months of class before Lorraine got wind of what was going on. Then, a week or so after her sixteenth birthday, Jo Ann got pregnant. She would later say she didn't realize this for months. Neither did her family. She attributed her morning sickness to the flu.

She says an adult member of their church congregation sexually assaulted her.

By then, Lorraine's reconciliation attempts with her husband had collapsed. He began threatening to break into the house and to take their son away to Colorado, Lorraine later recalled. She said she had to change the locks on the front door to fend him off. Divorce proceedings soon followed.

Jo Ann's pregnancy, meanwhile, proceeded for nearly eight months without anyone noticing that it was more than a mix of flu, a bad cold, and overeating. She looked somewhat stouter, but she had been struggling with her weight for years. A few extra pounds, along with her penchant to be out of the house more than in, helped preserve the general cluelessness. She even recalls having what she thought were periods throughout that time. The serious downside of this sub-rosa pregnancy was that she had zero prenatal care and became severely ill with toxemia in the final month, when the secret finally was revealed. With medical care for both mother and baby belatedly begun, Jo Ann pulled through, and her son David, named for David Corrigan, arrived on time and in apparent good health on January 7, 1983.

Prior to his birth Jo Ann seemed adamant about giving up the baby for adoption. But in the end she insisted that she wanted David to come home with her. She recalls that her siblings were told not that she had been pregnant, but that she had been sick and had to be hospitalized for a few days. When David appeared, Lorraine offered a cover story: The family was just babysitting for a church member in need.

Lorraine, Jo Ann recalls, did not like or want the baby. She refused to hold him or to be responsible for his care. She said she did not consider him her grandson, according to Jo Ann, and perhaps sensing the hostility, David seemed to cry incessantly whenever his reluctant grandmother hovered nearby. Lorraine would not take off from her own studies to help with childcare, nor was she willing to help even when she was home and idle. Jo Ann had to take sole charge, an immature teen essentially left to her own devices with a newborn. Over the next few weeks, Lorraine continually urged her daughter to put David up for adoption as the best choice for all concerned.

Overwhelmed by motherhood, depressed about hiding it, and feeling bereft of her own mother's support, Jo Ann relented. She and Lorraine visited a Mormon attorney in Los Angeles—a prominent figure in the church hierarchy then, destined to become a leader in the church's national organization in the years ahead. He explained that there was a Latter-day Saints children's services agency that could find a good adoptive home for David with a Mormon family. Jo Ann thought the attorney was extremely kind and understanding, and she signed the papers he had prepared. David went to foster parents in a distant part of Los Angeles County, about sixty miles from Highland Park.

David's father, an adult member of the congregation, was sent away on a church mission. His name does not appear on David's birth certificate—no father was listed. Jo Ann, however, was placed on Mormon probation, a common form of discipline within the church for members who confess to having sex outside of marriage. In further punishment, Lorraine decided Jo Ann would have to live with a Mormon foster family, too, separated from both David and the rest of her family.

Although she had been under the age of legal consent, no police or county child welfare reports of sexual assault were ever made. It was all kept private, within the family and within the church.

Just a few weeks later, before any adoptive parents could be found, David died during the night while in the care of his new foster parents. The cause of death was reported variously as "crib death" and sudden infant death syndrome.

In the wake of David's death, Jo Ann began what would become a lifelong pattern. The lively child turned rebellious teenager turned distraught teen mother, described as friendly and outgoing by adults in her life up to that point, appeared emotionally numb when told of David's death. She seemed at first to take the news in stride, stoically, even mechanically. "Can you give me a ride now?" she asked Lorraine after her mother had broken the news. Jo Ann had made plans to see a movie that afternoon, she explained, and she didn't want to miss the showtime. Lorraine gave her the ride, and she watched the film as planned.

At the funeral days later, with flowers Jo Ann had chosen on display before a tiny coffin, the delayed grief finally seemed to find her. She seemed genuinely despondent at the lonely little service. But mostly she had felt disconnected from the entire pregnancy, birth, and death, as if it had happened to someone else, or she had been observing events in her life as if they were scenes in a movie, projected in front of her rather than inside her.

Years later, a psychologist would postulate that Jo Ann the teenager may have exhibited signs of a dissociative disorder similar to the post-traumatic stress disorder suffered by many combat veterans and other trauma survivors. Dissociative disorder affects about 2 percent of the population, primarily women. Such a diagnosis, if correct, would not mean Jo Ann was mentally ill or eligible for a legal insanity plea as a defense against any crime, whether shoplifting or arson-murder. But such an ailment could appear to blunt a person's emotions and, at times, make even a caring person appear outwardly uncaring or unlikable. Or guilty.

> I have grown up behind walls. I was this naive little girl that whatever their husband said went. I couldn't stand and say how I felt or what I wanted. All I cared about was giving my babies everything they ever wanted. I wanted their lives to be different than mine. I didn't want them to grow up in a single-parent household like I did. Or to want something and couldn't have it. I wanted the best for them and I couldn't give that to them.

Within a few weeks of David's funeral, Jo Ann ran away from the foster home. She had asked if she could go home, but her mother said no. She describes this time as living "on the streets," but usually she would find friends who would let her stay the night and feed her. Then she would just roam.

One evening she walked into a Laundromat in search of a warm place to rest. A thirty-five-year-old man loading his clothes into a big tumble dryer struck up a conversation with her. She invented the name Josefina Garcia to introduce herself, and though she was barely seventeen years old and had not completed eleventh grade, "Josie" gave her age as nineteen. She ended up going for pizza with this man, and then to his home, and then into his bed.

When she was about to leave the next morning, he asked her to return at five o'clock that evening. She didn't question it. She simply said, "Okay."

When Jo Ann arrived at the appointed hour, the man awaited her with flowers and a ring. He would protect and care for her, he promised the seventeen-year-old grieving mother. He said he was in love.

"You'll never have to feel unwanted or unloved again," he vowed.

Jo Ann burst into tears. Then she slipped on the ring. The following day, she retrieved her things from her foster home, then ran out the door even as her foster mom phoned Lorraine to report, "Jo Ann's leaving with some man."

Three days later, they were married. The marriage was illegal, as it was under Jo Ann's false name and birth date. But she didn't want to think about that, or the fact that at the start of her marriage, her husband called her "Josie."

Did Jo Ann know even then that she had attached herself to the sort of man she always claimed she wished to avoid—someone who shared many of the qualities of her stepfather? Decades later, Jo Ann would reflect that she probably had known this was the case at some level, but that the love and protection and solidity of age he offered her seemed like the ultimate seductive narcotic.

Like her stepfather, Jo Ann's new husband started out pleasant and docile, full of plans for starting his own businesses and building a life for the two of them far more opulent than either of them had ever known. In front of others, he would always appear so. Over time, however, he transformed into a verbally abusive, then physically violent tyrant when they were alone, Jo Ann would later say. But by the time she allowed herself to see this aspect of his nature, their first baby was on the way.

Jo Ann's life with Ronald E. Parks had begun.

10

They Told Me I Couldn't

"Mommy, what do you do at a prison?" four-year-old August Cohen asked one evening.

The question jarred Raquel Cohen. She hadn't noticed her daughter sidle up as she carped to her husband, Ryan, about the daunting logistics of her first visit with Jo Ann Parks at the state women's prison in the California outback. She faced a seven-hour drive to Chowchilla, the desolate location for the world's largest women's penitentiary. The Cohens' previous five-hundred-square-foot apartment, though a step up from living in her in-laws' basement, had offered no opportunities to sneak up on anyone. Their new and deliciously spacious two-story house in suburban San Diego, however, offered endless hiding, tripping, falling, spilling, and listening locations for a precocious pre-schooler, and August made it her mission to find and use them all. She is her mom in miniature.

Cohen's mind raced. She had never really tried to explain her all-consuming, frequently maddening job to her preschooler. How could she make her work on behalf of a person wrongly convicted of murder comprehensible without stripping away a child's innocence and confidence and optimism?

"Prison is like a place for adults who have to go in time-out," Cohen finally said. August's eyes grew almost comically wide at this, while Cohen cast about wildly for a way to be honest without terrifying her girl. "Now, for some of them, it's like if you were put in time-out but you didn't do anything wrong and you don't think it's fair. So my job is to get those people out of time-out."

August laughed with delight at the notion of her mommy, provider of juice boxes, bedtime stories, and reminders to go potty before sleep, as a human get-out-of-jail-free card. From that day on, whenever she saw some cartoon character or human actor land in jail, August would shriek some variation of "Mommy, go help them! Make them your friend and get them out of time-out!"

"It's actually not a bad description of what we do," Cohen mused later. "Except it leaves out the horrific parts. You know, the stuff that has me watching endless repeats of *Elf* or *SpongeBob*, just to block out the horror for a while."

Innocence work, the art of getting convicts out of the most soul-killing time-out ever devised—being guiltless while imprisoned and surrounded by predators—was not what Raquel Cohen envisioned for herself as a kid. Growing up in the heart of Las Vegas, young Raquel Barilla was immersed instead in the world of gymnastics and cheerleading, always training for a meet, traveling to a meet, or competing in one. She excelled at tumbling and vault, gazed at the balance beam as if it were a monster from a child's nightmare, and generally loved the sport until a shoulder injury sidelined her at age sixteen. Instead of a year of tedious, iffy, and painful rehab, she turned to coaching, finding that she loved that nearly as well as performing.

Then an undergrad class at the University of Nevada, Las Vegas shook her focus and, ultimately, her career plans. She was assigned to research a paper on death row inmates who turned out to be innocent. This was in the early 2000s, a time when news of wrongful convictions, once a rarity, had become a daily news staple. The maturing technology of DNA testing, initially touted as the ultimate search engine for the guilty, had emerged as the unexpected savior of the innocent, shattering decades of complacency about a justice system thought to have been far better at policing its own errors than it turned out to be. Through her research, Cohen became aware of the growing network of innocence projects clamoring for the systematic use of DNA testing to exonerate the wrongfully convicted.

A short time later, the local judge who had taken on Cohen as a student intern recommended a law school for her: the judge's alma mater, California Western School of Law in San Diego. Cohen already knew and loved California's southernmost beach town from frequent gymnastics competitions held there. When she requested more information from Cal Western, the material she received included a pitch from the California Innocence Project based at the school, outlining the project's need for volunteers, interns, and applicants for its clinical law program.

Reading that pamphlet, Cohen felt as if everything she had been doing, from gymnastics to her internship to her undergraduate classes, had converged and pointed her toward San Diego and innocence work. She applied and was accepted, starting law school and work with the project in 2007, with the goal of being hired on as a staff attorney after graduation.

Her introduction to the practical side of innocence project work came within a few weeks of the start of her first year in law school, when she was assigned to investigate the case of Jason Rivera. "Thrown into the deep end of the swamp," is how Cohen would later describe the experience. "I was scared to death." She later realized that this was the innocence project's modus operandi, because it revealed fairly quickly which students were a good fit for the work, and which weren't.

The Rivera investigation grabbed, enthralled, and horrified Cohen from the start. Little about the murder case made sense to her, least of all the catalyst for the destruction of multiple lives: One person died, one was gravely injured, and Rivera's freedom ended, all because of a ludicrous fight over a girl at a high school party.

When arrested, Rivera was an eighteen-year-old varsity soccer player who had never been in trouble in his life, the college-bound son of a prosperous and prominent family in the inland city of Riverside, California. Teamed with second-year student Alissa Bjerkhoel, Cohen met her first client on her first-ever visit to a prison. Rivera had just turned thirty-one years old at that point, thirteen years into his life sentence for murder.

The chain of poor choices and fatal coincidences that put him there started on the evening of March 18, 1994. Rivera had gone to Riverside's poshest neighborhood, Hawarden Hills, for a raucous "Celebrate Friday" party, which also doubled as a birthday party for his younger sister, Jennifer. Shortly after arriving, he encountered Dominic Luna, a formidable 220-pound sophomore football player with a grudge against Rivera. Luna disliked what he considered to be the disrespectful way Rivera had dumped his girlfriend, who happened to be a friend of the football player's. The confrontation turned into a fistfight. Bouncers patrolling the party quickly broke it up and ordered both young men to leave.

That should have been the end of it. But for his sister's sake, Rivera decided to return later, along with three other students. Two of the other teens were Rivera's friends, Richard and Paul. But Richard brought a third student, eighteen-year-old Manuel

Martin Navarette, introduced to Rivera for the first time that evening. Navarette had a gun in his jacket pocket.

The timing of Rivera's return could not have been worse. As he and the other students walked toward the house, a car came roaring up from behind and Dominic Luna jumped out. He grabbed Rivera and threw him to the ground between two parked cars. Then the husky football player—who outweighed Rivera by more than sixty pounds—crouched over his target, punching him hard enough to give him a concussion. Dominic's twenty-year-old brother, Albert Luna, stopped other partygoers from interfering with the fight even as Rivera cried out to his friends for help. Witnesses heard someone yell, "Blast him!" Then Navarette pulled out his gun and started firing. When he was done, Dominic writhed on the ground, seriously wounded. Albert Luna lay dying.

When the police arrived to sort out the mess, there was no doubt about Navarette's guilt. He ended up with consecutive life sentences, which meant he could not even apply for parole until he was nearly sixty years old. But witnesses gave conflicting accounts about other aspects of the fight, the shooting, and who shouted "Blast him," with one person testifying that it had been Rivera who called out those fateful words during the confusion and violence.

Prosecutors charged and tried Rivera and Navarette together, weaving a theory that the boys conspired with each other to return to the party to seek revenge on Dominic for the first fight. No one actually testified that there was such a plan, but prosecutors argued that Rivera must have known Navarette had a gun, otherwise he would never have shouted those words, *Blast him.* And if that were true, the law holds him as responsible for murder as the triggerman.

Rivera denied all of this, saying he and his friends had returned to the party with nothing more felonious in mind than picking up his little sister, so they could take her home and then move on to another party where they would be welcome. They had no reason to believe Luna would even be there, since he had been kicked out as well. Rivera swore he only met Navarette that night and had no idea he carried a gun.

Even prosecutors harbored doubts about their case before the trial. They offered Rivera a plea bargain in which he'd have to admit responsibility but would be spared hard prison time. Insisting on his innocence and unwilling to be saddled with a criminal record, Rivera turned down the offer. There are no do-overs when it comes to plea bargains. He literally rolled the dice with his future.

At trial, jurors believed the prosecution's narrative of conspiracy and revenge and found Rivera guilty. He received a single life sentence, with parole eligibility available only after at least fifteen years' hard time.

Cohen and Bjerkhoel dug into the case at once, spending many hours with Rivera and his family. They re-interviewed witnesses about the fight and the shooting—what was seen, what was heard, what was done, who said what. The two young lawyers were learning the art of how to be "reverse detectives." Cohen soon realized they were good at this, playing off each other, keeping witnesses off balance with pointed questions and sudden shifts in topic. The innocence project cannot afford staff investigators—it relies on the attorneys and a battalion of students to do the legwork—and the process is a fascinating analog to police work. Instead of building a case, the two law students were searching for holes, preferably new ones, to break down the narrative so assiduously constructed by the government. Reverse detective work is like deconstructing a building, exposing foundations that might be solid as a rock, leaving little room for appeal, or uncovering a rotting core, unable to support the assumptions laid over them that led to a conviction.

And Cohen and Bjerkhoel found those holes in the foundation of *People v. Rivera*. First they cracked Rivera's friend Richard, the only one in the group who knew Navarette before that night. Cohen reported that Richard even admitted to being the one who shouted, "Blast him!" That utterance had been the key to convicting Rivera, and it turned out someone else had shouted the fateful words.

Navarette confirmed this when Bjerkhoel appeared in his prison visiting room. He also grudgingly admitted Rivera had no idea he was armed that night. But when it came to signing a sworn affidavit, the convicted killer asked, "What's in it for me?" He'd only swear to it, he said, if the innocence project could help him get out of prison as well. That, the attorney knew, they could not do. And even if they could, it wouldn't help, because prosecutors would argue—correctly—that a convict in Navarette's position had no credibility. He would say anything if it gave him a shot at freedom.

When the innocence project cobbled together a habeas corpus petition based on Cohen and Bjerkhoel's findings, it got nowhere in the courts. The official reason the courts rejected the plea was "untimeliness," meaning it was too little, too late. The lasting lesson for Cohen was that, in any innocence case, the new revelations have to be overwhelmingly compelling or no judge was going to cut a convicted killer loose. It didn't matter that Rivera was a nice guy with enormous potential before prison, a model inmate once he was behind bars, or that there were some new holes in the original case against him. Absent a newly discovered videotape or some other incontrovertible proof that the government used false information to win the case, Rivera's habeas petition had little chance. The basic facts remained unchanged even after Richard's and Navarette's revelations: Rivera still came back to a party from which he had been ejected for fighting; he brought a posse for backup; one student in this posse of four had a gun; and the witness who said Rivera yelled, "Blast him," remained adamant that Rivera was the culprit. Those facts alone provided any appeals court more than sufficient reason to leave in place the jury's decision to convict Rivera and embrace the prosecution's revenge narrative over the defense's wrong-place-at-the-wrong-time interpretation of the facts.

Even so, Cohen and Bjerkhoel stayed with the case. Cohen worked on it through three years in law school, another year in a civil law practice while she waited for the innocence project to find enough grant money to hire her, and then continued when she was finally hired as a staff attorney in 2011. (Like a parolee facing a review board, every year Cohen anxiously awaits word on whether her grant will be renewed again, guaranteeing her one more year on the job.)

Throughout these years and job changes, she continued to visit Rivera, investigating and searching for new holes in the case against him. She also helped him seek freedom through parole as he continued his college studies and received counseling in prison that helped him overcome his bitterness from what he saw as his wrongful conviction for being the victim of a beating. Gradually, he accepted that he was not blameless—that his decision to return to a party he could have easily avoided had precipitated a needless death. Parole boards don't necessarily require a literal confession to a crime, but they do insist that potential parolees admit responsibility, and Cohen helped him understand that his choices led not just to his own loss of freedom, but also to another family's grief. His expression of remorse even persuaded members of the Luna family to support his parole. Rivera was released in December

2014, twenty years after the shooting and eight years after Bjerkhoel and Cohen first began working the case.

A few months before Rivera walked out of prison, DNA testing cleared another of Cohen's clients in a very different sort of case—a man convicted of three separate sexual assaults in 1998. All three involved attacks on young Latina women on their way to work or school early in the morning, all accosted in the same general area of Los Angeles. All three women pointed to Luis Vargas as their assailant, but only after much prodding by police detectives turned shaky descriptions into firm identifications. Based on that eyewitness testimony and despite his employer swearing Vargas was at work on his regular shift at the time of the rapes, he was convicted and sentenced to fifty-five years in prison. Meanwhile, the police remained silent about the fact that the same area of Los Angeles was being stalked by a serial rapist nicknamed the Teardrop Rapist, for a tattoo of a tear under one eye, who was linked to more than thirty rapes exactly like the ones Vargas had been convicted of committing. Vargas had a very faded teardrop tattoo of his own, from when he was thirteen years old and homeless. But after he was jailed, the real Teardrop Rapist continued his reign of terror for fourteen years after Vargas's arrest. More years passed before Cohen finally won a court order for DNA testing. The results showed the real Teardrop Rapist, who was never caught, was responsible for the crimes that sent Vargas to prison.

Yet it would take Cohen two more years to get him exonerated. And that was with a district attorney's office that *agreed*—eventually—that he should go free. In other cases, when prosecutors ignore even compelling evidence of innocence and fight to uphold convictions, many more years can pass before the molasses movement of the legal system finally lets the cell door creak open. William Richards, accused of murdering his wife on the basis of false testimony about his bite mark being found on the corpse, was cleared by the California Innocence Project in 2007, but he remained in prison ten more years due to the dogged opposition of prosecutors in San Bernardino, California.

From a legal standpoint, Cohen felt, Jo Ann Parks fell somewhere between the Rivera and Vargas cases. On one end of the spectrum was Rivera, whose case raised questions but lacked irrefutable proof of innocence. At the other end of the spectrum lay the DNA evidence that cleared Vargas, which, even according to the prosecutor on the case, pointed "unerringly to innocence."

The Parks case was muddled somewhere in the middle. Cohen felt she had science on her side in the Parks case, too, but unlike DNA analysis, which left no doubt when it excluded Vargas as the culprit, fire science relied on interpretation and opinion. Once Cohen had settled on exactly what sort of legal attack would be right for Parks, she would try to convince the DA's office to do what it did with Vargas: admit that a mistake had been made and Jo Ann Parks should go free. Cohen thought there was some chance of that happening. More likely, the DA would consult an expert who agreed with the original conclusion that put Parks in prison for committing a monstrous crime. In that case, a pitched and nerve-wracking courtroom battle would ensue. Then anything could happen.

One thing gave Cohen heart at the outset: The judge assigned to the case was Los Angeles County Superior Court Judge William Ryan. This judge did not have a regular court trial calendar. Instead, he specialized in deep-dive post-trial cases like Parks's, and he had a reputation for being thorough and independent, even if he tended to be unforgiving of lawyers who showed up unprepared.

Cohen was not sorry he had the case. It meant the judge who set Luis Vargas free would also determine Jo Ann Parks's fate.

Raquel Cohen prides herself on being tough. She is fueled by outrage at the system's failings and what she firmly believes is an inflated sense of certainty about its outcomes. This is not unique in her office and others like it around the world: Outrage is basically a founding principle and motivation for those who make innocence work their careers. "It's certainly not the money," she says.

But Cohen soon realized that the Parks case was not like any of her others. The outrage was there, but the toughness, the nothing-gets-to-me posture, had begun to fail her. It started with the pictures.

The Parks case file was filled with pictures. They were the heart of her case, because there was no physical fire scene left for her or any expert to examine. The apartment had been torn down decades ago. Its contents were long gone, thrown out or destroyed, the bodies long ago buried. Only photos were left.

So, using the big monitor on her desk at the innocence project, Cohen had begun a painstaking study of each crime scene photograph supplied in the original disclosure file. The disclosure file is the collection of police reports, images, interviews, witness statements, search warrants, and forensic analyses that are produced during the investigation of a crime. Most disclosure files are minuscule, because most cases don't generate much investigative work product. Many get scant consideration by the lawyers on either side who plea-bargain the results without a trial, the summary approximation of justice that keeps an overburdened system hobbling along. But in the minority of cases that do go to trial—the big cases and especially the capital cases—the disclosure materials become voluminous. Prosecutors are legally required to turn over all of it to the accused, even if—especially if—some of that material hurts the state's case and helps the defendant.

In theory this is a straightforward matter. The government has been required to show its hand ever since prosecutors in Maryland hid evidence that a convicted killer by the name of John Leo Brady hadn't actually committed the murder. This sufficiently outraged the US Supreme Court in 1964 to lead the justices to instruct all prosecutors everywhere that in the future, they were obliged to turn over all helpful evidence to defendants. These disclosures are now universally referred to as "Brady materials," and judges have the authority to punish prosecutors and free defendants when there are major violations. Many guilty verdicts have been overturned because prosecutors or police concealed important disclosures by accident or design. The State of California recently made it a felony for prosecutors to deliberately withhold evidence of possible innocence.

Nothing was missing from the Parks disclosure file Cohen received. But the digital photographs in the case, as is typical in any disclosure dump, were a disorganized mess mixed in with all the other files. Each photo was labeled by a computer-generated file name rather than a name that actually described the subject of the photograph, which meant Cohen had to sort through every one, looking to see if the actual image matched up with prosecutors' claims. So "12.jpg" turned out to be an exterior shot of the burnt-out hull of the Parkses' old apartment after the sun rose on the day of the fire. Photo "01h.jpg" showed the allegedly sabotaged extension cord lying on the floor amid ash and debris. Cataloguing all this proved a slow process, as Cohen kept clicking through, frowning at images that the prosecution claimed held incriminating burn patterns, where she only saw general devastation, char, and ash. She made notes of photos she wanted her expert to examine closely. And then came photo "AA029.jpg."

Cohen froze, at first not quite sure what she was seeing. The fire had distorted the form and coloration of the subject of the photo, which showed a portion of a fire-ravaged kids' bedroom. Then the charred objects at the center of the photo resolved into something recognizable and Cohen recoiled. She had stumbled on a photo of one of the dead little girls, RoAnn, sprawled across her burned twin-size bed. And this battle-tested lawyer, who blithely marches into the nation's most dangerous prisons to interview convicted killers, who faces off with seasoned prosecutors and cops with far more experience and resources at their disposal, had to fumble to clear the screen and flee the room—anything to avoid looking at any more of those images of Parks's dead children.

She would try very hard never to look at them again. And she would have nightmares for weeks about seeing the one.

That's when Cohen started to realize *People v. Parks* might differ from her other cases. There were several reasons for this. There was her own family history and its slight parallels with Parks's, in the form of a disappointing and dysfunctional father figure. Cohen's biological father had been an alcoholic and an abuser who left the household when Cohen was five. In the years that followed he would regularly promise to visit, or to attend one of his daughter's competitions. And each time, she'd wait, looking through the window for his car to pull in the driveway, or craning her neck in some gymnasium, peering over the crowd to see if she could spot her dad in the stands. Almost every time, he disappointed her. Only later did she learn that he had lived just two long Vegas blocks from the family for five years, yet he never let them know, never came by. His final act, after announcing to a sixteen-year-old

Raquel that he was dying of cancer and promising a lavish inheritance for her and her two brothers, was to leave behind an old wallet with five dollars inside, to be split three ways.

Her mom, like Parks's mother and Parks herself, ended up marrying the first man who came along after the divorce—the real estate agent who sold the family home after the breakup. But there the parallel to Parks's experiences ends: Cohen adores her stepdad, and after thirty years, he and her mom are still happily married. Cohen ended up with the nurturing, loving, happily chaotic extended family Jo Ann could never find for herself—which only heightened Cohen's sympathies.

Then there was the sheer trauma Parks suffered by losing her three small children, compounded by being accused and convicted of causing those deaths, made all the worse if she was actually innocent, then exacerbated once again by feelings of guilt and remorse for not doing more to save those kids. What greater hell could there be for a mother? How, Cohen wondered, do you even go on?

Soon Cohen found herself worrying about the wiring in her own house. She checked and rechecked the batteries in the smoke alarms, pushing the test buttons repeatedly to make them emit their earsplitting shrieks. She hired an electrician to check the house wiring for fire risks. Next she labored into the night drawing up escape plans for the family should fire ever break out, then worried that she had become obsessed. "That's just common sense," Ryan Cohen reassured his wife. "We should have done that long ago. It's a good thing."

Around that same time, a pair of San Diego–based therapists volunteered free services to all the innocence project's exonerated clients. The stressed-out staff attorneys also had the option of six free weekly sessions. When this was announced at a staff meeting,

Cohen clapped and shouted out happily, "Ooooh, I'll go! Everybody needs a little therapy."

Telling herself it was a lark, more out of curiosity than any perceived need, Cohen started her free sessions, determined to keep it to the six freebies. "Then I'll just stop and get on with my life," she told Bjerkhoel.

Sure enough, six weeks later, Cohen walked into the therapist's office in downtown San Diego, confident that it would be her last visit, and that she would make her counselor feel comfortable with that as well.

"Instead, it was a total disaster," Cohen told her husband when she came home that night. "I started bawling my eyes out, and all this stuff from the Parks case came up. I didn't realize how much it was weighing on me."

Far from presenting herself as the impervious professional ready to say goodbye to therapy, she embarked on an emotional, tearful discussion with her therapist about her sorrow for her client, her worry about raising Parks's hopes too high then letting her down, and her intense fears that there would be a house fire in her own home (a recent air conditioner installation, she admitted, devolved into a virtual inquisition of the electrician on the job). Finally, Cohen spoke of the parallels between her life and Parks's, how Cohen was a relatively new mother herself, a second child on the way, her first almost exactly the same age as Ronnie Parks at the time of the fire. Despite her best efforts to build boundaries between her personal feelings and her work, this case had bored through her professional armor like no other, and the thought of losing terrified her. And because she genuinely believed Parks should be exonerated, Cohen knew a loss would be devastating.

When Cohen finally fell silent, the therapist had looked at her and said, "Why don't we keep coming once a week." Then she promised the attorney discounted sessions for the duration of the Parks case. It's been more than two years since then.

"Hopefully we win," Cohen says, "and then I really can get on with my life."

Meanwhile, every time Cohen cracked open the file in the first few months of working on the habeas petition, she seemed to find a new source of outrage.

"Look at this!" Cohen jabbed at her computer screen, then banged her keyboard. "No matter what she said or did, they put a guilty spin on it. It's unbelievable."

She had finally finished her initial review of the massive Parks file, and she took exception to the original trial prosecutor's interpretation of Jo Ann's decision to have her tubes tied after giving birth to her third child with Ron Parks. He had made it into a motive for murder, and Cohen was fuming. "It's such bullshit!" she said aloud to no one in particular.

Cohen ticked off the reasons behind her client's decision. The Parkses were impoverished at the time. They had lost their home. Their car had been repossessed. They were behind on every bill. She had first asked about the possibility of tubal ligation right after the middle child, RoAnn, was born. She did this out of fear: She had been ill during the latter stages of that pregnancy, as she had been with David, the baby she lost. But then she changed her mind. She was only a few months past her twentieth birthday at the time, and she agreed with her doctor and Ron that she was too young for permanent sterilization. After Jessica's birth, she decided it was the right time. They were more broke and behind than ever, the marriage stressed, the bill collectors dogging them. After three kids, she said she was done and had the surgery.

"So Jo Ann is trying to be a responsible parent, to seek birth control and not have more children they can't afford and can't take care of properly," Cohen griped to her colleague Bjerkhoel, who was composing a brief about shaken baby syndrome on her desktop computer and listening at the same time. "And what does the prosecutor do? He argues that this perfectly reasonable choice is proof that she never really wanted children in the first place, that she viewed them as a cost and a burden and wished they had never been born at all. So she set the fire to get rid of them at last."

Bjerkhoel rolled her eyes at the official spin. The two attorneys long ago slipped into an easy relationship allowing them to work, vent, and share their outrage over bag lunches, all pretty much simultaneously. They say this mutual griping is a vital survival tactic inside a seven-lawyer operation battling juggernauts like the Los Angeles County District Attorney's Office, which has more than 2,100 attorneys, investigators, and staffers and a three-hundred-million-dollar budget.

"They really don't get how outrageous they're being," Bjerkhoel said of the DA's position in the Parks case. "They think they're on God's side, the good side. So anything goes."

Even as the two women shook their heads both in mock wonder and in agreement, Cohen smiled. She knew this almost precisely mirrored how prosecutors and police speak of the innocence project attorneys and experts, assuming they would be willing to say or do anything to win freedom for a client or cast doubt on police work because they are biased against authority. They are, in the words of one prosecution expert in the Parks case, "in the exoneration business."

"They're being ridiculous!" Cohen added some choice swear words to Bjerkhoel's assessment. Her husband, Ryan, who met Cohen at the project as a fellow intern and law student, likes to say he fell in love with her because she lights up any room she enters. Cohen glares whenever he says this. "I don't light up any room now," she would tell him during the height of the Parks case. "I'm like a dark cloud now."

This cobbling together of a motive out of seemingly innocuous, arguably praiseworthy information about a person's past may have outraged Cohen, but it didn't really surprise her. She knew this was how most criminal trials worked. Almost any fact can and will be spun to suit one side's narrative or the other's. If the Parkses had bought fire insurance right before the fire, that would have been cited as hard evidence of motive for arson. It's one of the first things investigators look for in any potential arson case, and the lack of any sort of pathway to profit from a fire would normally give them pause. In this case, instead of accepting the absence of insurance as evidence of possible innocence, police and prosecutors spun that fact as proof of a *guilty* state of mind: Jo Ann Parks must have thought if she bought insurance she would make herself a suspect. So choosing not to buy insurance became possible evidence of guilt, too. This was the adversarial legal process at work, Cohen knew. It was a given. And, after all, she would try to shape her own narrative, too, with the firm belief that her view of reality was the correct one.

Cohen rose stiffly from her chair, easing the pressure on her back, raising the cantilevered desk surface upward with her so she could stand while working. Photos, mementos of cases, clippings, and mottos on typed bits of paper surrounded her tiny workspace like a colorful, comforting reef. A framed picture of her daughter, Mia, at age one, held by a smiling Cohen, bears the label, XONR8N MAMA, a play on the California Innocence Project's phonetic abbreviation for *exonerate*, XONR8. Another photo portrays a broadly grinning Jason Rivera, flanked by Cohen and Bjerkhoel, on the day of his parole. There's a courtroom shot on the day another of the duo's clients, Kimberly Long, won a new trial in her murder case, with a tiny quote from Ecclesiastes taped below, THE END OF A MATTER IS BETTER THAN ITS BEGINNING. Nearby, handwritten cards bear these:

Strong people stand up for themselves but . . . stronger people stand up for others.

There is no force more powerful than a woman determined to rise.

They told me I couldn't.

Cohen gazed at the mottos without really seeing them. The government spin in the Parks case had suddenly grasped her full attention, not as a source of outrage, but insight. It wasn't just that this bending of the facts was a stretch. It seemed over the top to Cohen, more than the usual gamesmanship. Maybe the spinning went deeper, she thought. More importantly, it seemed that it came far earlier in the case than the trial, perhaps to the point where it influenced and even biased the investigation itself. Had the arson investigators marched through the burned-down house amped by a tale of cough medicine and murder, anticipating evidence of a monstrous crime and then seeing exactly what they expected to see? Had theory preceded evidence instead of vice versa? Would there even be a case if Kathy Dodge had never made that fateful call, then mysteriously disappeared from the case? Did that call lead the investigators to simply look harder for the telltale signs of arson, as they would surely argue? Or did that call lead them to see what they wanted to see, rather than what was there?

Cohen wondered if this spin, this possible bias, might provide a new and possibly powerful line of attack beyond the more obvious claim of fire science gone wrong. Might this be a case of an investigation so blinded at the outset that detectives had detected a crime that never actually happened?

Now that would make a great story to tell the judge, Cohen thought. If she could only prove it.

11

It's All Gonna Come Out in the End

It made her think of old episodes of *Father Knows Best.*

From the start, Ron insisted he wanted to be the family's provider, which was what Jo Ann craved—to be cared for, looked after, protected. She loved that he said he wanted her to be a stay-at-home mom.

But his commitment to this vision wavered and then collapsed. Life with Ron Parks devolved into an endless series of moves, evictions, jobs found, jobs lost, and cars repossessed.

The problem was not a lack of marketable work skills—Ron Parks had been trained by the US Army as an electrician while serving in the Vietnam War, where he strung power and communications lines in the combat zone. Yet he habitually left or lost the skilled factory jobs that capably supported his family, instead nurturing his ambition to start his own business while also fantasizing about becoming a professional singer. The closest he came to reaching his entrepreneurial goal was selling used household goods at swap meets, an enterprise that consistently failed to cover the bills even as it sucked up his time with strike-it-rich deals that never came through. And his hopes of singing for a living didn't even come that close.

Eventually, Ron shifted from his sole-provider stance to demanding Jo Ann abandon plans to resume her own education in favor of working a series of part-time jobs, mostly waitressing, to keep the family afloat. She would have to take on shifts that did not overlap with his, allowing the two of them to juggle childcare. Their time together became scant. When they were at home at the same time, she would needle him about his work habits or his failure to do his share of the housework. She would do this in front of friends or neighbors while he seethed and replied with a simple, "Yes, dear."

It would be his turn to shout and strike out later, once they were alone, although Jo Ann recalls he always took pains to hit her only when the children were out of the room.

A pattern soon emerged: Each time Ron's pursuit of his career dreams forced Jo Ann out of the home to work, they would accuse each other of neglecting home and children. Ron especially railed against his wife for spending too much money on clothes and toys for the kids. Even Jo Ann conceded that she had packed their home with the "Magic Kingdom" toys and dolls she had envied when she was a child.

"You're obsessed with Disney," Ron complained one day. "You love Disney more than you love me!"

This taunt spiraled into accusations that she was sleeping with coworkers or customers at her restaurant jobs.

"At least I have a job," she lashed back. Next, as Jo Ann alleges, Ron beat her with car keys in his fist till she bled. Then he ordered her to quit her job.

A week later, as money dwindled and his swap-meet sales faltered, the cycle began anew and she had to find a new place to work.

> We first got married by a preacher under my wrong name . . . then got married legally in Las Vegas with my mother's permission. My mother never liked Ron because he was her age. Plus, he tried to pick up on my mom, or at least that's what she said. That's the last time I saw my mom until after Ronnie Jr. and RoAnn were born. . . .

Friends, family, and neighbors had mixed opinions about the dynamics of the Parkses' marriage, with some concluding the older husband totally dominated his young wife, while others thought the reverse—in part because Jo Ann's many complaints about him were the most public part of their relationship. Their Christian Science practitioner, Paul Garman, who knew Ron before he married Jo Ann and was close friends with him, felt Ron's religious devotion helped him change from an angry, depressed veteran whose first marriage had crumbled into a much happier, better partner for his second wife. He believed Ron frequently felt "henpecked" by a more dominant wife.

According to Jo Ann, Ron left that impression with many people because he would always bide his time when she yelled at him, appearing to placate her. Then he would lash out in private. He also kept her away from her mother and sisters if he could, limiting their exposure to his temper and treatment of Jo Ann. He would berate her when she visited her mother without his permission.

"Family always causes trouble," he told her. He justified this sentiment by recalling how Jo Ann's mother had banned him from her house, supposedly because of his behavior during his first visit.

She claimed he tried to stick his tongue in her mouth during a hello kiss.

"She's wrong, I was just trying to be friendly," Ron protested when Jo Ann had questioned him about it.

Later Jo Ann would learn that she was not the first person in Ron's life whom he told "family causes trouble." There had been a previous Mrs. Parks in Texas, and Ron had griped about his in-laws causing trouble then, too. They also accused him of acting inappropriately when kissing and touching other family members.

His marriage to Norma Parks had other parallels to his relationship with Jo Ann. Norma was five years younger than Ron when they married in a whirlwind courtship—which put her at exactly the same age as Jo Ann claimed to be when she married Ron. They barely knew each other when they exchanged vows. They had a son—also named Ron Parks—in 1972, then the couple separated a year later. Norma accused Ron of beating her, of beating their little boy for not succeeding in his potty training quickly enough, and of shooting at both of them while driving by the house in a pickup truck. When Ron and Norma split up, he took Ron Jr. with him against her wishes, Norma claimed. A few weeks later, he agreed to return the little boy in exchange for getting custody of their pickup truck.

Norma also claimed that several mysterious fires occurred around Ron during their marriage, including a grease fire in their kitchen that caused serious damage but did not consume the house or injure anyone.

There was one more parallel between the two marriages: According to Norma, Ron liked to give cough medicine or other drowsiness-inducing drugs to his son to make sure he slept through the night.

. . .

As a result of the constant churn in jobs and income, Ron and Jo Ann frequently could not pay their bills on time, when they could pay them at all. They lived a rootless existence of constant moves all over Southern California, as well as several migrations to Las Vegas, where they stayed with Ron's uncle and worked in casinos. By the time they returned from Nevada to California in the summer of 1987, their marriage had congealed into a pattern of fighting, abuse, flight, and reunification. Twice Jo Ann moved in with her mother but eventually had to leave each time, giving in to Ron's pleas, threats, and physical force.

In early 1988, a few months after Jessica's birth, their financial and living situation took a sudden turn for the better. Ron landed a job at the Darigold ice cream packing plant. This time, Jo Ann saw, he seemed to want to stick with it. He liked the overnight work shift and being home during the daytime.

With a steady salary and their monthly bills under control, the Parks family moved into a small, one-bedroom wood-frame house in the south Los Angeles community of Lynwood. The house was run-down—the six-hundred-dollar rent was derided years later by the Parkses' attorney as "standard slumlord rate"—and the kids had to use the living room as their cluttered bedroom.

A few weeks after moving in, the main shortcoming of the Lynwood house became apparent: The electrical system, with its old wiring and venerable fuse box, proved to be inadequate and decrepit. Whenever someone turned on more than one electrical appliance at once—the microwave, the coffeemaker, the blender, the air conditioner, or some other appliance—the electricity in the entire house would shut off. According to the Parkses, if they turned everything off and waited for five to ten minutes, the electricity would resume working but go out again if multiple appliances were switched on.

For nearly two months, they repeatedly called the landlord about the problem, receiving many promises but no repairs. Finally Ron offered to hire a friend who could do the work inexpensively and then bill the owner. The landlord said no, that his own workers would take care of any issues. No workers came. Visitors to the Lynwood house, including Paul Garman, later confirmed seeing the electrical-system issues firsthand. The Parks family just got by with the constant power outages, periodically calling, with nothing to show for their efforts.

Then, on April 26, 1988, Jo Ann later claimed, she screamed and cowered when an enormous electrical spark flashed in the kitchen like a lightning strike, filling the room with the distinctive blue light of arcing current. Then she smelled the sharply acrid odor of burned plastic insulation drifting out of the kitchen.

She called Ron at work to ask him what she should do. He suggested she contact the Lynwood fire department. Firefighters came out that afternoon to inspect the home, and they reported finding faulty wiring leading into the house, as well as a deteriorated outlet and wiring behind the kitchen stove.

The firefighters determined the electrical system in the home was a possible fire hazard. They turned off power to the house entirely at the fuse box and filed a complaint with the city's code enforcement department for possible action against the landlord. Finally the firefighters advised Jo Ann to leave the power off until repairs had been made. She called the landlord and property manager yet again, and they promised to have workers there early the following morning.

While next morning slipped toward noon, the Parks family

tired of waiting for the repair crew. Eventually Jo Ann went out and bought a pair of smoke detectors for the house, which the landlord had not installed as legally required. Then Ron turned the electricity on again so the refrigerator would stay cool and milk for the baby would not spoil. Jo Ann later told fire investigators that they kept their other appliances switched off, waited for a while, and when everything seemed fine, they decided to go out.

Ron took Ronnie Jr. and RoAnn to the neighborhood park. Jo Ann recalls that she stayed home with Jessica, later taking the car to get a box of fried chicken from a nearby drive-through. Then she planned to bring the food and baby Jessica to meet the rest of the family at the park so they could picnic together.

At 3:40 P.M. on April 27, Jerome Samuel, a fire prevention officer with the Lynwood fire department, saw smoke while driving on Imperial Highway. He called his department headquarters so they could dispatch a firefighting engine company, then he drove to the source of the smoke a few blocks off the highway. He found the Parks house fully engulfed in flames. No one was home. A neighbor told Samuel that the family had gone out, but that she was babysitting their youngest child, Jessica. (Later Jo Ann would recall that Jessica was with her at the time of the fire, but she also says her memory for details of traumatic events is not always reliable.)

A short time later, according to Samuel, the entire Parks family arrived home to find the house in flames. Before the fire could be put out, almost all of the Parkses' possessions and most of the interior of the house were destroyed as they stood by helplessly and watched.

Ron Ablott, the same Los Angeles County Sheriff's arson specialist who would investigate the origin and cause of the fatal fire a year later, arrived long after the Lynwood fire was extinguished. He worked alongside an assistant chief from the fire department to trace the start of the fire. After walking through the rubble and examining the home, Ablott decided this blaze had been accidental, and that it started in the bedroom where Ron and Jo Ann slept.

The window in that lone bedroom had shattered during the fire. Flames had shot out, scorching and burning the outside of the house near the window. From this, along with a corresponding burn pattern inside, Ablott concluded that the fire started in that bedroom. He decided that these fire patterns pointed to an extension cord that supplied power to a small air conditioner in the bedroom window, and that overheating of that cord caused the fire. The cord had been coiled, and Jo Ann or Ron had dropped clothing on top of it. The high current drawn by the air conditioner, combined with the coiling of the wire, generated enough heat to melt the cord into the carpeting, Ablott theorized. He then presumed this overheating became great enough to ignite the clothing piled on top of the cord, and the fire spread from there—a rare but possible means of starting a house fire. A companion report written by the assistant chief, which was supposed to summarize his and Ablott's conclusions, blamed a "short circuit" in the air conditioner cord. This was a different mechanism for starting a fire than cited by Ablott, as a short circuit requires the baring of the two metal wires inside an electrical cord, which then must touch each other to create sparks and heat.

Ablott recalled lecturing Jo Ann about not coiling or covering electrical cords in the future, though he was not sure at the time that she fully understood what he was talking about. Although the fire was classified as accidental, Ablott's report nevertheless blamed Jo Ann and Ron's "careless maintenance of appliances in the southeast bedroom."

Ablott's opinion was based primarily on the large V-pattern in the bedroom around the air conditioner, and the fact that the flames that shot out from the bedroom window did the most damage to the outside of the house. This is a standard method of determining the origin of a fire by locating the area of greatest damage. But that standard may lead to deceptive results in fires where flashover has occurred.

The building was "fully involved" when firefighters arrived—the last and most severe stage of a house fire, which is often preceded by flashover—yet the Lynwood fire reports do not address whether flashover occurred or how it could influence evaluation of fire patterns. Nor is there analysis of the effect of the bedroom window shattering during the fire, which allowed air to rush in and create an area of greatest damage even if the fire originated elsewhere. Ablott disregarded or didn't believe Jo Ann's statement that the air conditioner had been switched off when they left the house. And although he mentioned in his report that Jo Ann claimed the house had electrical problems before the fire, Ablott's report makes no mention of the fact that the fire department had been there the day before and confirmed Jo Ann's complaints, declaring the electrical system a possible fire hazard and code violation.

Ron Parks hired an attorney to sue their landlords. As the case involved minor damages because no one was hurt in the fire and the Parkses' personal property had relatively little monetary value (the most costly item was a child's bunk bed worth a few hundred dollars), the legal claim apparently went nowhere.

But this fire, as well as the manner in which it was investigated—with its focus on wiring, confusion about a short circuit, and disregard for flashover—would loom large a year later in the far more catastrophic fire to come.

. . .

A few weeks after the Lynwood fire, the Parks family moved fifty miles inland to the desert city of Fontana, where housing costs were low and a nearly new apartment complex, complete with swimming pool, awaited. The apartment was a find, clean and spacious and one of the nicest places Ron and Jo Ann would ever rent together. Unlike the Lynwood home, which put the family in a neighborhood frequented by street gangs, drug dealers, and plagued by high crime, Fontana felt safe to Jo Ann. Yet there was trouble from the start. She felt isolated in the new town, far from family and friends. Ron's commute to downtown Los Angeles was long, and the Parkses fought constantly over whether Jo Ann should keep the car in the evenings and drive Ron to and from work.

The move to Fontana also coincided with a change in three-and-a-half-year-old Ronnie's behavior. One morning Jo Ann woke up and found half the contents of the refrigerator on the floor. Ronnie had climbed out of bed before sunrise and raided the kitchen. Another night, Jo Ann recalls getting out of bed to investigate a noise she heard, only to find the front door open and Ronnie running around outside at three in the morning. More often he would just get up after everyone fell asleep, then turn on the battered old Zenith television. And one time, Ronnie turned up with a book of matches he had discovered outside in an old barbecue grill.

By phone and in person, Paul Garman repeatedly counseled Ronnie about his wanderings and about playing with matches. Garman recalls how bright, articulate, and responsive the little boy was during these chats.

"Okay, Uncle Paul," he promised. "I'll be good."

A deadbolt lock on the front door that required a key solved the problem of Ronnie leaving the house. But the other late-night wanderings, though diminished in numbers, did not stop completely.

Life took a turn for the better for Jo Ann, though, a few months after moving. She found a new friend: Kathy Dodge, who had just moved into the apartment next door.

They first met when Dodge's pit bull lunged at the Parkses' cocker spaniel outside the apartment while Ron was walking the dog. Jo Ann, standing in the doorway, panicked and shrieked, "Get that dog out of there." But her alarm dissipated when it became clear the bigger pit just wanted to play, not fight.

"She's okay, you just have to get to know her, she's just an animal nut," Ron whispered to Dodge, who was looking askance at the screaming woman in the doorway. Soon the new neighbor had been invited in, and the two women hit it off despite the jarring first impression. They found they shared a few things in common: Dodge had a son close to Jessica's age, she understood the struggles of a young mom on a tight budget, and the two women shared a passion for crafting, knitting, and crochet work. Soon they were spending three evenings a week making pillows, afghans, and baby blankets.

"We both liked each other right away," Dodge initially would tell police. Later, she would tell a different story: Jo Ann wasn't her type of person to hang out with, but she associated with her anyway because she "felt sorry for her."

Either way, they did hang out quite a bit. Besides spending evenings together crafting, on weekends they'd hit the swap meets together, kids in tow. Some nights they'd watch videos together at the Parkses' apartment, even the Disney movies Jo Ann liked to watch. Dodge had trouble deciding if she found Ron handsome and charming, or a "pervert" because something about his behavior around kids, his off-color comments at inappropriate times, left her uneasy. According to Jo Ann, one of the things that put Dodge off was a comment Ron made about the house fire in Lynwood: "If one of the kids had died in that fire, I'd be a rich man." Dodge would remember things very differently a year later, to Jo Ann's detriment. In any case, nothing seemed amiss between Dodge and Jo Ann during the summer, fall, and winter of 1988. The two women spent time together almost every day.

They were an unlikely duo. Dodge, though a mere three years older than Jo Ann, looked a decade older, harder, and far more streetwise. Though slight, only five-feet-one-inch tall, Dodge took pride in being tough, combative, and handy with a gun. She would go on to accumulate a record of minor scrapes with the law, including shoplifting.

If she was bothered by Jo Ann's messy house, her approach to childcare, or her persona of a young mother overwhelmed by life and responsibility, Dodge never let on—not then, at least. In response to her acceptance and friendship, Jo Ann confided in Dodge. She spoke of her unhappiness with her marriage to Ron. She spoke about the fire and the electrical malfunctions that plagued her last home. She even revealed her deepest secret: her rape, first pregnancy, and the birth and death of David. Jo Ann rarely shared her past with anyone. She could not speak of David without weeping, not even to her mother. Yet she found herself telling Dodge, able to unburden herself with her new best friend.

Then one afternoon, early in December 1988, the friendship ended—over money.

Dodge babysat for the Parkses that day. When Jo Ann returned, Dodge grinned from her living room chair and held up an American Express money order she had purchased for five hundred dollars. Like the Parks family, Dodge often lived paycheck to paycheck, and when she did have more cash reserves than usual, she could not resist boasting about it. "I'm stupid," she'd later explain, "but I kind of show off money." She had received a settlement from a complaint against a restaurant chain, and she had converted a portion of it to a money order she intended to use as payment to join a travel time-share. It was an old-school money order, thick with copies and carbon paper, and Dodge waved it around dramatically.

"God, look at all the carbons, Jo Ann," she said. "How come they need so many carbons?"

Jo Ann smiled and nodded. They chatted briefly, then Dodge got up to check on the kids playing outside. Before she walked out, Dodge would later recall, she placed the money order inside her purse and left it in the living room. A minute or two later, Jo Ann soon followed her outside, saying she had to go home. Jo Ann would recall that there were other people in the house at the same time, including a pair of teenage boys she didn't know.

A short time later someone from the time-share arrived to pick up the money order. But when Dodge went to her purse, the money order had vanished. A minute later, Jo Ann heard loud banging on her front door, and the sound of Dodge cursing her out.

"Get out here, Jo Ann!" Dodge shouted. "Were you in my purse? Did you take it? Give me back the money order!"

Jo Ann opened the door and started to say she had not touched the purse and didn't steal the money order, but Dodge cut her off, screaming, "I'm saying you did steal it!"

Jo Ann slammed the door shut and shouted her denials through the wood as Dodge resumed banging. Then Jo Ann surprised Dodge by throwing open the door again, this time dumping a glass of water on her head. This did not cool things down. Dodge responded by grabbing Jo Ann and repeatedly punching her. Then she called 911 to report the theft and to request a patrol car to swing by to get her money back.

When Dodge told the police Jo Ann had stolen the money order, one of the officers asked if she had witnessed the theft. Dodge shook her head. Did anyone see it? Again, no. Jo Ann, standing there listening, invited the police in to search her apartment for the money order. They declined and soon left.

Dodge wagged a finger and said, "Only God and you know who did it. And it's all gonna come out in the end."

She stormed off. Over the course of the next few days, a bizarre apartment-complex siege began. Someone flattened the four tires on the Parkses' van. Christmas decorations Jo Ann had put up on the apartment front door were slashed with a knife. Jo Ann claimed Dodge walked up to her and flashed a handgun, then spoke threateningly about her three children.

Then it was Jo Ann's turn to phone the Fontana police—repeatedly. According to Dodge, officers first warned her that she could be arrested for harassment if she didn't back off. Then they told Dodge that anyone who left a young son home alone to go out to harass a neighbor could have her kid taken away by child protective services for neglect.

By the end of the week, Jo Ann and the kids had decamped to her mother's house in Los Angeles, their furniture and possessions taken to storage. Lorraine insisted Ron had to sleep outside in the van, so after a few days, the family moved to a cheap motel instead. Then after the holidays, Ron got laid off at the dairy, forcing the family into a homeless shelter. After two months there, Darigold rehired Ron. As soon as they had enough money for the first and last month's rent, they found their next rental house.

For the first time, there would be three separate bedrooms for the family, and a yard for the children to enjoy. "It's what we both long desired," he told his new landlord while making his rental agreement over the phone.

Rent of six hundred dollars and a deposit of another six hundred dollars secured the place, paid in cash to their new landlord, who met them near her home in the oceanfront enclave of Sunset Beach, many miles and millions of dollars from their new place in Bell. A day later, the Parks family began moving into the tiny converted garage at 6928 ½ Sherman Way.

With help from a friend and someone with a truck for hire, the Parkses carried their belongings into the cramped apartment's 528 square feet, with its tattered carpeting and yard overgrown with weeds. The windows in one of the back bedrooms were jammed or nailed shut, and Ron could not get them to open. There was no use in complaining, he told Jo Ann: The rental agreement made minor repairs and lawn care the tenants' responsibility. "I'm only charging you six hundred dollars' rent," the landlord had said. "You can afford to put some money into the place."

And so they did. Jo Ann bought and hung latex-lined floor-to-ceiling drapes for the living room. The curtains would prove to be nice-looking, inexpensive, and, it turned out, highly flammable. The old-school swap-meet television set with the big picture tube that had to warm up before viewing, along with its patched, taped, and extra-long electrical cord, came out of a dusty storage locker to be set up on a fiberboard TV stand in front of the living room windows and curtains. Ron stacked a brand-new videocassette recorder on top, with an electric window fan positioned next to it to ease the heat in the stifling apartment. All three appliances had to be plugged into the same outlet in a corner of the living room with the help of an extension cord. The cords ran along the wall to the outlet, where they may have gotten tangled in the drapes by accident, by small children playing, by the action of hoses and firefighters putting out the fire or, as the police would later allege, on purpose by an arsonist. Also under the window sat piles of cardboard boxes and plastic crates, filled with clothes and toys that awaited unpacking—or positioned as a fuel supply for an inferno. The Parkses recalled that they had placed the electrical and extension cords across the tops of the boxes; fire investigators would later claim the cords were placed dangerously—and deliberately—beneath the boxes, which created a fire hazard.

During the first week in the apartment, according to Jo Ann, she scolded little Ronnie twice for getting up late at night and turning on the old television set.

The family that had just experienced a devastating house fire a year earlier did not take the time to install the smoke alarms that their landlord had neglected to provide.

On April 8, 1989, Ron and Jo Ann would later say, they dropped the kids off at a babysitter's house. Then the couple spent the day at Universal Studios, where in 1989 the leading attractions were Earthquake: The Big One, which simulated an 8.3 magnitude quake, and Burning House, predecessor to Backdraft, a burning building attraction.

Then they left the park at six P.M., picked up the kids, and went home. While Jo Ann continued unpacking, Ron got ready for work, then tinkered with getting their new VCR to work with a television set built before there were such things as VCRs. He got it working just before he left a little before eight P.M. His time card shows he clocked in at Darigold at 8:24 P.M., but nothing else about the next four hours in the life of the Parks family can be known with certainty.

Did Jo Ann put her kids, then herself, to bed, only to be awakened hours later by screams, followed by the utter terror of being trapped inside a burning house? Or did she carefully stage the scene, drug and trap her kids, start multiple fires, then sit back and wait in safety for minutes or even hours until the house was engulfed, only then running next door, feigning terror? Can a witness, an investigation, a test, a burn pattern, or an experiment determine which is more likely, the accident or the crime?

All that is known for sure is that shortly after midnight, Bob Robison opened his front door to a seemingly frantic Jo Ann Parks pounding and begging for help, the night tinged orange by flames.

Three days later, Kathy Dodge made a horrifying and convincing phone call that seemed to fill those critical four hours with a chilling tale of murder by fire.

Jo Ann had no recollection of running into Dodge after leaving Fontana amid threats and fear. But Ron and Jo Ann did return there a few weeks later to pack up their hastily abandoned apartment, and Dodge would tell police the two women made amends at that time over the money order dispute.

"I'm not saying you did it, I'm not saying you didn't, but I'm gonna miss you and I do forgive you," Dodge recalled telling Jo Ann when they parted for good. She told the police that both women cried while saying their goodbyes. "It was sad," Dodge explained, "and I still do like her."

Yet Dodge's opinions about Jo Ann seemed to have changed radically in the four months between their fight over a money order and Dodge's call to the police about the death of the Parks children. In December 1988, it had been Jo Ann Parks whose call to the police led to talk of alleged child neglect by Dodge. It had been Ron who spoke of getting rich if only one of his children had died in an earlier fire and who had immediately responded to a newspaper ad guaranteeing "million dollar verdicts." And it had been Ron whose ex-wife claimed he doped his son with cough medicine to get him to sleep.

In April 1989, it was Dodge calling the police to level the same sort of allegations against Jo Ann, all the while assuring the detectives who interviewed her that she was "not doing this because I'm getting vengeance." Now it was Jo Ann who allegedly neglected her kids. It was Jo Ann dosing them with cough medicine. And now Dodge had Jo Ann as the "lawsuit happy" half of the couple and saying, "If Ron had come home five minutes later, Jessica would be dead and we'd be rich."

The police had little information on the Lynwood fire at that time, and so they had no way of knowing that this supposedly chilling comment Dodge recalled made no sense. Ron had not come home five minutes early or late on the day of the Lynwood fire—he had been at the park, waiting for Jo Ann to bring lunch. There is no evidence Jessica was ever in jeopardy that day. Dodge's account was wrong. Yet it would completely alter the course of a fire investigation, turning it into a murder mystery. Even the prosecution's own fire expert would later agree that the arson and murder case against Parks likely would never have happened without that accusatory call from Kathy Dodge.

As for the alleged theft of the money order that put Dodge and Parks at odds in the first place: If someone did steal it, the thief never tried to cash it. Dodge eventually got her money back from American Express.

12

Everything Which Is Not Law

There are nearly twenty thousand habeas corpus petitions filed in federal court each year in the United States, and several times that number in state courts—more than eight thousand in California's superior courts alone, where Jo Ann Parks's case resides. All of them are desperate, last-gasp pleas from men and women in prison. All claim to be victims of great injustice. And almost all of them fail. The courts reject them with breathtaking routineness, the guilt of those petitioning for relief under the ancient law deemed glaringly obvious, unworthy of the time and expense of a formal hearing to revisit old cases and causes. The sheer numbers alone demand a pitilessly high bar in a legal process Alexander Hamilton once described as America's great bulwark against tyranny, and that Thomas Jefferson praised as the ultimate legal protection for all:

"The Habeas Corpus secures every man here, alien or citizen, against everything which is not law, whatever shape it may assume."

The Founders had no idea what sheer numbers would do to

their lofty intentions, which is to render the habeas process into the courthouse equivalent of football's Hail Mary pass.

But the California Innocence Project's petitions are different. Inmates may churn out handwritten habeas pleas daily, or they hire jailhouse lawyers paid with cigarettes and canteen credits to do it for them. Only a select few, however, make their way through the innocence project's Pit to land before a judge, and that selectivity, coupled with the credibility that comes from past success at exonerating the wrongly convicted, means the courts will at least give a careful reading of the project's petitions.

Every staff lawyer at the California Innocence Project would be named as attorneys of record on Jo Ann Parks's habeas petition, but Raquel Cohen ran point on the case. It would be her reverse detective work that would have to convince a judge that a formal hearing had to be held for Jo Ann Parks, rather than the pro forma rejection that the vast majority of habeas petitioners face. To do that, to get a hearing, which is a much lower bar than *winning* a hearing, she would have to blow the government's case out of the water.

Cohen faced a tall order with that. Even in the sterile language of court filings, the facts of the Parks case—at least the four main lines of evidence that the jury chose to embrace—are undeniably ugly.

First there is the allegation that Parks tried to stage a fire in the little living room on Sherman Way by making small cuts in an extension cord, then wrapping the cord (though not the parts with the cuts) in a bit of the draperies. The prosecution persisted in calling this an "incendiary device," though it turned out to be incapable of actually starting a fire. Prosecutors said that wasn't the point; the failed device, just like a poor marksman's errant shot, showed criminal intent. When the "device" failed, arson investigators resorted to an age-old practice called "negative corpus," claiming no accidental causes could be found, and therefore Parks must have started it by hand with matches or some other open flame. Negative corpus is a play on the classic Latin term *corpus delicti,* the "body of the crime," from which is derived the legal principle that a person cannot be convicted of committing a crime unless that crime can be proven to have been committed. Negative corpus turns that principle on its head, holding that, even without actual evidence, the existence of a criminal act—such as setting a fire with matches—can be assumed to have occurred through the process of elimination. Negative corpus has long been a controversial tool in fire investigation because, unlike the lingering physical evidence often available in shootings, stabbings, rapes, and most other crimes, a deliberately set fire often consumes the evidence that can prove it was intentionally set . . . or that it started accidentally.

Next, the lead arson investigator on the Parks case swore that fire patterns on the walls, floor, and bed proved that a separate second fire had been set in the girls' bedroom, again by hand. Accidental house fires have single points of origin—the stove, a cigarette dropped on a couch, a faulty heater. But arsonists often start fires in several places in order to make sure an entire building burns.

The third and most chilling line of evidence is the investigator's expert opinion that burn patterns proved that Ronnie Jr. had been barricaded inside his bedroom closet during the fire. If jurors believed only one thing the prosecution offered, believing that little boy had been trapped deliberately in a closet to face a truly terrible and terrifying death would be enough to convict Jo Ann Parks all on its own.

The fourth and final line of evidence was designed to make

jurors *want* to believe the worst interpretations of the fire scene—to make them view Parks as capable of blocking her son in a closet as the house burned down. A parade of mostly police witnesses painted Parks as a liar and a cheat who changed her story about the fire multiple times. The prosecution used that information to construct a portrait of an unfeeling mother who didn't want her kids, who made insufficient and insincere efforts to save them, who showed too little grief when they died, and who sought to profit from her children's demise by filing lawsuits, seeking donations, and even pleading for free Disney tickets.

It sounded bad, Cohen knew. It sounded evil. And it had worked.

"For me, it was the arson evidence, the burn patterns, that convinced me," one of the jurors, Mario Trujillo—a firefighter himself—recalled many years later. "That, and her demeanor. There were witnesses who said she acted inappropriately."

Trujillo added that while the men on the jury were divided at first on her guilt or innocence, the two women on the panel felt strongly from the start of deliberations that she was guilty, based primarily on her demeanor, her leaving the scene with the police before her children's fate was known, and her failing to dash into the building and get burned herself. "No mother would act like that," Trujillo quoted one of the women on the panel. "She's guilty based on that alone."

Parks's freedom would be won or lost on countering the minutiae of the prosecution's case. Yet to get Parks a new day in court, Cohen had to grab the judge's attention with the big picture. She needed to offer a compelling narrative, a first act that portrayed the case not simply as a lone travesty of justice, but as just one dramatic example of a sweeping, nationwide scandal of bad science and bad faith in desperate need of reform. She needed the judge who would decide Jo Ann Parks's fate to see the case as both historic and emblematic. In the opening pages of the petition, the attorney wrote:

> In 1993, Jo Ann Parks was convicted of murdering her three children based on untested and outdated theories of arson science.
>
> The fire investigators falsely testified . . . to these conclusions by (1) using the outdated theory of negative corpus; (2) allowing their expectation bias and "junk science" to steer their investigation; and (3) basing their findings on the incorrect assumption that flashover did not occur.
>
> By today's methods, none of the allegedly incriminating evidence used at Parks' trial supports the prosecution's theory. Fundamentally speaking, the investigators and jury were misled by biases and "junk science."
>
> Tragically, Parks is now serving a sentence of life without the possibility of parole for a crime that never occurred. The death of the victims in this case were the product of an accidental fire.

In order to make such a sweeping attack stick, Cohen had to undermine the four main pillars of evidence that had convinced a jury to convict a young mother with no criminal record and no history of violence of three counts of premeditated murder. The key, she believed, was to go after the work of the lead fire investigator, Ron Ablott. His steady, deep-voiced, authoritative testimony had been critical at the original trial. If she discredited his findings, Cohen believed, there would be no case left standing against Parks except for the claims she hadn't been grief-stricken enough. And there were plenty of witnesses who had seen just the opposite. So Ablott's mastery of fire science—or his lack of it—would be key. Knock that down, Cohen reasoned, and there would be no evidence of Parks's guilt. There would be no evidence of any crime at all.

Most law schools don't teach their students how to re-investigate a fire scene. They test for and reward students who master matters of precedent and legal interpretation, who learn to argue the sufficiency of the evidence, and who can discern whether some line of testimony is relevant or improper, probative or inflammatory. The goal is to foster attorneys who can do battle with motions and memoranda and offers of proof—who can wage and win war, in short, with paper.

When first-year law students apply to the California Innocence Project, they are given a different sort of test. More of an audition, really.

One might be asked: "Go to the W Hotel and get the front desk clerk to tell you the most famous person who stayed there in the past six months."

Or: "Find out the elementary school that your professor's kid attends without asking directly."

Or there was the assignment first-year law student Raquel Cohen faced: "Obtain your professor's DNA without him knowing it." (Solution: She followed him to a restaurant and wrestled his water glass from the busboy after he left.)

"Yeah, nobody else does that," Justin Brooks, the founder and head of the California Innocence Project, explains. "But the idea is to see how tenacious they'll be in the field. We want to weed out people who are too shy or unimaginative or who don't put in the effort to complete the assignment."

Innocence work is lonely work, he says, and it requires maximum effort for uncertain and infrequent returns. So Brooks looks for a certain type each year to fill the ranks, as the students do much of the investigation in his shop, and the best of them join the ranks of the staff attorneys. More than good grades, high scores on the LSAT, or Ivy League pedigrees, Brooks is looking for tenacity and work ethic and a certain lack of deference for the official story—an essential trait for reverse detective work.

Brooks intentionally makes these pivotal application tests come due during the middle of finals, when the law students are crazy busy and stressed. "They have to really want this, have to be willing to make a sacrifice. Those are the kids I want."

The idea of working full-time as an innocence lawyer was unheard of until fairly recently. Up until the 1990s, those who ran and studied the justice system presumed that the innocent only rarely suffered wrongful convictions, a notion bolstered by modern legal protections for the accused such as Brady, Miranda (safeguarding the right to remain silent and have a lawyer upon arrest), and Gideon (the absolute right to a lawyer when on trial, regardless of means). Added to that was the evolution of modern forensic science for identifying the guilty through the technological wonders popularized by the TV show *CSI*—through which everything from hair and fibers to paint chips to bite marks to striations on bullets could be matched to suspects with unerring clarity. It seemed there was no room for error.

Even before those protections evolved, the idea that false convictions were rare was rooted in the system with more than a little arrogance. Learned Hand, one of the most quoted judges in history and generally known as a liberal defender of civil rights, wrote in 1923 that the system "has always been haunted by the ghost of the innocent man convicted. It is an unreal dream." Eighty-four years later, the late justice Antonin Scalia would echo those thoughts in a concurring opinion, adding a completely specious calculation of his own that the error rate in criminal convictions was vanishingly small, .027 percent, "or, to put it another way, a success rate of 99.973 percent." Scalia arrived at this number through the sleight of hand of counting all types of convictions, including the vast majority that are won by criminals pleading guilty. (In 2014, a more scientific calculation of error rates among men and women sentenced to death—the sort of case that gets the most scrutiny by appellate courts—found that four out of a hundred are actually innocent, an error rate one hundred and fifty times greater than Scalia suggested.)

The idea of justice system infallibility took a serious hit, however, in 1989. That was the year a new use was found for the ultimate forensic science breakthrough: DNA matching. Touted by police and prosecutors as the new gold standard for linking criminal to crime, it also turned out to be a powerful tool for setting the innocent free. Gary Dotson, serving a fifty-year sentence for a 1977 kidnapping and rape in Illinois, became the first person in the United States to be exonerated by DNA evidence. His conviction had been based on eyewitness testimony, a police sketch, and blood type matching that was "consistent" with the rapist (as well as with ten million other American men who had the same blood characteristics). A DNA analysis could, in theory, narrow down the true rapist to only a handful of people on the planet, and by voluntarily seeking DNA testing, Dotson ran the chance of that happening—of proving his guilt beyond any reasonable doubt. Instead, the analysis showed with certainty that he could not have been the rapist, proving all that other "solid" evidence against him had been completely false. The case also called particular attention to just how unreliable eyewitness testimony can be—or how easily witnesses can be swayed in the wrong direction by suggestive questioning or prodding from police or prosecutors.

By 1992, with a scattering of lawyers around the country pushing to repurpose the crime-fighting technology of DNA testing to free the innocent, ten imprisoned people had been exonerated through new DNA evidence. There was only one prominent innocence organization in the nation at the time, New Jersey–based Centurion Ministries, but then the floodgates opened. A pair of lawyers decided to build an entire law practice around DNA exonerations. They called it "The Innocence Project," the first of its name, founded at the Cardozo School of Law in New York by attorneys Peter Neufeld and Barry Scheck. Scheck would also be part of the "dream team" of lawyers involved with the successful defense of football great and murder defendant O. J. Simpson.

By 1999, four other innocence projects had opened, in Washington State, Illinois, Arizona, and California. Their leaders met in Chicago over pizza and plotted an innocence network to share information and tactics and to advocate laws to make reopening cases with DNA and other new evidence easier in the future, as many judges and prosecutors balked at the expense and inconvenience of testing evidence from old, long-settled cases. By 2018, the laws had changed in many (though not all) states, and sixty-six US-based innocence projects had launched, with another ten in other countries joining the "Innocence Network" as well.

These groups have been the driving force behind the more than 2,250 exonerations of the wrongly convicted by 2018—men and women who have collectively served nearly 20,000 years in prison for crimes they didn't commit. Faulty or erroneous forensic evidence was cited as a frequent contributor to these wrongful convictions.

Justin Brooks got his start in innocence work when he was still a tenured law professor raising a family, secure in his job and place in the world at a Michigan law school. As a first-year law student, he had gone with a class to visit a prison, which changed his perspective on the criminal justice system, leading him to focus on defense work. But it was an article about the plight of a young Chicago woman sentenced to death at age twenty-one that propelled him into innocence work. Accused of participating in a double gang killing with two other members of the Maniac Latin Disciples girl gang, she had been questioned for nine hours straight by police before confessing—a confession she later claimed was coerced. Her attorney did little investigation, interviewed no witnesses, and spoke with his client for about ten minutes before setting up a "blind" guilty plea to murder charges for her, with no specified sentence—virtually unheard of in a capital case. She was sentenced to die. Shortly after that, the lawyer gave up his practice and became a priest.

When he read about the case of Marilyn Mulero, Brooks decided to visit her in prison and walked away believing in her innocence. Had her attorney explored the crime scene, it would have been clear that the only eyewitness to the shooting had lied, that she could not possibly have seen what happened from her vantage point. Plus Mulero was a poor kid of Puerto Rican descent, which touched a chord in Brooks, who spent part of his childhood in Puerto Rico and graduated from high school there, courtesy of his professional tennis player father's wanderlust.

Back at the law school, he announced to his class, "There's a girl on death row who says she's innocent. Who wants to help me out?"

Four students raised their hands. Four years later, Brooks and his crew of student investigators succeeded in getting Mulero off death row and sentenced to life instead, even as he continued to work on getting her guilty plea tossed out as well. He remembers sitting out in his car that night, on a bitter cold Chicago street, exulting in the victory and possessed of the conviction that he was going to do innocence work for the rest of his life. Within the year, he gave up his tenured position to relocate to San Diego and, for half the pay and twice the cost of living, launched the new California Innocence Project at California Western Law School.

He has been representing Mulero for twenty-two years now. He flies to Illinois to visit her at least once a year. She has watched him walk twenty-seven wrongfully convicted men and women out of prison during that time. Those clients ranged from Brian Banks, a football star falsely accused of rape, to Michael Hanline, who served thirty-six years—the longest wrongful incarceration in California history at the time of his release—for a murder conviction won because police, prosecutors, and a judge buried evidence that the wrong man had been arrested. Brooks has used a range of tactics, too. Sometimes he works jointly with prosecutors to right wrongs without battling in court—a cooperative approach that makes him an outlier in the innocence business. But he has also marched more than six hundred miles with his staff from San Diego to the state capital of Sacramento to champion the "California 12," a group of project clients Brooks wants the governor to pardon. He also hounds, cajoles, and pokes Governor Jerry Brown daily on Twitter about the California 12, whose number includes Jo Ann Parks.

But for all his efforts, the courts have refused to grant a new trial for Mulero, his first innocence client. The reasons are technical and procedural: The evidence of innocence was available when she pleaded guilty, so it does not meet the test of "new evidence" of innocence, and the courts have rejected lawyerly incompetence as a grounds because Mulero pleaded guilty instead of going to trial. Never mind that it was her lawyer's bad advice that led her to accept the guilty plea in the first place. Now, unless the governor of Illinois commutes her sentence, she will die of old age in prison. Her appeals are exhausted.

The facts in the Jo Ann Parks case are completely different from Mulero's, and yet the same roll of the dice is in play, the same concern that procedure and technicality could take precedence over evidence of innocence. Cohen could assemble a team of fire experts who would say the original investigation led by Ronald Ablott got it all wrong. But the district attorney's office could simply argue that Parks's petition has been filed too late, or the new facts aren't really "new," that they were argued at the original trial by the original defense experts, which means the trial was fair and the jury made its choice: Game over. Such arguments have worked well for prosecutors in other cases. And so Brooks and Cohen can only wonder and worry: Will Parks be the next Michael Hanline or the next Marilyn Mulero?

By the time he first testified as the prosecution's primary fire expert in the *People v. Parks,* Ron Ablott had worked for the Los Angeles County Sheriff for twenty-eight years. Before joining the department, he served an army combat tour in Vietnam and a brief stint as a draftsman in the junior engineering program at North American Aviation, makers of the famed X-15 rocket jet and the Apollo space capsule. His aspirations to become an aerospace engineer ended with an industry downturn, and the resulting layoff led to a job working seventy hours a week delivering dry cleaning. Then he bumped into a high school friend's dad, a veteran Los Angeles County Sheriff's arson investigator, who said, "Why don't you apply to the sheriff's department? They don't lay off people."

Ablott took that advice and ended up graduating from the sheriff's academy with the next class of trainees. After a requisite tour of guard duty at the county jail, where all sheriff newbies begin, he worked his way up from patrol officer to detective rank, joined the homicide unit for ten years, then moved into the arson and explosives detail. There his friend's dad, Bob Bishop, became one of his mentors, part of an elite group of fire investigators who had been working the job since the 1940s and '50s. By the time of the Parks fire, Ablott had done thousands of origin and cause investigations, and had been qualified to testify as a fire expert in more than a hundred court hearings and criminal trials.

On April 17, 1989, eight days after the fire, Ablott and his partner made their first trip to the burnt-out shell of the Parks apartment. The Bell Police Department, sufficiently convinced by Kathy Dodge that they might have a murder-by-arson case on their hands, had requested help from the sheriff's arson unit.

They were met outside the apartment by Bell Police Sergeant William Talbott and Captain William Franklin of the Los Angeles County Fire Department, the initial fire investigator on the case, who had photographed the scene on the day of the fire. Franklin explained to Ablott how he and a novice investigator, Captain Lester "Fuzzy" Fuzell Sr., had used digging tools to excavate some electrical cords covered by a thick coating of ash that hose water had turned into a slurry, now dried. He said he was particularly concerned about the end of an extension cord that had several appliances plugged into it—the "octopus," as he called it—that was located near the largest V-pattern in the living room, beneath the windows. Franklin said he believed that was where the fire could have started—an accidental electrical fire. He had photographed the octopus of cords, then left them near where they were found. The photos show a couple of small cuts in the cord near the octopus, none of them wrapped in drapery, in an area where shovels had been used during overhaul.

Talbott then briefed the sheriff's fire experts on Kathy Dodge's allegations and on the fire a year ago in Lynwood that also involved an electrical cord. He had to remind Ablott that he had investigated that first Parks fire as well, and that he had ruled it accidental.

Decades later, Cohen would argue that, in this briefing, bias contaminated the fire scene investigation at its very start, leaving its findings questionable at best, fatally flawed at worst.

She did not mean bias in the common sense of the word, as a willful and malicious state of mind, synonymous with conscious racial, gender, or religious prejudice. Cohen would suggest an entirely different cognitive bias, a normal, instinctive, subconscious function of the brain. It is not an insult to be accused of cognitive bias. Everyone experiences it in some form every day, as part of the brain's pattern-recognition system that allows us to anticipate and prepare for events before they occur. One form, expectation bias, evolved as a survival mechanism—the brain filling in blanks in perception and information with what we expect from past experiences and other clues. But during subjective and abstract tasks, such as reading the meaning of fire patterns, the sort of information Franklin and Talbott provided can lead the human brain to perceive the patterns that a person *expects* to find, or that confirm an existing opinion—the closely related confirmation bias. This brain function explains why most people are so accepting of information—from news reports to political speeches—that supports what they already believe, while feeling deeply skeptical of even the most well-researched and verifiable information that challenges our existing assumptions and beliefs. Resisting such tendencies, keeping an open mind rather than succumbing to "tunnel vision," is a difficult challenge for anyone, but especially for expert investigators, who tend to be extremely confident in their opinions and abilities.

This common form of cognitive bias is the reason research scientists and medical researchers construct "blind" studies, so that neither their test subjects nor the researchers themselves can be influenced by knowing, for example, which subjects receive a medication and which are imbibing a placebo. Although the virtues of blind scientific studies have been understood for centuries, the pitfalls of not working "in the blind" in criminal investigations only became clear in recent years, with the FBI's disastrous examination of fingerprints related to the terrorist bombings in 2004 of four Madrid commuter trains that killed 192 people and injured more than 2,000. Three FBI fingerprint examiners separately concluded that a bag of detonators used by the bombers held fingerprints matching a Muslim American attorney in Oregon who had previously defended Al Qaeda terrorism suspects. Brandon Mayfield spent seventeen days in jail before Spanish authorities identified an Algerian terrorist as the true source of the prints. The Justice Department later concluded that "confirmation bias" and a "loss of objectivity" led examiners to see in the fingerprint comparison "similarities . . . that were not in fact present."

Divining the meaning of burn patterns at a fire scene requires even more subjective judgment than fingerprint comparison. In the Parks fire, Franklin, who initially saw an accidental fire, knew nothing about Kathy Dodge or Jo Ann Parks at the time he examined the physical evidence at the scene. Ablott, however, recalls walking into the house and immediately seeing signs of intent—of seeing that "something was wrong." A prosecution expert working to uphold the conviction decades after the crime asserted that Ablott also was likely already thinking during that first walk-through that the first nonfatal house fire in Lynwood had been arson, too, but that Jo Ann had fooled him into ruling it an accident.

The forensics community is divided on what can or should be done about the issue of cognitive bias. Those who favor a scientific approach believe investigators trying to determine the origin and cause of a fire should examine the scene without knowing anything about the personalities, motives, or suspicions in the case. That way the physical evidence can be interpreted free of bias. Why, they ask, does a fire expert need to know someone has been accused of being a poor parent in order to interpret a burn pattern? Why take the risk of bias creeping in?

Those who, like Ablott, come to forensics through detective work rather than lab training argue that such a blind approach is impractical—arson investigators must work the scene but also work the people, just like any detective. Omitting the human element, according to this view, would rob investigators of insights they need in order to know where to look and what to look for at a fire scene. Ablott needed to know about the previous fire, according to this view of the issue, because it alerted him to look more closely for signs of arson. Arson detectives say two house fires involving the same victims in the space of a year is a reliable indicator that they were not accidental. The scientists say the forensic analysis of each scene has to stand on its own; making assumptions about the physical evidence in one fire simply because there was an earlier fire is a demonstration not of acumen, but of bias. It is akin to the "Gambler's Fallacy," which is the false belief that in a game of chance, such as dicing, the odds of a winning roll increase after one or more losing rolls—the gambler assumes he "is due." In fact, prior dice rolls have no influence at all on future rolls—the mathematical probabilities on any given roll never vary. Likewise, the existence of an earlier fire may seem suspicious, but that doesn't change the nature of the physical evidence at the second fire, nor should it alter the scientific analysis of either fire scene.

Ablott would later say he resisted concluding that the Parks fire had been intentional for as long as he could, but that he finally had to accept the terrible reality of what the evidence revealed to him. Cohen asserts Ablott's perspective of "resisting the inevitable" before declaring Parks guilty is the very definition of cognitive bias; Ablott says his cautious deliberation before reaching a final conclusion demonstrates his unbiased approach.

"I just did not believe in my mind, coming from the family in which I was raised, that anybody could do that to their children," the seasoned former homicide detective would say years later. "It was just hard for me to fathom, but I finally had to conclude that was what happened."

Ablott, who retired from the sheriff's department in 1998 but still works as a private fire scene investigator, says he has always tried to avoid errors and bias by examining every fire scene in the same systematic way. He walks and examines the outside first, snapping pictures in sequence, then moves inside to inspect room by room. He's left-handed, and so he tried always to circle clockwise around each room, leading with his right side, so it felt a little uncomfortable for a lefty. He felt this kept him more alert to details and patterns that can indicate a larger area of origin for the fire, or allow him to narrow the field to a more specific point of origin.

During his walk-through of the Parks living room, he immediately seized on the power cords that Franklin had pointed out—the extension cord and other wires that had connected the TV, VCR, and fan to a single outlet in the corner. He found bits of charred drapery material wrapped around portions of the cord, most of which had been badly damaged in the blaze. Tracing the path of the cord along the living room wall, he found the remains of a blue plastic crate or basket and underneath it, a portion of the cord that had been protected from the flames. This was a section with small cuts in the cord's insulation. No drapery wrapped this portion. Ablott decided the various "modifications" to the cord couldn't have happened during the firefighting and overhaul with metal shovels and other tools. Instead, Ablott concluded that the fire probably had started with those wires—that insulation had been stripped away deliberately to cause a direct short circuit, and that the electrical system was purposely overloaded to heat up the damaged wire and start a fire. The draperies could then have become the fire's first fuel, allowing the flames to take root and spread, he concluded. This initial finding was remarkably similar to what he opined in the Lynwood fire a year earlier, except he had deemed that blaze accidental and the damage to the cords caused by fire and heat.

For more than a year, Ablott maintained his opinion that a deliberate short circuit caused the fatal fire, even though it should have been obvious from the start that a short circuit with those cut cords was highly unlikely if not impossible. The cuts to the wires were so small that only one conductor was exposed at any one spot on the cords. But both metal wires would have to be bared and touching for there to be a short circuit, heat, and sparks.

Furthermore, there is no evidence that the circuit breakers in the house tripped before the fire—which they are designed to do, automatically cutting power when there is either a short circuit or an overload. This should have suggested to Ablott that either there was no short circuit or, if he were correct about a short, that the breakers malfunctioned. That, in turn, would introduce another possible cause for the fire—deficiencies in the apartment's conditions. But despite the landlord's history—cited for violations more than two dozen times in four different cities, including Bell—and despite the absence of legally required smoke alarms in the apartment, no investigation of the landlord's maintenance practices was undertaken in the Parks investigation.

The only examination of the electrical system was done more than two months after the fire by an electrician hired by the landlord's insurance company, who found nothing wrong. His findings in favor of those who were paying him were accepted without question by the authorities. An arson expert hired by the landlord's insurer, a former Los Angeles Fire Department investigator named Steve Takach, was allowed to attend meetings with police investigators and to contribute his photos and opinions, which were so extreme that he concluded Parks had doused the girls' bedroom with a flammable liquid such as gasoline in order to accelerate the blaze. (That flammable-liquid idea has been rejected by every other expert and investigator involved with the case; Takach apparently relied on the sort of false indicators of arson that John Lentini exposed in the Lime Street fire experiment.)

As he formed his own theory of electrical sabotage, Ablott discounted alternative accidental causes for the living room fire, including the Parkses' old swap-meet television and other electrical appliances, recalling how he had found the TV outside the fire's area of origin during his first visit to the house on April 17. Only that sabotaged wire was in the right place to have sparked the fatal fire, he wrote in his arson investigation report.

But in the summer of 1990, Ablott's theory fell apart. That was when detectives pulled the wires out of evidence storage, got permission to x-ray them at the coroner's lab with equipment intended for autopsies, then had a forensic electrical engineer look at the X-rays and the wiring in order to confirm Ablott's opinion of deliberate short circuit. Instead, the engineer, William Armstrong, a former Jet Propulsion Laboratory rocket scientist given to wearing lab coats with the moniker MR. WIZARD on his name tag, said there was no way those wires started a fire. There had been no short circuit or overheating, just partial melting of the insulation from the heat of the house fire—burned or melted from the outside, rather than from the inside, as would occur during an electrical overload. Armstrong also confirmed that if someone deliberately wrapped draperies around the wires to start the fire, the saboteur had, oddly, neglected to wrap the parts of the wire that were cut. Which begs the question: If someone was constructing an incendiary device, wouldn't the logical step be to wrap the exposed wires with the flammable drapery material?

Investigators and prosecutors responded by rebranding the cords, calling them a *failed* incendiary device. Armstrong's report provided ammunition for that. Armstrong, whose expertise was electrical engineering, not edged weapons or differentiating cuts made with knives from those made by scissors or the edges of shovels, nevertheless rendered an opinion that the cuts had been done with a sharp knife. He also opined that a four-year-old child playing with a knife would certainly have cut himself in making such slices in the electrical cords. And none of the children had cuts on their hands. These opinions, though seemingly outside Armstrong's professional expertise, became key to the prosecution's argument that the wiring was sabotaged by Jo Ann Parks, despite its inability to actually start a fire. This nonexpert testimony from an electrical expert became gospel in the case, never seriously challenged when, arguably, it never should have been allowed in the first place.

With his original theory on the cause of the living room fire disproved, other experts who later reviewed the case on Parks's behalf have said Ablott should have reconsidered his area-of-origin determination at that point, given that the wires were at its center. Or he could have reconsidered other possible causes, such as the old television he had discounted at first. Ablott chose a different course. He used the process of negative corpus—after first assuming the absence of possible accidental causes—in order to allege that Parks had to have started the fire with matches or a lighter, because there was no other explanation.

A quarter century later, Cohen would argue that Ablott misused negative corpus, improperly discounted the TV set as a possible fire starter, then falsely testified that all possible accidental causes had been eliminated.

During Ablott's first walk-through of the house, he also found some unusual fire patterns in the girls' bedroom that showed flames burning low in the room next to RoAnn's bed, then moving out of the room into the kitchen. Meanwhile, patterns high on the wall showed fire moving into the room from the kitchen. There are numerous possible reasons for such conflicting fire patterns, including a separate fire set deliberately in the bedroom on the floor, or a separate low fire started by flammable ceiling tiles catching fire and falling to the floor near the bed. The window failing and providing new ventilation, triggering flashover, could also play a role in creating such patterns as the air currents churn and swirl.

In a handwritten report dated June 20, 1989, Ablott concluded that "investigators were unable to establish this area as an area of origin since the damage could have been caused by a secondary fire as a result of radiated heat and flame impingement from the living room fire."

A typewritten version of the same report, also dated June 20,

1989, included some key edits. Despite the identical dates on the reports, Ablott said the typed version was actually finished in July, a few weeks after the handwritten version. Early that month, Ablott visited the Parks fire scene again with Bell police officers, fire investigators, and the insurance investigator Takach, who was adamant that an arson fire had started in the girls' bedroom and that the landlords therefore had no liability for the fatal blaze. Ablott's typed version of the report agreed with Takach: "Investigators established this as a separate area of origin and was caused by the application of an open flame."

All of these opinions on where and how the fire (or fires) started in the apartment rested on a single keystone finding of Ablott's: He testified that flashover did not occur in any room of the Parks house, which, if true, would make reading the fire patterns much simpler. Yet every other expert who has looked at the case since, including those hired by the prosecution, says flashover can and does create false indications of areas of origin and should always be taken into consideration in a fire investigation. Those experts include John Lentini, who proved this effect of flashover with his experiments in the Lime Street fire and his observation of false indicators of arson in the Oakland firestorm.

And in the Parks fire, all of those same experts now say flashover occurred in the living room and both back bedrooms where the children's bodies were found.

Even Dinko Bozanich, the prosecutor who tried Parks and who insisted there was no flashover that night, believed a contrary finding could devastate his case. "If a flashover occurred," he told the judge in arguing to limit one witness's testimony about the topic, "that changes everything with regard to the arson investigation presented in this case so far."

Decades later, Cohen would argue that falsely telling the jury that flashover never occurred had rendered the trial fundamentally unfair and invalidated Ablott's key findings about the origin and cause of the fire. That mistaken expert opinion alone merited an overturning of the guilty verdict, as Cohen saw it.

But there was one significant finding by Ablott in which the issue of flashover did not really apply, and it was arguably the most devastating testimony against Parks: Ablott's opinion that Ronnie Jr. had been barricaded inside his bedroom closet.

Ablott spent more time in that bedroom than any other part of the house during the investigation, as he tried, with the help of several investigators and firefighter Dirk Wegner, the first nozzleman to enter the house, to reconstruct the scene in Ronnie's room during the fire. Reconstruction is always a challenge because of the destructive effects of firefighting and overhaul, but Ablott felt it was essential to understanding how and why Ronnie died in his closet.

Few of the firefighters or policemen who responded to the fire that night could say definitively whether the closet door was open or shut when they entered the house. Prosecutor Bozanich admitted as much during the trial—he said there was no reliable human testimony to say if the door was open or closed. Figuring out the position of the door during the fire was complicated by the fact that high-pressure fire hoses, air movement when windows fail, search and rescue efforts, and the post-fire overhaul to remove smoldering debris each could have altered the position of the door several times, opening or closing it. The two first responders who seemed certain it was closed during the fire repeatedly contradicted each other and themselves in their accounts, and also incorrectly remembered the door being completely intact when the fire was put out. Photos show most of the three panels that made up the bulk of the door's surface were burned away, leaving little more than the rails and stiles—the outer edges of the door—in place. Photos of the door in a closed position still provide a clear view of the inside of the closet, although the very first picture taken of the scene depicts the closet door wide open with debris piled in front and inside. This photo, part of a series taken to document evidence in the bedroom, was snapped shortly after the fire was extinguished and before the boy's body was found.

In his reconstruction efforts, Ablott sought proof of two things: that the door was shut during the fire, and that something had been placed in front of the door that blocked Ronnie Jr. inside and prevented him from escaping. Ablott swore he finally found what he was looking for.

To prove the door was shut during the fire, the prosecution relied upon the condition of the boy's body—his burns were less severe than his sisters', suggesting he was protected by a closed door—and on the condition of the door hinges. The hinge plates showed mirror image patterns of oxidation, Ablott asserted, which he said could only occur if the door was shut, pressing the plates together. However, the door itself was not preserved by investigators. It had been treated carelessly, thrown to the floor, marked by ashy boot prints that show it was walked on, and Ablott took no measurements to see whether the inside or the outside surfaces were more deeply burned and charred. Few photos were even taken of the inner side of the closet door, so that only witness memories—police and firefighter witness memories—can attest to which side was more burned. Only the hinges were preserved for examination.

Ablott next claimed to have found powerful evidence that there was something in front of the closet during the fire that had protected the carpeting from burning, allowing little more than soot and smoke damage underneath. He and his helpers spent hours trying to find objects that had been thrown around the house or taken outside during overhaul, trying to fit them into the roughly rectangular protected pattern on the carpeting in front of the closet threshold. After trying many objects and furnishings that might fit that spot like a jigsaw puzzle piece, they came up with the rectangular base of a wicker clothes hamper, most of which had been consumed in the fire, though the surviving base with its plastic corners seemed to fit the shape on the carpet. One of the plastic corners on the base had melted, and the plastic looked like it had flowed onto and adhered to a pet bowl that fit another protected area on the carpet near the closet. This, Ablott concluded, meant the hamper had been placed in front of the closed closet door to form a barricade, blocking the door from opening and trapping the child inside. The closed door had provided some protection from the flames, but not from deadly fumes and smoke that ultimately killed him.

A closed closet door by itself meant nothing. Children often hide in closets and shut the doors during fires. And if the four-year-old had surreptitiously gotten out of bed and either turned on the TV, which then caught fire, or had been playing with matches and accidentally started the fire, he would have been even more likely to hide because he had misbehaved. That was one of the reasons a police search party had combed the neighborhood before his body was found—under the theory he might have run away out of guilt or fear of getting in trouble.

Similarly, a clothes hamper standing in front of the closet by itself meant nothing, either. If the closet door had been left open, the hamper's placement provided no evidence of criminal intent.

Only the two together—proof of a door closed *and* a hamper pushed against it—could be used to suggest an intent to kill.

Ablott would later reconstruct this scene in the courtroom, with the side of the jury box serving as a simulated closet door. Why such a pivotal piece of evidence as the door itself was not saved has never been explained.

Cohen argued that it is impossible to tell from the available evidence and testimony whether the closet door was open or closed during the fire. She also believed that the validity of Ablott's reconstruction was dubious at best, and that other rectangular objects, even falling ceiling tiles, could just as readily explain the protected areas of the carpeting. The problem was, unlike other elements of the government's case against Parks, the damaging claims about the hamper and the closet could not be undermined by claiming that the evolving understanding of flashover and fire science invalidated Ablott's findings. All Cohen had—so far—were dueling expert opinions. Unless she found some overlooked piece of evidence that crushed the prosecution's theories about the closet door, this would remain her greatest challenge to overcome in trying to free Parks. The attorney feared she could prevail on all the other points, but still lose if the judge accepted that part of the prosecution's case.

Bozanich, the trial prosecutor, had come up with an ingenious summation at the end of the case that piqued her fears, because he avoided the conventional argument that the sum of the proof and testimony was overwhelming. Instead, the prosecutor suggested each line of evidence was more than sufficient to convict on its own. Even if the jury distrusted Ablott and his findings on the cause of the fire, Bozanich argued, there was more than enough other evidence to convict:

I refuse to be hamstrung or bound by this contention that Ablott is the People's case, and without him it is zilch. To show you what I'm talking about, take Ablott out and throw him away, and just say, it's inconclusive from the arson expert evidence as to how many fires were set, one or two.

But if you find that there was a prior fire in Lynwood, there was a sabotaged wire, and the boy was in the closet with something in front, and her total lack of explanation for [her absence of smoke and fire exposure], you don't even need an arson expert opinion, ladies and gentlemen.

Those facts, if they have been established, conclusively prove beyond any reasonable doubt that the defendant is guilty as charged. . . . If you take the sabotaged wire, just by itself, it starts telling us someone wanted to start a fire. . . . Even if you had no expert opinion, no evidence about the defendant's lack of fire damage, no evidence about that closet door and hamper, and that's all you had . . . you could conclude there is no other reasonable conclusion than arson occurred.

If you just find a blocked closet door, and the fire occurring, that's enough to conclude beyond a reasonable doubt it's arson, without anything else.

Forget the closet door. The defendant not having any fire damage. That cries out to you, she set it.

But when you start combining all these things . . . you convict her, absolutely. An overwhelming case. No arson expert opinion needed, none.

. . .

Decades later, the district attorney's office was still quoting this summation as justification for denying the habeas corpus petition. Each time Cohen read it, the reasoning made her shudder a bit. If the new judge bought into that old argument, she knew, her case and Jo Ann Parks would be done.

13

"If I Am Wrong, Then Everything I Have Ever Been Taught . . . Would All Be Wrong."

Inviting jurors to feel free to disregard key pieces of evidence sounds like a bold expression of confidence. In truth, Deputy District Attorney Dinko Bozanich had been engaging in a bit of creative damage control. He was deeply worried that the jurors already might be disregarding major parts of his case.

"This was not a slam dunk for me. Far from it. It was a close case," Bozanich recalled many years after the trial. He felt that "one more scintilla" of evidence for the defense could have tipped the scales the other way.

"So I wanted to make it clear that any of those facts on its own would be enough to convict. The sabotaged wires. Her lack of fire injury or smell of smoke. The boy blocked in the closet. You believe any one of those beyond a reasonable doubt, and it's full stop. Enough to convict. And I think making that clear to the jury helped them arrive at the correct verdict."

Bozanich spent nearly thirty years as a career prosecutor for the Los Angeles County District Attorney. He charged and convicted defendants with high-enough profiles to earn such nicknames in the media as the Sleepwalker Killer and the Alphabet Bomber, responsible for twenty-five murders and multiple bombings.

The Parks triple-murder trial convened on October 13, 1992, in the Norwalk branch of the Los Angeles County Superior Court, which serves the southeast section of Los Angeles County, where the fatal fire occurred in the city of Bell. Prosecutors liked trying cases in Norwalk because the defense attorneys always griped that jurors there seemed particularly tough and more law-and-order minded. Their nickname for the courthouse was "No Walk"—a "walk" being slang for a non-guilty verdict. Whether it was true or merely urban legend, prosecutors loved that their opponents felt that way.

Bozanich believed in his case and in Jo Ann Parks's guilt, but even in No Walk, he feared he might lose the battle of the arson experts with his jurors. He thought the defense might kick up enough doubt and confusion about Ablott's story to make it a draw or, perhaps, to win outright. He ended up spending so much time flapping his arms and pacing the courtroom as he traded barbs with Parks's arson expert that the defense team quietly nicknamed him "the Stork."

Under the best of circumstances, the scientific and technical testimony about any fire and arson case can confuse jurors, if not put them to sleep. Investigator Ablott, large and shambling and a bit intimidating, had done well on the stand under Bozanich's friendly questioning. But during cross-examination, the prosecutor's nemesis, Deputy Public Defender Charles Gessler, had caught Ablott in a credibility-damaging contradiction—bad enough that Bozanich worried it could cost him the case.

Ablott had provided a detailed account of how he examined the Parks's badly burned TV set during the same April 17 survey of the house in which he discovered the seemingly sabotaged wires.

In his testimony at Parks's trial, he swore he made that examination in the living room, where he also saw pieces of glass from the shattered television screen scattered on the floor. After looking over the sagging, gutted electronics and shattered picture tube, he ruled out the television as a possible cause of the fire because, he said, he determined it had stood outside the area of origin. He also found that the picture tube had imploded, indicating that the television had been attacked by fire from the outside. Had the fire begun inside the television, Ablott explained, the cathode-ray picture tube would have exploded, and the damage from that would differ from what he had observed at the fire scene. He confidently told jurors that the television had nothing to do with starting the fire.

There was a problem with this pivotal testimony. According to evidence photographs and the testimony of county fire investigator Bill Franklin and his trainee, Fuzzy Fuzell, firefighters removed the burned hulk of the television from the living room and dumped it outside at the back of the house the day after the fire. The glass Ablott so vividly remembered was swept up long before he ever visited. He never saw where the TV had been set up before the fire. The police diagram of where the television had been before the fire shows it close to and in front of the windows and the flammable draperies—close to or within Ablott's hypothetical area of origin in that one-hundred-square-foot living room. Finally, wherever Ablott might have examined the TV, his beliefs about imploding and exploding televisions are based on a theory that, according to other experts in the case, was shown to be junk science several years before the Parks fire.

Bozanich spent considerable energy and time attacking Jo Ann Parks's credibility for contradicting herself and changing her account of events, so it was both embarrassing and damaging to have his key witness tarred in the same way. And if Bozanich tried to explain away those contradictions as simple, innocent lapses in memory on Ablott's part, he knew it would open the door for Gessler to ask jurors to give the same benefit of the doubt to the woman he was condemning for every misstatement she ever made, including lying about her age on her marriage certificate. Worse, the defense attorney would now happily argue that if Ablott was wrong about that key point, what else might he be mistaken about? The incorrect information about the television and Ablott's dismissal of it as a potential ignition source for the fire created a possible bombshell, and it wasn't the only one. The defense attorney went after Ablott for also suggesting he had discovered the sabotaged wires, although they had been partially excavated more than a week earlier by Franklin and Fuzell. The defense attorney wondered aloud—for the benefit of jurors—if Ablott might suffer from memory problems. What, the lawyer speculated, did that imply about Ablott's habit of sticking his penknife into charred wood to measure how deeply and long it burned, without ever writing down his findings—just keeping track of them in his head? Such methods are considered inaccurate and unacceptable by modern standards—which is why arson investigators today use special gauges to measure the depth of char, and they keep detailed records and charts as each measurement is made, providing a kind of road map that helps uncover the movement of a fire.

On the other side, Gessler had a secret weapon to counter Ablott: his own arson expert, Robert Lowe. Dapper in his cardigan and tie, tall and silver-haired, he was, as even Ablott described him, "everybody's favorite uncle—everybody just automatically believes him, whether he's right or not."

With a long career that began as a navy aviator in World War II, Lowe had left military service to become a Los Angeles City firefighter, then a Los Angeles County Fire Department captain, and, finally, an arson investigator. He retired from the fire department after twenty-two years and more than thirty-five hundred fire origin and cause investigations. Then he went to work as a private fire investigator, accumulating two more decades of experience analyzing everything from house fires to automotive defects to rocket engine explosions. In the Parks case, Lowe provided plausible and innocent explanations for evidence that Ablott had used to form his opinion that the fire had been arson and murder.

Ahead of his time in terms of abandoning arson myths and embracing new ideas about fire behavior, Lowe argued even back in 1992 that flashover played an important role in the Parks fire, despite Ablott's contrary opinion. He believed the effects of flashover explained the burn patterns Ablott thought were so suspicious. He played a dramatic training video for the jury depicting a chair fire and a television fire to show how quickly a room can be engulfed by flashover—from a tiny flame to an inferno in less than five minutes.

Many arson investigators and prosecutors at that time were pushing back against what was being referred to mockingly as "the flashover defense" in criminal cases. The new understanding of flashover and burn patterns being championed by experts such as Lowe and John Lentini was viewed by many police fire investigators as out of the mainstream and a bit of a joke. They felt the critics were trying to erect obstacles and deal setbacks to those whose business was catching fire bugs.

Bozanich, taken by surprise by Lowe's flashover conclusions, took a similarly mocking tack, trying to dismiss Lowe as a dishonest kook, calling his theories "ridiculous" and the product of a "slam bang approach" by a "big crackerjack one-man investigative team." Bozanich tried to sully Lowe's reputation further by digging up an old appellate court opinion that criticized him for filing an incomplete fire report in a civil suit over an insurance claim. Lowe explained that his partner had filed the report behind his back before Lowe had completed it, because his final conclusions would have alienated their client in the case, cutting off a lucrative source of income.

Then Lowe fought back. He further shook Bozanich with his testimony about his experiences with older models of television sets that were far more prone to starting fires than more modern designs. Their high-voltage transformers and cathode-ray tubes created electromagnetic fields that attracted dust and lint—blankets of it that coated the old-school electronics inside the TV cabinet. Lowe said this allowed heat to build, eventually causing parts to fail and throw sparks out of the ventilation slots in back of the television cabinet, or to cause outright fires inside the TV cabinet. Lowe explained how either development could have set the living room draperies aflame on the night of the fire, starting a blaze that spread to other flammable items in the room, after which the flames could spread quickly through the tiny house. According to Lowe, the patterns and traces left behind on walls and objects by such a fire in that heavily damaged living room would have been indistinguishable from the patterns Ablott insisted could only have been created by Jo Ann and her matches.

He couldn't prove that the television started the fire, Lowe admitted. But, given Ablott's specious reasons for ruling out the TV as a possible cause, Lowe argued, there was no way the prosecution could prove the television did *not* start the fire. He said Ablott's use of negative corpus to claim that Parks had to have started the fire by hand was therefore unacceptable. The cause of the fire should officially be "undetermined," Lowe said.

Bozanich responded by successfully drawing Lowe and Gessler into an argument about what model television had been in that apartment—a Zenith, RCA, or Magnavox brand TV. Ron and Jo Ann Parks had been unsure and contradictory in their statements about the brand of the swap-meet TV. Some old models of Zenith had been recalled as a fire hazard, and the two attorneys each brought in a TV expert to argue about which TV was which. The bottom line was that no one could say for sure, because the police had not saved the television as evidence. This whole TV-brand issue was a red herring—all those old models posed a small but real fire risk, whether recalled or not. But Bozanich had succeeded in shifting focus to a confusing side issue about TV models, distracting from what should have been the only issue that mattered: the possibility that any television fire, regardless of brand or year of manufacture, had been improperly ruled out in order to support Ablott's finding of arson.

Lowe also remained equally adamant that there had been no sabotaged wiring. He pointed to the photos of the discovery of the cut cords and showed how the copper wiring below the supposedly suspicious cuts in the insulation was bright and shiny, like new. Had they been exposed during the fire and buried in chemically harsh wet ash overnight, they should have looked blackened or tarnished. Their pristine condition suggested to Lowe that the fire overhaul, or the digging up of the wires the next day with a metal rake, could have caused those nicks in the cords.

Finally, Lowe argued that the closet door in little Ronnie's room was open during the fire and that the hamper could not have been barricading it. The wicker hamper had burned completely down to the base. The prosecution asserted that the hamper protected the bottom of the closet door during the fire, which is why that part of the door appeared in photos to be less burned than the rest. But Lowe said that protection theory would be true only if the hamper had *not* burned. Photos taken by Ablott during the reconstruction, however, showed a hamper that had been consumed almost completely, down to its base. And that, Lowe pointed out, meant the burning wicker hamper was pouring out heat and flames as it was consumed. If it really had been right next to the closet door, the bottom of the door should have been *more* burned than other areas of the door, not protected.

If the authorities had preserved the best piece of evidence, the closet door itself, and if they had competently examined or at least kept the television set, these questions might be answered definitively, Lowe said. Perhaps they would have proved Parks's guilt, or perhaps they would have set her free. But those key pieces of evidence had been destroyed by the government, Lowe said, either through negligence or deliberate choice. By the time charges were filed and defense experts had come along, the authorities had allowed the house to be torn down. When Lowe drove out to see the place, only the concrete slab remained. Only police and the landlord's insurance investigators ever had the chance to examine the actual fire scene and evidence.

By the time Lowe was done testifying, Bozanich worried that the jury might call the battle of the arson experts a wash, or perhaps decide it slightly in Lowe's favor. And so he continued to relentlessly go after Parks's credibility and character. He called witnesses who had never been interviewed until years after the fire to say Jo Ann appeared unemotional or unconcerned about the loss of her children. When neighbor Shirley Robison, who was with Jo Ann for hours on the night of the fire and who had been interviewed by police early on, described her as "very upset," Bozanich shot back, "Do you know she was upset or did she just *appear* to be upset?" He peppered every witness who thought Jo

Ann had been sad, crying, or emotional during the fire with pointed, sometimes sarcastic questions. He particularly challenged Shirley Robison's account of restraining Jo Ann from running back into the burning house. She didn't try very hard, Bozanich asked, did she? Isn't she much bigger than you? Could she have gotten away if she wanted to? By the end of the case, Bozanich referred to that moment as Jo Ann's "halfhearted" attempt to *appear* to want to run in and save her kids. This courtroom warfare to frame and reframe events was relentless and, it would turn out, quite effective.

Of course, Jo Ann Parks had been her own worst enemy. Had she stuck with her first account to police describing the night of the fire, Bozanich would have had a much harder time of it. She said she heard screams, opened her bedroom door, faced a wall of flame, and immediately turned and ran outside for help. Bozanich speculated that her lack of any sign she was near a burning house, the fact that she had no injuries or smell of smoke on her, fit his arson theory better than any other scenario: She had set two small fires inside and then left the house and her kids to meet their fate, returning only when the apartment was fully engulfed, just in time to bang on the neighbor's door and pretend she had just run out of the house.

Lowe offered another explanation for her lack of fire injury or smoky smell: backdraft. He said every part of the house was aflame or filling with smoke when Parks awoke to a child's screams—except for the master bedroom, where she slept. This room was an add-on to the original garage structure, connected by a single door to the rest of the apartment, with a solid, formerly exterior wall separating the room from the rest of the flaming apartment. Jo Ann and Ron had a water bed; it was their habit to keep the door shut at night, so the cat didn't come in and puncture the bed with its claws. When she opened the door to see why Ronnie was screaming, the master bedroom offered a fresh source of oxygen for the fire. Eventually that would cause the fire to spread rapidly into the master bedroom. But the first thing that would happen, Lowe said, was that air would rush from the bedroom past Parks in the doorway and into the burning house. This initial backdraft meant no smoke or flames moved into the master bedroom or toward Parks in those first seconds. She would still have felt a blast of radiant heat, however, as if standing near a furnace, but she would not necessarily get burned or smell of smoke unless she lingered or tried to advance into the burning apartment.

Leaving that door open, then running out through the exterior door and leaving it open, too, fed the existing fire and allowed it to spread quickly into the master bedroom as well, Lowe explained. This is why neighbor Bill Robison could run into the master bedroom once roused by Parks, but could not go farther into the house.

Had she stuck with that original story, Gessler later explained in his summation to the jury, there might have been a very different ending to the investigation. Instead, after that horrible scene at the police station in which Ron Parks accused his wife of killing the children (or letting them die), Jo Ann changed her story, saying she tried to crawl through the flames on the night of the fire but finally had to turn back and run for help.

"That is a lie. She didn't do that," Gessler told the jury. "This is why we are here. It's because Mrs. Parks is not a heroine. Mrs. Parks did not die in that fire with her children. And Mrs. Parks did not make what would have turned out to be a heroic but futile effort to save her children and die of the carbon monoxide and smoke inhalation and heat . . .

"It is understandable with Mr. Parks on her case, she would

make up a version that was a little more heroic than the truth. Is that so sinister that she should be convicted of three counts of murder?"

Gessler compared this fake story Parks told about crawling to save the children to Ablott's "reconstructive memory of a television set in the living room that he never saw," as well as claiming he carefully dug up sabotaged wires another investigator had excavated a week earlier.

"I guess that clues you in a little bit," Gessler said, "about a man who is reaching, who wants to be right, and who will grab the facts to support his opinion."

The long trial stretched across eight months, with numerous delays and holiday breaks. The atmosphere remained testy throughout. Bozanich has an in-your-face aggressive style even on his best days, but with such a close-fought battle, he and Gessler spent much of the trial accusing each other of misconduct of one kind or another. Gessler's co-counsel thought they were about to come to blows one afternoon. Bozanich grew incensed when a paralegal on the defense team kept running up from the gallery on breaks to comfort Parks and to provide tissues to dry her tears while jurors were still in the courtroom. The prosecutor railed aloud about the defense wasting scarce taxpayer dollars to pay an employee for useless comfort duty. Then he begged any news reporters in the courtroom to investigate the propriety of paying a paralegal to facilitate crocodile tears.

If arson expert Robert Lowe was Gessler's secret weapon, Bozanich's nuclear bomb on the witness list was Kathy Dodge. She was the one witness with the potential to devastate the defense with her claim that Parks had longingly talked about the millions she could have made if their first apartment fire in 1988 had killed little Jessica. If she were persuasive on the witness stand, Dodge's appearance in the case could almost guarantee a trip to death row for Parks. She was literally the last person in the world Gessler wanted to see walk into the courtroom.

A highly respected defense attorney, Gessler specialized in defending against the death penalty and had tried many high-profile murder cases, including representing Lyle Menendez, one of the two brothers charged in Los Angeles's most famous case of parricide. In thirteen death-penalty trials, not a single one of his clients ended up on death row.

In the twilight of his thirty-year career at the Los Angeles County Public Defender's office, he did not want Jo Ann Parks to become the first of his clients to be sentenced to die. Each day he dreaded finding out that Bozanich would be calling Kathy Dodge to the stand to provide what no other witness on the list could: evidence of premeditation and motive for murder. Would she also blurt out something about the alleged five-hundred-dollar money order theft as evidence of Parks's alleged avariciousness or bad character? Worse, would the judge permit Bozanich to ask her about the allegations of child neglect and dosing the kids with cough syrup? Even with autopsy results that showed no signs of cough medicine in their bodies, and no physical injuries to suggest abuse in the past or on the night of the fire, Dodge's accusations would be a home run for the prosecution. Without Dodge, the only explanation for RoAnn to die unrestrained in her bed with the door open was that she had succumbed in her sleep to carbon monoxide poisoning. But that only tracks if the fire was accidental. The prosecution's theory that her mother started a separate fire right next to the girl's bed, without restraining her or locking her in the room, seems inexplicable. Nearly three years old, healthy and active, she would have just run out, perhaps even helping little Jessica escape her crib, too, the moment fire-setting mom left the room. The girls' seeming unfettered ability to flee also made the alleged barricading of Ronnie in the closet anomalous: Why restrain one child but not the other? It made no sense.

The cough medicine accusation would bring a more sinister explanation to these inconsistencies. The unlikely scenario of starting a fire in the girls' room without waking them suddenly would make terrible sense if the children had been drugged.

The specter of Kathy Dodge had a marked effect on Gessler's trial strategy. A capital case is divided into two parts: the guilt or innocence trial and then, if there is a guilty verdict of first-degree murder, a penalty phase provides the big finish. In most states, the jury makes the call after each side presents a case for execution or mercy (in the form of a life sentence without parole in California). But Gessler, like all defense attorneys skilled at death-penalty cases, crafted a defense against a death sentence in both phases of the trial, evoking from the witness's trial phase not only information to support innocence, but also to give jurors reasons for sparing the life of the client. And so Gessler did just that—pushed into it by Bozanich when the prosecutor somewhat surprisingly called a hostile witness to the stand early in the trial: Ronald Parks.

The very first question Gessler put to him when he was invited to begin cross-examination was intended to be a shocker: "Mr. Parks, are you trying to kill your wife now because you didn't succeed in April 1989?"

Long silence. Blank stare. Then: "No. I am not trying to do anything."

Gessler went on to build a portrait of a vile, uncaring father who had the electrician's skills and the sociopathic tendencies that could lead him to create an incendiary device to kill his family, then attempt to profit from it.

But in doing so, Gessler had set the terms of his defense. He had reserved his opening statement for later in the case, which meant the jury had heard nothing but the prosecution's version of events before the first witness took the stand. Until Gessler hurled that accusation at Ron Parks, jurors had no idea what direction the defense would take. The first message in defense of Jo Ann Parks sent their way was not that the fire was accidental, but that someone started it on purpose. The only distinction Gessler suggested was just that the culprit was the husband, not the wife.

It was, in short, an endorsement of the prosecution's arson theory.

Later in the trial, of course, a second defense—accident, not arson—would be raised as well. But when Lowe learned of this dual approach, he was furious. He felt his entire role in the case, his careful analysis aimed at convincing the jury that the fire had been accidental, not criminal, had been undermined before he set foot in the courtroom. His opinion would be just one choice in a buffet of options Gessler was offering up.

Lowe later said this was the moment Parks lost the case. But it appears Gessler felt he could not depend on Lowe alone to sway jurors to acquit. Had the death penalty been off the table, the defense attorney might have just pushed the accidental-fire theory of the case. But that would have been a risky move. If the jurors decided there was arson and murder, Gessler's fallback strategy was to make them think Ron was getting away with murder. That would make it very hard for them to impose the death penalty on Jo Ann if they thought a much more callous and abhorrent husband walked free.

If the goal of that tense and unpleasant cross-examination was to showcase just what sort of person Ron Parks was, Gessler certainly accomplished that. The jury had heard neighbor Shirley Robison's account of what he said at the police station on the night of the fire, blaming his wife for the deaths of their children. But on the witness stand, Parks gave a new version: "I told her, 'Honey, you did everything you possibly could to help them children. It's not your fault.' "

Next, he explained how, shortly after the fire, he responded to a newspaper advertisement by a lawyer who promised "million dollar verdicts." He immediately retained the attorney to sue his landlords for the deaths of his children. He said he and his wife dropped the suit, as well as an earlier one filed over the Lynwood fire, because a subsequent attorney warned them they would "look like fire bugs."

Asked to talk about his children, Ron Parks could not remember either of his daughters' birthdays—just the years of their births. He confidently named his son's birthday, but he got it wrong, eleven months off—wrong day, wrong month.

"I'm going by recall," he said with a shrug. "My children have been dead three years, and I don't celebrate birthdays."

He could not remember their bedtimes, either, or kissing them good night or any other bedtime rituals, explaining that he had to "move on." He offered an even more nakedly cold assessment of this moving-on process than he had during the TV interview he gave shortly after the fire.

"I've dropped them out of my life. I have a new life now," he testified. "I mean, it's like spilt milk, you've got to let it go. You can't wipe up and carry it with you the rest of your life."

Even Gessler, veteran of thirteen gut-wrenching death-penalty trials, seemed taken aback as Jo Ann Parks burst into tears at the defense table. "The memories of your children are like spilt milk?"

Ron Parks nodded. "That's what I'm saying."

Meanwhile, in anticipation of Kathy Dodge testifying, the defense team began preparing an emotionally fragile and easily rattled client to testify on her own behalf. If she risked taking the stand and going toe-to-toe with the pugnacious Dinko Bozanich, Parks could give her version of events on the night of the fire. She could explain why she exaggerated her attempts to save her kids after recounting in her first official statement that she simply turned and ran. She could explain her difficult relationship with Ron. And she could try to explain away Kathy Dodge as a vindictive ex-friend. Eager to tell jurors her side of the story, she even sat for a mock cross-examination in the county jail visiting room. Parks recalls that she "passed with flying colors," but there was always the possibility that Bozanich might destroy her on the witness stand, creating a dilemma for Gessler. But if Kathy Dodge testified, the defense attorney might have little choice—he'd have to put Parks on the stand.

Then, in a surprise move, Bozanich rested his case without calling Kathy Dodge. It turns out she had become a disaster of a witness, changing her story repeatedly, forgetting key facts, and barely able to speak in coherent sentences when detectives tape-recorded an interview with her to prepare for trial. She went from saying in her first statements to police that she had seen Parks give cough medicine to her youngest child three times to saying she had seen her give it to all her kids all the time. Her initial damning statement about getting rich off Jessica's death in the first fire had six months later morphed into Parks saying something more ambiguous: "I would've got money out of that, you know, I would've sued but Jessica would've died." In her next statement, she could no longer remember who said what, Ron or Jo Ann, about the first fire. She no longer believed Jessica was left in the house at all that day, or if anything like that had been said at all. The person who first put Jo Ann Parks under the investigative microscope turned out to have little value as a credible witness.

Her most damaging statement three days after the fire had turned by the time of the trial into this: "I don't remember if they left Jess—I don't think they left Jessica in there, but they said that if they did or they didn't—if they would, then she would have got burned. Then they could have either got a big—they would have got the money out of there. They could have got a lawsuit. And I was thinking—I don't know if she meant it where, darn, she should have left Jessica in there or, you know, she didn't leave her in there, she's happy, she doesn't—I don't know."

Worse still for the prosecution, Dodge trashed the credibility of two of her friends who might have corroborated portions of her accusations against Parks. Dodge told police one of them was actually a dangerous and violent methamphetamine addict—she actually warned two sheriff's homicide detectives that they should bring backup if they decided to visit her. She said the other friend had recruited her to participate in a welfare fraud scam and couldn't be trusted, either. A third person from the same circle of acquaintances wrote a letter to authorities detailing similar allegations of child neglect but then later admitted little of it was true.

During a hearing with the jury not present, the judge looked at the transcript of Dodge's latest recorded statement to detectives and pronounced it "gibberish." The danger of bringing such a witness into court for Bozanich was that it could undermine the credibility of his entire case. So he cut his losses and rested the people's case without calling her, although she could still be called as a rebuttal witness later if necessary, to refute any claims Parks might make on the witness stand.

The defense team appeared beyond relieved. The jury would

never hear about Dodge, or about allegations of neglect or drugging, or that damning quote Parks allegedly made. Gessler could now focus the defense case on the accidental-fire theory. And he told his client she need not testify. That way there would be no risk of Parks melting down on the stand, he said, or that her testimony would provoke Bozanich to call Dodge in as a rebuttal witness, warts and all.

Reluctantly, Jo Ann Parks recalls, she agreed to remain silent and not testify, for better or worse. The jury would not hear Dodge's incendiary allegations, but neither would they hear from the mother of three dead children, which would surely disappoint them. Gessler, however, appeared confident to Parks. The defense team had dodged a bullet and argued to the jury that there were way too many doubts about the prosecution's case to sustain a conviction.

But the last word those jurors would hear at the end of the case was the word Bozanich chose to describe Jo Ann Parks: *executioner.* No one wants to think of a mother that way, he said, but that is the word that fits.

After ten days of talking it over, the jury agreed. The ten men and two women pronounced her guilty.

Afterward, several jurors explained their verdict. In part, it had been Bozanich's portrait of Parks that swayed them into believing she behaved more like a killer than a mother. Yet the key detail was something the defense hadn't anticipated, a bit of information that seemed to help rather than harm Jo Ann's case: the testimony of Bell police officer Pete Cacheiro.

Cacheiro had repeatedly misled Parks by telling her the kids were okay as she stood watching the burning house. He told her that everything was and would be fine. The defense was based on the calculation that jurors would feel that no concerned mother would leave the scene if she thought her kids remained in jeopardy. So Cacheiro's false assurances would provide an explanation for why she would be willing to leave the scene to go to the police department to make a statement: She thought the danger had passed. Add to that the fact that she was in shock, a passive, traumatized person used to deferring to others, and the defense lawyer seemed to have the bases covered. The jurors plausibly could conclude that Parks simply did what the nice policeman told her to do—wait for her kids in the police station just blocks away.

But the jurors didn't see it that way. Some of them, at least, felt there was no way any mother—any mother who wasn't a killer, that is—would hear her kids were okay and then leave the scene without first seeing them for herself, grabbing them up, and hugging and kissing them.

No lawyer had argued this particular point. No witness testified about it. Some of the jurors just felt this behavior was wrong. And for them, everything flowed from that small yet huge moment, the lens through which they viewed the rest of the evidence. For those particular jurors, the key wasn't just about the battle of the experts. Or the puzzle-piece reconstruction of the closet. Or whether a second fire was set in the girls' room. It was about how Jo Ann Parks acted that night.

Why, they asked, would a mother leave that fire scene without first making certain her kids were really okay—unless she already knew they were dead?

To be sure, not all jurors felt that way. Others said they found her behavior suspicious but not definitive. They needed the arson and fire evidence to be there, too.

Gessler had been right in part about one thing, however. His tactics may not have kept Jo Ann Parks out of prison, but his targeting of Ron Parks likely saved her from a death sentence. A majority of jurors reported that they thought the husband was involved, and may have been the instigator. They would not sentence a mother to death when the man they thought might ultimately be responsible walked free.

Bob Lowe remained furious with the defense attorney for undermining him as a witness. He fervently believed Parks should have been exonerated. He thought Kathy Dodge should have testified, so jurors would understand that her bogus allegations had biased the fire investigation and turned a tentative finding of an accidental blaze into an arson case.

He also felt it was a fatal error not to call Bell police officer Jeff Bruce to testify. Bruce was the first responder who pounded on a back bedroom window with his flashlight in order to break through to rescue the children, instead triggering a sudden increase of ventilation and a flare-up of flame that Lowe believed had sent the girls' bedroom into flashover. Lowe believed Bruce's testimony was key because it contradicted Ablott's theory that Parks had set a separate fire in the bedroom. Bruce saw a room filled with black smoke; Lowe believed the fire didn't start in earnest in that room until the window broke and fresh air flooded in.

But in his police report, Bruce seemed to overstate his actions, claiming he entered the room and searched for the girls before the flames drove him out. Later he admitted that he never managed to get fully into the room. The explosion of flame drove him back. Scheduled to testify for the defense at the trial, Bruce had been flown into town from Wyoming, where he had taken a job as a small-town police chief after leaving Bell. But then Gessler chose not to call him as a witness.

Bozanich maintained that Bruce had no credibility and, thirty years later, the district attorney's office continued to maintain that Bruce's testimony had no value and could not be believed. However, all the key parts of his account of the night of the fire were corroborated by a neighbor whom detectives interviewed, and who saw a police officer do everything Bruce claimed except for entering the house through the back bedroom window.

Crushed by Parks's conviction, Lowe began a correspondence with her in prison that lasted the rest of his life, as he gathered all the documents and evidence in the case—more than ten thousand pages of material—and worked tirelessly to get the Parks case reopened, writing the governor, the media, even Oprah Winfrey.

Lowe provided the basic theories, timeline, and discoveries that eventually helped persuade the California Innocence Project to take on Parks as a client. Lowe died of cancer in 2013, but his daughter Mary Ross has continued in his place, serving with her sister and nieces and Lowe's widow as a surrogate family for Parks, attending her hearings, visiting her, writing her, and helping her lay plans for her freedom, if it should come.

After two decades of effort, it seemed Lowe's advocacy finally had borne fruit. Raquel Cohen and her colleagues at the innocence project had put together the habeas petition for Parks, and had also informally provided background information to the Los Angeles County District Attorney in order to discuss a possible settlement. If they could convince prosecutors that a mistake had been made—as they had done with Luis Vargas, falsely accused of being the Teardrop Rapist—they could work something out without court proceedings. The project had done this before in other cases and jurisdictions: There would be a joint press conference, prosecutors standing together with innocence project attorneys, together righting a wrong from long ago. Instead of smearing one another with accusations and hostility, this would be a chance for everyone to look good. "No blame," Justin Brooks promised, "just sharing credit for doing something right."

Cohen thought the initial talks with the DA, though preliminary, seemed promising. The prosecutor on the case, Deputy District Attorney Erika Jerez, seemed willing to consider the possibility that the case against Jo Ann Parks was flawed. It's not an entirely comfortable position for prosecutors, who by nature tend to consider themselves a force for fighting crime, the one bright line between public safety and societal chaos. At the same time, even on the best of days, being a career DA in Los Angeles is a mostly stressful, messy, and thankless job. You're expected to win all the time, whereas defense attorneys are considered successful for winning only a handful of their cases. The workload can be numbing, routine, and far out of the public eye. There are rewarding moments, of course, the ones that keep you going—the lives you improve or even save, the bad guys you put away, the mom or dad or wife or husband who embraces you as a savior. Maybe after twenty or thirty years of these infrequent moments there's a judgeship waiting for you. But the fact is, a lot of the cases suck: You have reluctant witnesses, reluctant victims, witnesses who lie or forget or change their stories and make you look like an idiot, or who just don't show up. Prosecuting domestic violence can shift from vital cause to minefield in a heartbeat: You meet the bruised and battered victim at the start of the case, she wants the bastard who broke her jaw in jail, thank you, and throw away the key while you're at it, but by the time of the trial months later she has yielded to his pleas for forgiveness and wants her husband back, and suddenly you're the enemy trying to destroy a family. It takes a level of commitment few people possess to slog it out in these trenches and to champion the people's point of view in such cases—which is to say, the 99.99 percent of criminal actions that never make the eleven o'clock news.

Jerez came up through these trenches to the habeas section in the Los Angeles County District Attorney's Office, where her job usually amounted to defending convictions from being overturned. Occasionally there were cases in which she found herself accepting that mistakes had been made and that an exoneration or a sentence reduction was warranted. But if the tendency of innocence lawyers is to see potential exonerations as plentiful, a veritable ocean of injustices, the tendency of prosecutors is to see a very small wading pool of possible exonerations, with the rest viewed as gimmicks and lies. And so it grates on many prosecutors when innocence cases draw headlines and condemnations for the authorities. Jerez complains of feeling vilified just for doing her duty of seeing justice done as she balances twin school-age boys with a job that, for the most part, consists of upholding criminal convictions.

She was willing to hear out the innocence project attorneys on the merits of their petition to free Jo Ann Parks. First, though, she wanted to have a current sheriff's arson expert look over the file and give his take on the case. If he thought an injustice had been done, they could start serious talks about a deal to release Parks. The arson expert accepted the files and the assignment, assuming he was going to find a problem-filled investigation that might be difficult to defend.

Instead, the new investigator came back with a surprising opinion: Jo Ann Parks was a serial arsonist and murderer.

Edward Nordskog is a twenty-year veteran arson investigator with the Los Angeles County Sheriff's Arson/Explosives Detail, with a storied career investigating serial fire-starters and bombers, as well as thousands of more mundane arson investigations. Coincidentally, he took over Ron Ablott's job when Ablott retired in 1998, though the two never worked cases together. Nordskog is the author of several nonfiction books on arsonists, and he lectures on the behavior of fire setters, which has become a specialty of his. He is a gifted storyteller with a collection of fascinating cases to talk about and truly horrifying accounts of serial arsonists who managed to get away with setting fire after fire without getting caught.

Nordskog believes Jo Ann Parks is such a person: a serial arsonist whose true nature was not even exposed by her trial and conviction for murder in 1993.

In his report on the case and the innocence project's claims, he endorsed all of Ablott's findings about arson, and described his original investigation as exemplary, careful, and unbiased.

As for his take on the fire itself, Nordskog concluded that Jo Ann Parks's crimes are far worse than anyone previously discerned. He asserted that the first fire in Lynwood was no accident but simply Parks's first failed attempt to murder at least one of her children by staging a seemingly accidental fire. Part of that staging included making phony complaints about electrical problems at the house in advance of the fire. Nordskog believes she deliberately arranged the air conditioner cord to start the first fire. The Nordskog report neglects to mention that the fire department verified Parks's reports of dangerous electrical problems that posed a fire risk and a possible code violation one day before the first fire. He also failed to include in his report the fact that, during Parks's trial, Deputy DA Bozanich assured the court in a legally binding stipulation that the first fire was definitely an accident and that Parks was not responsible.

"This first case fooled all the investigators and was not examined or investigated in a detailed manner," Nordskog countered in his report. In other words, Nordskog was asserting that Ron Ablott, whose work he deemed first-rate in the second fire, was fooled and slipshod in the first.

Nordskog asserted that Parks finally succeeded in committing murder by fire through staging a successful blaze at the Sherman Way apartment. He then vividly described what he believes happened, going far beyond anything presented at Parks's trial, constructing a diabolical portrait of a remorseless killer who wanted to get rid of her kids, then cash in by lawsuit. He described the incendiary device made of cut wires and drapery as crude and ineffective, but exactly the sort of sabotage that an unskilled person might construct. He described the failed incendiary device as consisting of an eighteen-inch-long section of wiring that had been stripped by Parks of all insulation, then wrapped in drapery and placed under boxes and clothing baskets in order to spark a fire. (No evidence of such a dramatically obvious incendiary device was ever mentioned by any witness at the trial.)

Though he cited no evidence to support the contention, Nordskog believed the autopsy findings were wrong, that Parks must have drugged her children—at least the two girls—into a state of incapacitation for her plot to succeed. The tests are not infallible, he suggested, or the samples may have deteriorated.

When the incendiary device failed, Nordskog theorized, Parks started several fires by hand, left the house (explaining her lack of injuries, soot stains, and smoky smell), delayed seeking help while the fire spread throughout the house, then staged a fake rescue attempt for a neighbor to witness.

"The motive for this attack is based within the phenomenon of filicide [the act of a parent killing his or her children] and possibly Munchausen's by proxy [a mental disorder in which a person seeks attention by inducing illness in another, typically a child]," Nordskog wrote. "Parks had unwanted children. . . . This is a fairly well documented phenomenon among female fire setters. My own books document several similar cases. Jo Ann Parks was not the first, nor the last housewife/mother to arrange such an evil plot. Like the others, she fooled investigators at her first fire, but then was subsequently caught."

Nordskog also dismissed the innocence project's claims supporting a new trial for Jo Ann Parks as coming from experts whose livelihood and fame rests on their being "in the exoneration business" and requires them to ignore evidence in a way Nordskog finds "distressing and ethically challenged." He particularly mocked the idea of cognitive bias in the Parks case (and any other arson case) as unscientific and insulting. When Ron Ablott walked into that apartment for the first time, his immediate suspicions that something wasn't right weren't due to bias, Nordskog wrote. "It is good detective work."

Missing from the report is any mention of what others believe was Ablott's poor detective work: his failure to take into account flashover during the fire, the single most important claim by the innocence project, or his testimony about examining the Parks's television and why he ruled it out as a possible accidental cause.

When this report arrived from the DA's office, it shocked Raquel Cohen and her colleagues—for its tone, for the inflammatory serial fire-setter allegation, and for the errors of fact and science she believed it contained. Part of her couldn't wait to get Nordskog on the witness stand. Cognitive bias unscientific? There had been hundreds of scientific papers published on it since the FBI's Madrid bombing fiasco. An eighteen-inch bared wire wrapped in drapery? Where was that coming from? What about the flashover claims? She knew the prosecution's expert had left himself open to withering questions on the witness stand. That part, at least, Cohen thought was good.

But another part of her was daunted and disappointed. She had wondered why her opponent at the district attorney's office had suddenly gotten more businesslike and less amenable to even discussing a possible settlement. This report had to be the reason. This was Nordskog's way of telling the prosecutor that the Parks conviction was righteous, and that the DA should do everything to keep the perpetrator of this evil plot in prison.

Cohen walked the report over to her boss, telling Justin Brooks there would be no settlement. They laughed a little at the accusation of being in the "exoneration business," knowing that almost no one involved as experts in these cases made any money at all, because the innocence project had next to nothing to pay them. But it was a halfhearted laugh. The most prominent expert witness Cohen wanted to testify, John Lentini, was targeted for particular criticism in the report as a flawed and outrageous character who "has a strong personal bias against the very job and title that the [arson] investigators hold," and who works as an "exoneration advocate . . . profiting quite well from his work in this sector." Lentini, suggesting such attacks would become a distraction, told Cohen he'd prefer not to take the stand in the Parks case, and suggested she call on one of his co-authors who worked on the Parks report instead.

Cohen and Brooks are used to skepticism, hostility, and pushback from law enforcement when the attorneys claim there were flaws in a particular investigation. It becomes even more strident when they point to systemic flaws, such as Cohen's claims about problems with the underlying forensic science in the Parks case. Making Parks a sort of "patient zero" for new lines of attack against cognitive bias and negative corpus was always likely to generate vigorous opposition. His young attorneys, Cohen especially, fume about this, but Brooks is unexpectedly sympathetic.

"Imagine you're a prosecutor," he said. "You spent months, maybe years, trying to put a person behind bars. And you are fundamentally a good person. . . . Most DAs are good people, trying to do their jobs every day. They view themselves as protecting the public, and they do that. Then think about the psychology of having us waltz in and say, 'Hey, you were wrong.' What's it like to be told you put someone away for ten or twenty or thirty years, and you were just doing your job, just putting the evidence out there and getting a conviction, acting in good faith? But it just so happens the evidence was wrong. How do you persuade yourself to accept that? Some do. Some can't."

Ron Ablott unintentionally described the nature of this dilemma, and the barrier between law enforcement and the innocence project, in just a few poignant words. Asked while testifying against Jo Ann Parks if he could be wrong in his evaluation of the fire and its cause, he said no.

"If I am wrong," he said, "then everything I have ever been taught and those people that have been taught before me would all be wrong."

And that is, in effect, what the California Innocence Project attorneys were claiming in the Parks case: the assumptions fire investigators made then, and in some cases continue to make today, have been wrong. The new report from Nordskog doubling down on the original findings in the case, and upping the ante with claims of serial fire setting, made it clear that the prosecution was not going to take that lying down.

There would be no easy settlement in the Jo Ann Parks case, Cohen knew. They'd have to go to court. They'd have to go to war.

PART THREE

FIRE ON TRIAL

14

Sherlock Was Wrong

Clarence Hiller's wife awoke with a start and shook him from sleep, sensing something amiss before she realized what it was: The room was too dark.

The hallway light outside their daughter's room, the one they always kept burning through the night, had gone out. And so the dutiful husband and father of four rose from bed to have a look, to make sure all was well, and to begin the last thirty seconds of his life.

Near the top of the stairs Hiller met an unexpected obstacle: the shadowy form of a man. The intruder lunged and the two men, shoving and flailing, fell thudding down the staircase. At the landing, the stranger wrestled a pistol free from his waistband and fired two quick shots. Clarence Hiller, a man who simply wanted to put on the night-light so his daughter would feel safe in the dark, sighed once and died in his nightclothes, his wife's shrieks still in the air. The burglar-turned-murderer pounded out the front door and onto the empty streets of predawn Chicago.

The police soon arrived and pieced together what had happened. The killer had climbed through the Hillers' kitchen window, entering quietly but leaving behind a key bit of evidence: On a freshly painted railing beneath the window, investigators found the vivid imprints of four fingers of someone's left hand embedded in the still-soft paint.

At 2:38 A.M., a police patrol spotted Thomas Jennings, a paroled burglar, limping in the darkness not far from the Hiller home. They frisked him and found a revolver in his pocket. None of the surviving Hillers got a good look at his face, but it made little difference. Four police experts agreed that, without doubt, Jennings's left hand had grabbed that wooden rail—a clean, simple, straightforward resolution, case closed.

So when Simon Cole, a social sciences professor at the University of California, Irvine, began his lonely campaign almost two decades ago to prove that the science of fingerprint analysis is missing a crucial element—namely, the science part—he wasn't merely going up against the police, the FBI, decades of television cop show heroes, and pretty much every black-robed judge in the land. Cole was taking on Clarence Hiller's ghost.

For Hiller has both empowered and haunted the justice system for more than a century, his murder by Thomas Jennings in 1910 a seminal moment in the history of law enforcement. Jennings became the first person in America to be arrested, convicted, sentenced to death, and hanged through the triumph of dactylography—also known as the analysis of fingerprints. Hiller's murder ushered in a new era of modern law enforcement, making possible the millions of fingerprint comparisons and cases that followed, from the Lindbergh kidnapping to the Night Stalker serial killings to the prosecution of the Al Qaeda operative who planned the millennium bombing of LAX.

But according to Cole—and a growing number of scientists, scholars, and legal experts horrified at high-profile fingerprint blunders—the courts have gotten it wrong for the past century. Since Clarence Hiller's murder, the legal system has treated fingerprint comparisons as not simply invaluable, which they unquestionably are, but as essentially infallible—when they are anything but. Just ask Lana Canen of Elkhart, Indiana, convicted of murdering her neighbor in 2002 based on a botched fingerprint comparison. Or Stephan Cowans of Roxbury, Massachusetts, who spent six and a half years in prison for a 1998 murder after the killer's fingerprints were falsely identified as his. And then there's Brandon Mayfield, the Oregon lawyer who was arrested when FBI experts mistakenly linked his fingerprint to the 2004 Madrid terrorist train bombing—notwithstanding the fact that Mayfield has never been to Madrid in his life, and the fingerprints were subsequently found by Spanish experts to match a known foreign terrorist.

Had the bombing occurred in the United States, the error almost certainly would not have been detected. Mayfield would still be in prison because, as everyone seemed to believe up until then, FBI fingerprint examiners were infallible. That was literally both the bureau's official position and the state of the law.

Cole, however, had been warning the FBI and other law-enforcement agencies for years that this would happen—that, in fact, it had been happening in lower-profile cases around the country since the day Hiller was hanged. The ability to match a known fingerprint to a partial, smudged, or faint latent lifted from a crime scene is an imperfect art at best, Cole says. It can only be deemed scientific and reliable after we know the error rate and also take steps to protect examiners from the sort of cognitive bias that infected the Madrid bombing fiasco, where the examiners knew supposedly incriminating details about Mayfield in advance, or knew that a match had been declared by other examiners already.

Fingerprint examiners, even top ones, can err when the pressure is great and the partial fingerprints are spotty. Yet their findings have been viewed as so persuasive and so overwhelming that even other fingerprint examiners are psychologically affected and tend to verify a declared match when they know another examiner they trust has found one. This is a classic example of expectation bias.

Although it's done in courtrooms on a daily basis, there is no scientific basis for saying any one fingerprint match is 100 percent certain. Not even DNA matching makes such a radical claim, instead expressing a match in terms of probabilities—one in a hundred, one in a million, one in a billion. Those calculations are based on extensive genetic research on human populations and the frequency of certain genetic markers. DNA matching, then, is true science. Fingerprint matching, not so much.

Long written off as an outlier for challenging the conventional wisdom about fingerprints, Cole has gained respect over the years and his arguments have gained traction, particularly in the wake of the FBI's embarrassment over the Madrid case. The errors were all the more humiliating because the FBI had just headed off several legal challenges to fingerprint evidence by convincing federal judges that its procedures had never yielded such a mistake, and that Cole's concerns, therefore, were of little consequence.

"There was a fallacy at work: the belief that, because all fingerprints are unique, therefore fingerprint evidence is inherently reliable," Cole has said. "It makes sense at first blush, but think about it: No two faces are alike, yet eyewitness identification is difficult and problem plagued. . . . The real question is not whether all fingerprints are different, but how accurate are fingerprint examiners at matching the small, fragmentary prints you find at crime scenes."

Fingerprint examiners long countered that argument by saying there's more than a century of "empirical research" to back up fingerprint accuracy. But the "empirical research" they are referring to is nothing more than the day-to-day use of fingerprint evidence by police agencies and its longstanding acceptance by the courts. That makes Cole's point: Science is designed to uncover errors and find the truth; the courts are designed to follow precedent, which means judges will admit evidence not because it's scientifically sound, but because some other court admitted the same sort of evidence in the past.

If the Madrid case raised questions about the dependability of the most ubiquitous and seemingly certain forensic science of fingerprinting, the release of a forensic science critique by the National Academy of Sciences in 2009, followed by an even more scathing federal report in 2016, created a sensation. Other forensic disciplines turned out to be in far worse shape than fingerprinting, those reports found. In the 2016 report, the President's Council of Advisors on Science and Technology also looked at the "science" of bite-mark analysis, hair and fiber comparisons, shoe-print matching, and a host of other commonly used methods of tying criminals to crimes and found serious problems with all of them. Suddenly Cole looked less like a gadfly and more like a prophet. He is now a respected voice for forensic reforms and head of the National Registry of Exonerations, the nation's leading clearinghouse for statistics and research on wrongful convictions, based at his Irvine campus.

As Cole had long argued, the presidential commission found there was no science in many of those "pattern matching" forensic practices—no analysis of how often the "experts" were mistaken, no guidelines for how to consistently make a match versus an exclusion, no data to show that, for example, bite marks left in a victim's skin, or tire tread marks at a murder scene, or shirt fibers caught in a gun's trigger guard, can validly be matched to a suspect in a crime. Without such foundational research, the subjective human process of matching fingerprints or bites or bullet markings or burn patterns can never be truly scientific, and the absence of scientific backing invites biased comparisons and junk science into the courtroom. Only DNA comparisons were deemed by the commission to be on sound scientific footing.

There were no significant studies of errors in fingerprint matching before 2011, and the efforts to make fingerprinting fully reliable and scientific have a long way to go. According to the 2016 report of the presidential commission, an FBI study found that false fingerprint matches could occur in one out of every 306 cases; another study found a stunning error rate as great as one out of eighteen cases.

The reason for the lack of scientific rigor is simple: Most forensic methods did not arise from scientific research but through a prosecutor's or policeman's need. Sir Arthur Ignatius Conan Doyle's fictional consulting detective, Sherlock Holmes, popularized the idea of using scientific techniques to solve crimes, including fingerprints, and inspired some real police investigators to try to do the same. Or consider the history of bite-mark evidence, first used rather inauspiciously in the United States during the Salem witch trials. In the modern era, in 1974 in California, a detective noticed a homicide victim had a bite mark on his nose. The detective had a bright idea: Get a dentist in to see if he could match a suspect to the bite. He found three dentists to match teeth to marks on the victim's nose. Walter Edgar Marx was then convicted of manslaughter. When he appealed, the California appellate courts held that bite-mark evidence was admissible despite what everyone, including the judges hearing the case, agreed was a complete lack of scientific backing for the technique. There was no controlled research, no real data, no testing, no validation, no blind testing for errors, no proof that human skin can accurately record a bite mark that can be matched to anyone. All the case had was a couple of dentists saying, yep, those teeth made that bite mark—a claim uttered with confidence and certainty, without ambiguity. And yet the wildly illogical judicial opinion in that case opened the floodgates for bite-mark prosecutions nationwide, with subsequent courts simply following California's precedent and eventually asserting that the original case had established the validity of bite-mark "science," though it established nothing of the kind. Such is the mesmerizing power of precedent, which is basically the court system's way of saying, if we did it before, it must be correct, and history is all the proof we need. This is why the law is the opposite of science, which welcomes and encourages proof that history is wrong, which is why we no longer envision a flat earth being orbited by the sun. Meanwhile, the Marx case spawned not only a new and dubious tool for imprisoning people, but it also created a lucrative cottage industry for dentists who claimed a new specialty: forensic dentistry, which figured prominently in, among other big cases, the prosecution of serial killer Ted Bundy.

The junk science pedigree of bite-mark evidence led the California Innocence Project to take up the case of Bill Richards, who spent twenty-two years in prison for the murder of his wife at their Mojave Desert home. A prominent bite-mark expert matched a mark on his wife's hand to Richards's crooked teeth. The expert, Dr. Norman "Skip" Sperber, claimed no more than two out of a hundred people would have a bite anything like Richards's. The testimony was enough to convict him.

The innocence project attorneys requested testing of DNA samples from the murder weapon, which did not belong to either

Richards or his wife. Then Sperber recanted his testimony and admitted there was no scientific basis for his findings. There was literally no case left after that. But the San Bernardino County District Attorney fought and appealed for the next eight years to keep Richards behind bars anyway, arguing—successfully—that the courts should ignore claims that the bite-mark evidence was false because it had been an opinion, not direct testimony, and an opinion technically cannot be false. Therefore Richards's trial technically had been "fair" under California law. The California Supreme Court went along with this reasoning—which meant there was no legal recourse for Richards, even though he had been proved innocent. It was so outrageous that Alex Simpson, associate director of the California Innocence Project, was able to lobby the state legislature successfully for a new law that allows appeals based on false scientific expert testimony. Without that change, Richards would be in prison to this day. He finally walked out of prison in 2016.

Without that change in the law, Jo Ann Parks would have no case, either.

Meanwhile, bite-mark comparisons are now widely regarded by the scientific community as junk science at its worst. The presidential commission report opined that it would probably never become a legitimate science. And yet courts still admit bite-mark evidence around the country on a regular basis—because there is legal precedent to do so.

The history of fingerprints is just as science-free as bite marks. A prosaic presence in every B-movie murder plot and rerun of *Law & Order*, fingerprinting is so ubiquitous today that it is virtually synonymous with the concept of identity itself. Fingerprinting certainly represented a revolution when the handcuffs snapped onto

Tom Jennings's wrists after the 1910 murder of Clarence Hiller. The discovery that fingerprints could be read in a way that rendered people as unique as snowflakes did as much for crime detection as penicillin would do three decades later for health care.

Perhaps it's not surprising, then, that the scientific reasoning, factual findings, even the wording of the venerable landmark legal opinion affirming the reliability of fingerprint evidence in the murder case against Jennings has been quoted, paraphrased, and depended upon ever since. The court gave an epic review of fingerprint history, how the ancient Egyptians used the pharaoh's thumbprint as an official identifier, how contract signers and courts in India for decades had relied upon fingerprints as binding identifications, how the system of fingerprint analysis invented by Sir Francis Galton, cousin to Charles Darwin, had a firm scientific basis and, by 1911, had been used by the British police in "thousands of cases without error."

"This method of identification is in such general and common use that the courts cannot refuse to take judicial cognizance of it," the Illinois Supreme Court boldly concluded in the Jennings case, reciting what seemed to be, even then, the long and solidly established history of dactylography. And in the years that followed, every state, federal, and local court has agreed in untold millions of cases, embracing fingerprint comparisons as a kind of forensic Holy Grail that has withstood the test of time.

The problem is, none of the original reasoning, which has been relied upon by the courts ever since, holds water: The ancient Egyptians didn't use fingerprints as identifiers, but as royal seals, no more relevant to the Jennings case than hieroglyphics.

The practice of using fingerprints on contracts in India was not based on science, but on superstition, undertaken on a whim by a British magistrate in Jungipoor, who felt his Indian subjects would believe their personal imprint on a document was more mystically binding than a mere signature.

As for Galton, he did invent a revolutionary system of analyzing the loops and whorls of fingerprints that is still in use today (and that bears his name), though he conceived of it not as a crime-busting tool, but as a means of classifying the genetically superior among us. Galton, in his most-remembered work, was the father of eugenics, his theory of controlled breeding and noble birth that has been used over the years to justify such human travesties as forced sterilizations, pogroms, genocide, and the Holocaust.

And as for those thousands of cases in Britain in which fingerprints were used without error prior to 1911? The truth is, no one knew then—or now—if there were any errors or not. The police experts were simply taken at their word. No one checked, other than like-minded police examiners already told that a match had been found.

One of the few serious courtroom challenges in the modern era to the validity of fingerprint comparisons took place in Philadelphia in 2002 under relatively new federal rules for admitting scientific testimony, the Daubert test. *Daubert v. Merrell Dow Pharmaceuticals* was a products liability lawsuit in which the parents of two children born with serious birth defects sued the drug maker, blaming their children's condition on the anti-nausea drug Bendectin. In 1993, the Supreme Court helped resolve the case by crafting a new legal test to allow evidence Merrell had sought to exclude under old courtroom standards that considered only whether a scientific principle was generally accepted (a standard that favors old science over cutting edge). The Daubert test required a more detailed scientific inquiry by trial judges, including whether a forensic method can be or has been tested, whether it's been peer reviewed, and whether error rates have been established.

The new standard, which applies to all federal courts and has been adopted by some states, has been used to expose systemic errors in forensics—fallacies and frauds that almost always favored prosecutors over defendants. Crime lab scandals were uncovered around the country—a serologist in West Virginia who falsified hundreds of tests to help sustain convictions, a pathologist who faked autopsy results in more than twenty death-penalty cases, even a host of lab problems at the FBI. Since 1993, Daubert has been used to challenge the validity of virtually every branch of forensics, including the first re-examination of the reliability of fingerprint evidence since the Hiller murder.

It came in a fairly run-of-the-mill cocaine-trafficking case against a Philadelphia man named Llera Plaza. US district judge Louis Pollak, considering testimony from a number of experts, including Simon Cole, ruled that while FBI fingerprint examiners could testify in the case, they were barred from claiming that any particular person absolutely matched a particular print. There would be no more claims of 100 percent accuracy. More scientific study was needed, the judge decided, before the luster could be restored to fingerprint matching.

This was as mild a slap as the judge could have delivered. Because no error rates for fingerprint comparisons had ever been calculated—indeed, the FBI was in denial that errors ever even happened—the judge conceivably could have thrown fingerprint evidence out of court completely if Daubert standards were followed to the letter. Yet fingerprint examiners nationwide were flabbergasted by this seemingly modest and scientifically sound ruling. If sustained on appeal, it could undo hundreds, if not thousands, of criminal cases, they feared. The FBI mounted a concerted effort to overturn the decision, bringing in a legion of experts to argue that in eight decades of fingerprint matching, the FBI had never made a false match, that fingerprint errors discussed by Cole and others had been made by police agencies other than the FBI, and that Pollak's decision would have disastrous consequences for public safety.

In a rare move three months later, Pollak overturned himself, saying he had been wrong in his initial decision and that the FBI examiners could continue to make their usual, full-certainty fingerprint identifications in court. The Madrid bombing case showed Pollak had been right the first time—this was exactly the sort of error the FBI had previously said could not happen when pressuring Judge Pollak to overturn himself and to abandon the requirements of the Daubert test. So Daubert, intended to balance the power of old precedent with the tendency of new science to disprove old ideas, is not really doing the job. Judges are no better than juries at telling junk science from sound science, and when they are skeptical, that skepticism is usually aimed at experts for defendants more than for the prosecution. In 2017, Judge Donald Shelton of Michigan told the sixty-ninth annual conference of the American Academy of Forensic Sciences that most judges allow any and all prosecution expert testimony without question, and are reluctant to block even the most specious forensic evidence, such as bite-mark comparisons, so long as other courts are allowing it. "If it was left to judges," Shelton said, "the earth would still be flat."

Now the other pattern-matching forensic disciplines, none of them on as firm a footing as fingerprints and many of them as weak as bite marks, face all the same problems and questions: Nonscientific and mythic origins. Lack of error rates. Lack of data. Vulnerability to bias. According to the data gathered by the National Registry of Exonerations, of the 2,250 men and women wrongfully convicted then exonerated of murder or other serious felonies between 1989 and 2018, 541 were convicted with flawed or misleading forensic evidence—about one out of four.

Almost all of the fancy technology and forensic acumen that has been lionized and romanticized for years by such Hollywood concoctions as the CSI television empire have been shown to be seriously flawed. In that fantasy world, every case is solved in sixty minutes by the certainty of science. In the real world, the science of hair and fibers, bite-mark comparisons, ballistic comparisons, footprint matching, fingerprint matching, and arson investigations has been tainted by systematic error, false assumptions, and theories that turned out to have never been scientifically tested. Ironically, the newest, most powerful, and most scientifically rigorous forensic technology—DNA fingerprinting, one of the only forensic practices that actually arose from the world of science instead of police work—has unintentionally highlighted the lack of scientific rigor in other forensic disciplines.

The dirty secret of forensic science's flaws has left the justice system alternately in a quiet panic or in massive denial over the implications of the vanishing aura of CSI infallibility. So far, the only checks on bad science in the courtroom are individual, one-case-at-a-time legal challenges mounted by individual defendants and innocence projects. Unlike medical science, where every drug, device, procedure, and method faces years of regulation, peer review, testing, and proof of efficacy, forensic science remains an unregulated wild west. Law-enforcement agencies control it all, with no central agency or authority to separate real science from junk science, and no incentive for police or prosecutors to ban even the most outlandish forensic experts so long as they help win cases. Indeed, law-enforcement organizations, including the US

Department of Justice and the National District Attorneys Association, have fought forensic reforms, just as the FBI pushed back against Judge Pollak's ruling.

The field of arson investigation is no exception.

The same year Jo Ann Parks's trial began, a group of experienced fire and police arson investigators from around the country assembled at the Federal Law Enforcement Training Center in Glynco, Georgia, for a new kind of advanced training on determining areas of origin at fire scenes. The goal was to expose fire investigators to the challenge posed by flashover, which suddenly had become a source of controversy and legal wrangling.

Two "burn cells" had been set up outside—stand-alone fake rooms, twelve-by-fourteen feet with a standard door used in homes across America, eight-foot ceilings, and plywood and gypsum board construction. These compartments were equipped to be set aflame, to reach 600 degrees, to achieve flashover and full-room involvement, then burn for two minutes before being extinguished. The trainees were kept away until the fire had been put out, just as they might arrive to investigate a house fire after firefighters had put out the blaze.

The blackened burn cells looked eerily like the small, charred rooms inside the Parks house. With the smell of burnt wood still heavy in the air, the trainees were asked to walk into the burn cells, observe the damage, and determine which quadrant—which fourth of the room—contained the area of origin for the fire. That was it: not the area of origin itself, but just the quarter of the room that contained it.

Most of the trainees felt it was child's play.

Later in the training, instead of empty burn cells, the test rooms were furnished as living rooms, bedrooms, and kitchens.

In each exercise, fewer than one out of ten of these veteran investigators got the right quadrant. Consider that: Some of the nation's leading local arson investigators, asked to identify where a fire started in an empty room, failed to do so more than nine out of ten times.

This was not because their execution of techniques and principles was bad. They did what they'd been taught to do. It was because the techniques themselves failed most of the time when flashover occurred. Severe damage that occurred long after the fire started was time and again mistaken for the area of origin, because that's what flashover can do.

These results were not an anomaly. Similar exercises were conducted twice a year for the next twelve years, and the classes consistently produced the same results. According to the instructors, the odds of just guessing at random would produce better results (one out of four) than the application of traditional fire investigation methods using the area of greatest damage as the likely origin.

That's remarkably consistent terrible performance—not by neophytes, but by journeyman investigators who were doing real-world arson investigations as a full-time job, drawing conclusions about fires using the very same methods that failed so miserably at Glynco. Except back home and out in the field, people were being denied insurance coverage, charged with crimes, and sent to prison based on the work of these same investigators using these same techniques.

Yet no detailed records of the failures in those burn cells were kept, and no one thought to inform the wider world of fire investigators—and convicts like Parks—that the conventional methods of fire investigation appeared to be broken when it came to flashover and building rooms that are fully involved with flames.

Finally, a now-retired fire investigation instructor with the Bureau of Alcohol, Tobacco, Firearms and Explosives, Steve Carman, sounded the alarm. He published an article in 2008 about the problem that flashover posed for traditional methods of fire investigation, which included the high number of errors in identifying the correct area of origin in the training center's burn cells. He described a 2005 exercise at Glynco with the burn cells in which only three out of fifty-three trained fire investigators identified the correct area of origin. When the same group repeated the exercise, again only three got it right—a different three. That's a success rate of only 5.7 percent in identifying the area of origin; no one nailed the actual point of origin.

Carman said these results showed there was a desperate need for additional research and training for investigators in how to correctly analyze a post-flashover fire scene, and that failure to take flashover into account—as happened in the original Parks investigation—invited errors.

A typically law-and-order ATF career guy, Carman had been investigating fires and training fire investigators for decades, and had been widely respected by his colleagues. Yet after he published his article about the burn-cell exercises, many of his peers treated him as a traitor for airing the dirty laundry.

"Oh my, a lot of guys were really pissed off at me," Carman recalls of the aftermath. "There was backlash about going public with this. But it was time for people to take their heads out of the sand and wake the heck up. We had a problem."

The fact that systemic problems existed with arson investigations, particularly with practices in wide use at the time of the

Parks fire and for a decade or more after it, seemed obvious to Carman and others. Reforms that began with the National Fire Protection Association's guidelines, which have been updated every few years, have been imposed on arson investigators since that time, often over the objections of many field investigators. Right around the time of the Parks fire, an entire laundry list of arson myths was exposed as junk science—myths that had been used for many years to convict people of crimes or deny them insurance payouts for lost homes and property. This included the glass crazing and bedspring melting that John Lentini exposed in the Oakland firestorm, but also other indicators of arson that turned out to be false: concrete spalling, pour patterns on floors, "alligatoring" of wood surfaces, the depth of charring as a reliable way to calculate how fast a fire burned. All of these indicators were used as proof that an accelerant had been used to make a fire burn faster and hotter, but it turned out that all of these "indicators of arson" could also be caused by flashover and other noncriminal causes. It has taken decades for these myths to be put aside, and the question of how to properly investigate a flashover fire remains highly controversial and a source of bitter legal battles. It was predicted that the end of discredited methods and indicators of arson and the creation of new guidelines would make it harder to determine a precise cause in many fires, leading to more findings of "undetermined" causes. FBI crime statistics show this may be happening: The number of fires found to be arson in the United States declined by 44 percent between 2001 and 2016. But if law-enforcement officials and prosecutors are looking at new cases differently, they have been opposed to reopening old cases and releasing convicts sent to prison on the basis of old arson myths. Admitting systematic errors would risk exposing tens of thousands of criminal and civil arson cases to the possibility of being reopened all at once. So each case has to be fought one at a time—if it gets fought at all.

Even so, similar concerns about flashover effects and other questionable arson investigation practices being raised in the Jo Ann Parks case have led to exonerations in other arson cases in Texas, Massachusetts, Pennsylvania, New York, Florida, and elsewhere. Cases are being reopened involving men, women, and juveniles imprisoned for years for arson and murder on scientific principles that have turned out to be unscientific. There have been at least thirty-six exonerations in felony arson cases so far, a majority of them murder cases, in which up-to-date science revealed no crime had been committed at all. There might have been a thirty-seventh, but the determination came posthumously—after Cameron Todd Willingham, in a Texas case with eerie similarities to Parks's experience, was executed in 2004. Nine prominent fire experts later reported that the case against Willingham had no basis in science. One expert hired by the Texas Forensic Science Commission, Craig Beyler, found that the key expert witness in Willingham's trial gave evidence that was "hardly consistent with a scientific mind-set and is more characteristic of mystics or psychics."

The arson prosecution of Kristine Bunch of Decatur County, Indiana, is a classic example of blunders, bias, and myth in arson investigation—a case that also has remarkable similarities to the Parks case. Bunch was exonerated after serving seventeen years of a sixty-year prison sentence after being convicted of killing her three-year-old son by locking him in a bedroom and setting their home on fire.

At the time of the fire in 1995, Bunch was a single twenty-one-year-old mother living with her son in a mobile home. She suffered mild injuries in the blaze, but her son perished. As in the Parks case, an allegedly halfhearted rescue attempt by a young mother was a key element of the case against Bunch.

Three days after the fire, she was arrested. A state fire investigator had ruled out potential accidental causes, did not consider flashover in his analysis, and determined that there were two separate points of origin based on his reading of burn patterns. He used negative corpus to find that Bunch started the blaze with matches or a lighter and used charcoal lighter fluid or some other accelerant to make sure the fire spread. A laboratory analysis was said to have confirmed the presence of a petroleum-based accelerant at both the points of origin.

The evidence at the time was deemed by the authorities to be overwhelming. Bunch, who had become pregnant before the start of her trial, was treated in court like a monster. The incensed trial judge accused Bunch of arranging the pregnancy because she thought it would boost her chances of receiving leniency. "It will not," the judge assured her. "You will not raise that child."

Bunch not only lost a child in a fire. She lost another to seventeen years in prison, as the judge's assurance was prophetic: Bunch's sister raised her son.

With the help of two private attorneys and the staff of the Center on Wrongful Convictions, an innocence project based at Northwestern University in Illinois, the entire arson case against Bunch finally was revealed to be baseless. The laboratory tests for accelerants were flat-out wrong—the fire was not started with petroleum products, and evidence in a later civil suit suggests it was fabricated by the authorities. Three other fire experts said the burn pattern analysis was wrong and that the correct ruling on the origin and cause of the fire could only be "undetermined." The original trial judge scoffed at these findings and upheld the conviction. Years more of appeals were needed to finally set Bunch free.

The most striking similarity to the Parks case, however, was in the prosecutorial portrait of a murderous mom, which helped drive the jury to convict Bunch. That portrait also may explain why the trial judge remained unmoved by new evidence of innocence that appellate judges new to the case found to be powerful. The official attack on Bunch's character was virtually the same as the portrait of Jo Ann Parks drawn by Deputy District Attorney Dinko Bozanich. At Bunch's trial, the prosecutor argued that she was a neglectful mother who had barely tried to save her son from the burning mobile home, if she'd tried at all. After the fire, the prosecutor said she showed little or no remorse—she didn't cry enough, or sincerely enough. The prosecutor also claimed (despite testimony to the contrary) that Bunch had wanted to give up custody of her son before the fire. The prosecutor argued that this desire to be rid of parental responsibilities demonstrated a motive for murder—not unlike the prosecution's take on tubal ligation in the Parks case as demonstrating motive to kill.

According to a study by attorneys Andrea L. Lewis and Sara L. Sommervold of the Center on Wrongful Convictions, this sort of attack on women defendants in arson murders and other "heinous" criminal cases is very common and extremely effective. They found:

"Two types of flawed mothers are portrayed within the criminal justice system: the 'mad' mother, the superior caretaker who has conformed to traditional gender roles but merely committed an irrational act because she was mentally ill; and the 'bad' mother, who simply is a cold, callous woman incapable of caregiving and is therefore non-feminine.

"The bad mother falls into the cultural archetype of the Female Monster."

Kristine Bunch was lucky, a Female Monster released after just seventeen years in prison.

Jo Ann Parks is in her twenty-eighth year as resident Female Monster.

15

The Monster Speaks

"I try not to hope," Jo Ann Parks whispers into a grimy visitor's-room telephone. "I have resigned myself to life in prison. To working here. To friends here. Hoping and then still not getting out, that would be too much. Too hard."

But a moment later, the woman in the rumpled blue county jail overalls, her long, dark hair plaited and streaked with gray, admits this isn't quite true. She does hope. After two decades of seeing every roommate, friend, coworker, and enemy come and go as she remained, the LWOP on her file—Life Without Parole—giving her every reason never to hope again, she has given in. She has a habeas hearing under way, which she never really believed would happen. She has been visited by a representative of California governor Jerry Brown to see if she'd be worthy of a pardon, something she never thought possible. And her former roommate and girlfriend has gotten out and found a job in Hawaii, and given Parks a standing invitation to join her there if she wins her freedom.

"So, yeah, I am hopeful," she says reluctantly, without a smile, almost without expression, but eyes pressed closed. "To be honest, I'm on pins and needles."

It is Christmastime at the cheerless, slit-windowed twin towers of Los Angeles County's Century Regional Detention Facility. The main holding place for LA's women inmates, it is tucked next to a feverishly busy elevated freeway in an industrial zone of the city of Lynwood, across the highway from an auto dismantling plant. If there were views available to inmates at the top of its West Tower—which there are not—the neighborhood where Jo Ann Parks's first house fire took place would be visible a couple of miles up the road. The West Tower is Parks's home away from home while her habeas corpus hearing is held. She has spent half her life at the state's largest penitentiary for women, 265 miles north in rural Chowchilla, California. The distance is too great to keep shuttling her back and forth to hearings in downtown Los Angeles, so she is in the jail indefinitely. And jail time is hard time: She misses her job, her meds, her friends, the ability to walk the yard, to be on familiar ground, to know what to expect. County jail means most hours spent in a cell, with little to do but worry.

The jail visitor's center is decorated for Christmas with a sad gaudiness. Big tempera Christmas trees, elves, and snowmen are painted on the windows behind the front desk, which is festooned with shiny gold garlands. The airport-style metal detector to safeguard against visitors bringing in contraband has been decorated with white and red candy-cane stripes. A small silver Christmas tree is set up on top of a display warning visitors against bringing forbidden items into jail (prescription drugs, makeup, ballpoint pens—the list is extensive and not very merry). Another poster urges visitors to tell someone in authority if they witness severe signs of depression in an inmate. YOU COULD SAVE SOMEONE'S LIFE!

The visitor line is long at the women's lockup. It is always long, but the holidays bring the hordes and a special air of desperation.

The queue is filled with children gripping the hands of their grandmothers or fathers, waiting to be ushered through the candy-striped metal detector. Then they must follow painted lines on the floor that match a colored ticket the guards hand each visitor. This leads them to the correct bank of elevators to be whisked up the tower, where Mommy waits behind a visiting booth's thick glass window.

Parks gets few visitors. Her mother stopped coming just two years after she was imprisoned. Her siblings have never visited. Her lawyer visits regularly now that she is in Los Angeles, as well as Mary Ross, daughter of fire investigator Robert Lowe, a principal link to the outside world. Parks has been sick with flu-like symptoms that everyone in the jail seems to have. She worked for years in prison in a facility that makes dentures, but here in the jail she says she has been put to work counseling younger inmates on how to prepare for prison life. She had certainly learned the hard way, targeted at first by other inmates for being a convicted child killer, learning over time how to avoid confrontation, keeping her background quiet, gradually building friendships and trust with a few other lifers.

She has taken classes and jobs that she felt would make her marketable if she ever got out.

After all these years, she still finds it hard to talk about the fire without tearing up—quiet tears, not sobbing. She is still emotionally flat outwardly. "It's just who I am." She shrugs.

She says she regrets not testifying at her trial, not telling her story to the jurors. She is tortured by the possibility that it might have made a difference, but her attorney assured her it was an unnecessary risk, that "We don't need it." She says she wanted to jump up time and again and shout, "No, that's not true!" during the prosecution's case, but all she did was stare straight ahead, not making eye contact with jurors, as her attorney had instructed. The hardest part was listening to her husband, Ron, describe the children as "spilt milk."

"He made me feel like he didn't love the kids at all," she said. "That they meant nothing to him."

Yet she refused entreaties to implicate Ron, who died of cancer in 2011, having divorced Jo Ann and married again in 2009. When the guilty verdict came in and the penalty phase that would determine a life or death sentence was about to begin, Parks had a choice. As she tells it, her defense team pointed out that if it were true, she could save her own life by saying she knew Ron had set up some sort of device to start a fire that night. Did he want to sue the landlords? Was it her job to save the kids, but the plan backfired?

According to Parks, she refused to say anything of the kind. "It's not true. I couldn't say that. I wouldn't."

She says she's taken responsibility for what happened in another way. "Even though I didn't set the fire, I felt like I shouldn't be alive. If anybody should have died that night, it should have been me, not them."

The habeas hearing has been hard, she says. The holding cells in the court building are intensely uncomfortable, long waits on hard benches in handcuffs. She arrives in court stiff and limping, hands cuffed to belly chain, but that's not the worst of it, she says. The worst part is the hearing. Each day in court consists of hours of delay and waiting, bracketed by interminable stretches of technical testimony. And then, just when everyone in the court is fighting to maintain focus, eyes heavy, seat aching, some riveting and terrible bit of information will surface: a description of the 911 call, a reference to Ronnie's closet, or a projection of some chilling photographs of her old burned house. That's all it takes to trigger the old shock, the old memories of that night. She buries her face in her hands. When pictures of her burned children flash up on the courtroom's big screen, Raquel Cohen rubs her back and murmurs, "Stay calm, it'll be okay." The prosecution team eyes her with steely resolve and suspects it's all theater.

"I just want it be over," she says. "I loved my babies. I didn't set the fire. But I didn't save them, either."

While at the jail, Parks took an English class to pass the time and try to learn something instead of worrying and pacing. The teacher was so impressed with Parks's work on an essay on prison life he assigned that he entered it into an annual talent show contest sponsored by the posh, old-money Los Angeles Athletic Club. She would get to read her work at the club—if she earned her release in time. The essay was entitled "Inside/Outside."

INSIDE

When you first go to prison you are scared of the unknown. You see nothing but chain-link fences, buildings, dead grass, dirt, and bushes. You notice all the different gangs for they are all separated in groups and by color. The women are talking, laughing, some are even crying. You hear alarms going off and see the women get to the ground. You hear the clanging of keys all around you. Your senses are on overdrive because there is so much going on around you that you are not used to seeing or hearing, it takes a minute to adjust. The smells are strange to you. You're outside, you smell dirt in the air or the stench of the porta pottys being cleaned, the traps from the kitchen being cleaned. You even get the smell of death because there is an animal that hid and died somewhere near. The unit's swamp coolers have this fishy-moldy smell. You even get the smells from the kitchen. When the food is being cooked, sometimes it smells good, sometimes it smells like rotten meat. Over the years of being there the unknown becomes normal to you. You get used to the smells and sights all around you. This is your new normal.

It's normal to hear loud intercoms all day long of all kinds of announcements, or deputies yelling. It's normal to hear a locker slam or drawer to a door being slammed. Hearing women yelling down the halls or even screaming. To see fights or even to witness someone getting beat by more than one person at a time. You adjust quickly because it's a different world and you have to survive. So you watch everything that everyone is doing. You see more than you like to at times. You see women selling or doing drugs, tattooing being done, women having sex in the dayroom or on yards. You notice arguments starting and you know you need to get away. You are scared and shocked at first but with time it becomes normal. You get schooled by the lifers that have been there longer than you. They show you how to survive and the unspoken rules of prison.

The unspoken rules are: 1. You don't tell anything you see. 2. You don't get involved. 3. You never cosign for anyone. 4. Never buy anything you can't pay for because they will beat you up and steal all your property, canteen, and boxes that your family sends and you will still owe them. 5. Never stop a fight, you may end up taking the beating for the girl you tried to save. 6. You tell, you are considered a snitch and sometimes they will slit your face from ear to mouth as a sign that, "you hear, you tell."

So you have choices and decisions you need to make. You can run the yard with the gangbangers and help them to do their dirty work. You can do drugs or pills, stay high and in trouble. You can make pruno (alcohol), stay drunk, sick, and fighting. You can even fight your way around prison. All of this gets you write-ups, jail (the hole), [or administrative segregation] c/c (you get out only two hours a day).

Or you can make the decision that you are going to do something positive with your time. . . .

16

The Bias Man

The battle over bias in the forensic sciences—and fire investigation in particular—is the justice system's holy war. It's not just about finding the best way to investigate flashover fires, or arguing the scientific reliability of using dogs to sniff out accelerants used by arsonists. (As to that: The National Fire Protection Association says that canine alerts are useful but too error prone unless confirmed by lab tests, though some jurisdictions insist on prosecuting based on dog evidence alone.)

The question of investigative bias is something else entirely, striking at the fallibility of the humans who employ the technique and technology of forensics and crime-fighting. And that is anything but impersonal. The divide over bias has grown as absolute as a religious schism, as evolution versus creationism, as nature versus nurture, or baseball versus football. There is little common ground between the purists, who say the scientific determination of the origin and cause at a fire scene should focus solely on the physical evidence at the scene, and the practicalists, who say a proper analysis must be informed by the totality of the circumstances, from the character of the suspect to their potential motives for causing a fire.

The two sides are so far apart that they often seem to speak different languages during the ritual confrontations of the courtroom. Observing one of them testify while the other side sits and watches is a distinctive spectacle, marked by the constant shaking of heads on one side or the other.

The very first witness in the Jo Ann Parks habeas corpus hearing sits squarely in the purist camp, an absolutist whose views earn scorn from many in law enforcement. But Paul Bieber argues that the facts are on his side. The former San Francisco firefighter turned fire investigator turned expert witness has researched wrongful arson convictions in the United States and has found that a large majority were contaminated by cognitive bias that, he believes, affected the outcome of the investigation. And the source of that bias, Bieber argues, is investigators' exposure to information that has nothing to do with the scientific analysis of a fire scene.

"It is not an insult to say cognitive bias is present in an investigation, though many investigators take it that way," Bieber says. "Here's the problem: Once you make up your mind, it is violently contrary to human behavior to change your mind. . . . That is the challenge. That is the starting point of cognitive bias."

Bieber argues this tendency exists in even the most well-intentioned experts, which is why he believes fire investigators need to be a blank slate when they walk into the remains of a house fire. In his view, the only information that should contribute to a scientific opinion on how a fire started should be the burn patterns and other physical evidence present at the scene. Eyewitness accounts of fire behavior, whether from firefighters, occupants of the house, or neighbors, can also be considered. And that's it. No exceptions.

He believes the Parks case is a textbook example of how failure to exclude extraneous information can lead an investigation astray. Consider, he suggests, the electrical cords deemed to be an incendiary device by the lead arson investigator in the Parks fire.

"Let's say you go into the Jo Ann Parks home without any knowledge of the background. You don't know she had a previous fire. You don't know she has a friend talking about dosing kids with cough medicine. You're simply performing a forensic investigation of a fire scene, which means you are applying scientific, engineering, and technical principles to the investigation of physical and empirical evidence. That's what it is supposed to be.

"Now, say you have five experts of equal experience, but they go in in blind, shielded circumstances, never hearing any of this extraneous bullshit about the mom or the case, because they don't need to know that to examine the physical evidence. How many of those five experts look at those wires and say, *I don't know what that is; it looks like a bunch of wires?* And how many say, *This is clearly a failed incendiary device?*

"What value is that opinion scientifically if I can't reach it without adding in extraneous information? Because without that extraneous information, all I see there is a bunch of wires."

A classic example of an arson finding based on expectation bias instead of a scientific analysis was described years ago by author and fire investigator Shelly Reuben, in an essay recalling a nonfatal house fire on the Jersey shore in the 1980s. Before the origin and cause investigation of the fire scene had begun, insurance and police detectives had determined that the house had been burned down deliberately by the owner. They had compiled an extensive list of "red flags" that seemed to make an arson finding inevitable:

— The owner had a criminal record, bad debts, and had lost his job.
— He had taken out fire insurance on the house.
— Furniture had been taken out of the house just before the fire.
— The family pet had been taken from the house before the fire.
— The owner was home at the time of the fire, but his car was not in its customary place in the driveway or garage.
— Many of the family clothes were missing from the closets rather than lying burned inside the ruin of the house.
— The owner of the house seemed overly distraught.

The insurance investigator and police detectives saw in this information an obvious case of a homeowner setting a fire to resolve a financial crisis, with the arsonist taking pains to preserve prized possessions just before setting the fire. This was grounds to deny an insurance payout and to issue an arrest warrant, they decided.

But before an arrest could be made, Reuben conducted the actual origin and cause investigation, relying on fire science instead of the list of red flags. Burn patterns led her to a possible area of origin, and once that was pinpointed, she found the fire had started with a short circuit hidden inside a wall, caused when a nail used to attach exterior shingles had pierced internal wiring. The fire was accidental, she concluded, and all those red flags turned out to be red herrings.

In the end, a closer look at the supposedly suspicious behavior led to benign explanations: The bad credit was from a mortgage payment that had been just a few days late. The owner had been laid off temporarily, but had been told by his employer he'd be rehired shortly. The couch had been put in the garage because the new family dog had been chewing it. The dog was missing because he had been dropped at the veterinarian. The clothes were gone because they were being laundered in advance of a family vacation. And the car was gone from its customary place because the owner's wife had taken it and their kids to visit their grandparents.

"Unlike burn patterns, red flags are indicators," she wrote, ". . . and like wind socks and weather vanes, can blow this way or that."

Bieber's proposed solution to such biased investigations, as simple as it is despised, is for fire investigators—at least those conducting a science-based examination of a fire scene—to work "in the blind" as Reuben did. To not look for or become aware of such "red flags." They should not consider or even know about other reasons to suspect that a crime had been committed until after the origin and cause investigation is complete. Anything short of that allows bias to influence the outcome.

In his report on the Parks case, Ed Nordskog dismisses cognitive bias as "the latest negative buzz phrase used when nothing else can be proven . . . akin to calling someone 'racist' and then putting the burden on them to prove otherwise." He derides the idea of making arson investigators work in the blind as ridiculous and impractical. "Only someone who has no idea how fires are actually investigated would say that," Nordskog says.

"Just consider the history," counters Bieber. "It's what the scientific method requires."

The notion of blind investigations in general is neither new nor outlandish. The first documented example of a blind scientific investigation was a successful probe of fraudulent claims commissioned by King Louis XVI of France in 1784. Louis wanted to verify or disprove the miracle-cure claims of one of the most famous physicians of his era, Franz Mesmer, who had captivated such luminaries of the day as Wolfgang Amadeus Mozart and the last queen of France, Louis's wife, Marie Antoinette. Now regarded as the father of hypnosis, from whom the term *mesmerize* originates, Mesmer claimed he could use magnets and other techniques to manipulate invisible vital fluids inside all living creatures in order to cure physical and mental ailments. He called this property of living things "animal magnetism," and Mesmer claimed his mastery of it had, among other feats, cured a well-known musician's hysterical blindness. What Mesmer was actually doing was using music, lighting, and spoken cadences to place individuals and groups into a hypnotic trance, then using hypnotic suggestion to effect cures.

The king appointed four members of the French Academy of Sciences to investigate Mesmer, led by the US ambassador to France at the time, America's sardonic and clever founding father, raconteur, and inventor, Benjamin Franklin. Among the commissioners was Dr. Joseph Guillotin, inventor of the world's most famous beheading device, which would be used after the Revolution to execute Louis, Marie Antoinette, and, ironically, the two other members of the Mesmer commission.

The commission asked Mesmer's trainees to don blindfolds, then attempt to distinguish objects, including a tree and a flask, that supposedly had been filled with vital fluids. They failed to do so. The commissioners also tested subjects who believed they had been cured of various ailments, whether or not they had actually received the animal magnetism treatments. The commission considered the resulting cures as a form of self-delusion or imagination, identifying what would later come to be known as the placebo effect.

The debunking of animal magnetism as a cure or a boon to sound minds and bodies brought an end to Mesmer's star turns with the royalty and Europe's wealthy elite, although his practices remained in vogue for the next century.

A few years later, blind testing was used in Britain to ascertain the effects of nitrous oxide—laughing gas—on humans (with subjects unaware whether they were breathing different concentrations of the gas or just plain air), and to compare the sound quality of a Stradivarius violin to a new guitar-like instrument crafted by a naval engineer, François Chanot. The committee, listening from another room, chose the new violin design.

In more modern applications, blind auditions are used by most symphony orchestras, with prospective players hidden behind screens. The probability of women landing a chair in America's symphony orchestras rose by 50 percent since the practice of blind auditions became commonplace, according to a 2001 gender bias study by researchers at Princeton and Harvard universities. Cognitive bias has been recognized as a factor even in pop culture—the television show *The Voice* has its judges sit in chairs facing away from singing contestants while judging their performances. Testing of new medicines is routinely done in "double blind" experiments, in which one group gets the real drug and one group gets a placebo, and neither the test subjects nor those administering the drugs know which is which.

The goal of blind testing is to avoid introducing information that could bias the test results. Seeing the legendary Stradivarius (or the marine scientist's equally distinct rival creation) while comparing their sound would be an obvious way of biasing judges of violin quality. Less obvious is the possible biasing of drug testing that can occur when lab workers know they are giving out placebos, which creates the risk of purposely, accidentally, or unconsciously providing cues to test subjects that they are not receiving the actual medicine, as well as the risk of data and observations being misreported.

For the same reasons, the criminal justice system is also beginning to recognize the value of blind practices in non-forensic practices: Double-blind methods for securing eyewitness identification of suspects are being adopted by some police departments. The most common characteristic in cases where DNA evidence overturns wrongful convictions are faulty eyewitness identifications (a factor in seven out of ten convictions of the innocent). Multiple studies across decades have shown eyewitness identifications have an error rate of at least one out of five in cases where witnesses are asked to identify strangers in traditional police lineups. In many of the wrongful convictions cases, initially uncertain witnesses were cajoled, coerced, or given subtle, even unconscious cues by police detectives, which led the witnesses to identify the suspects that investigators preferred, rather than relying strictly on memory. As time passed and through repeated retellings, witnesses would also begin to express more confidence in their recollections, though most researchers have found memories become less, not more, accurate over time. In some cases, eyewitnesses are led to alter their descriptions of suspects to better match the detectives' preferred suspect—though this also can be an unintended and subconscious process rather than deliberate corruption. Double-blind procedures seek to reduce bad eyewitness identifications by keeping both the witnesses and those administering the lineup from knowing which person on display is the actual suspect. The San Diego police, for example, have begun showing witnesses randomly generated photos on a computer screen that the police officers in the room cannot even see. Then the potential witness is asked to select the person most resembling the culprit. In contrast, the Los Angeles Police Department uses the venerable "six-pack" method of lineup identification—a group of six photos chosen by investigating officers and shown to eyewitnesses with the investigators present. LA police agencies have had to pay out several multimillion-dollar lawsuit verdicts for wrongful conviction based on bad eyewitness identifications in recent years, but have resisted changing their methods.

The way forensic science is deployed by law enforcement seems at times to be designed to introduce bias into the process. It is both permissible and common for a police investigator or prosecutor to introduce a case to a forensic analyst by explaining who a suspect is, what crimes are alleged, and what results are needed to "make" the case—be it a fingerprint or DNA or fiber or ballistics comparison. In other words, a forensics specialist often is told what the "right" answer is before the testing even begins, before they compare that smudgy partial fingerprint to the "right" suspect's fingerprint card, or before an arson investigator peers at a single burn pattern in a house where foul play is suspected before the fire scene is fully examined.

In his testimony in the Parks case, Paul Bieber said he first became aware of the role cognitive bias can play in the criminal justice system through a case he analyzed for the Northern California Innocence Project. George Souliotes of Modesto, California, had been convicted of setting a fire in 1997 that burned down a home he owned and rented out. A mother and her two children died in the fire.

Investigators assigned to the fire began by assembling information that seemed suspicious to them, but had nothing to do with fire science: a for-sale sign on the lawn; Souliotes's desire to evict his tenants; erroneous information that the house was going into foreclosure; and questionable eyewitness testimony from a distraught woman who thought she saw a vehicle like Souliotes's near the house at the time of the fire. This information suggested a financial motive, hostility toward the victims, and presence at the scene of the crime. The investigators suspected arson before any detailed investigation of the fire scene. Once inside, they quickly concluded burn patterns and melted metal door thresholds proved the use of gasoline or other flammable liquids to make the house burn hotter and faster than a normal fire. These conclusions were based on ideas that had been discredited as junk science by 1997, Bieber testified, "yet there was a tremendous amount of certainty."

It took sixteen years to finally free Souliotes from prison at age seventy-two. The judge who overturned Souliotes's conviction singled out "tunnel vision" and confirmation bias as key elements behind the wrongful conviction.

"I thought at the time that this must be a unique circumstance," Bieber told Judge Ryan on day one of the Parks hearing. "But I learned that [this] is actually a common occurrence."

He added that the sorts of errors he saw in the Souliotes case and in the Parks investigation were "not an example of poor investigator integrity, or that they are not honest about their conclusions. They believe they are correct."

But cognitive bias, he added, led investigators astray in both cases.

In a perfect world, he argued, the fire science experts searching for clues to how a fire started could be protected from such errors—as could the suspects their work implicates—if they were kept away from the nonscientific detective work, and were kept in the dark about the results of the larger criminal investigation. Noting that ten pages of a twelve-page fire investigation report in the Souliotes case detailed non-fire-related information, Bieber said the problems in that case could have been avoided by working in the blind. The presidential commission on forensic science agreed with this idea, Bieber said, finding that only "task relevant" information should be given to the forensic examiners to shield them from possible bias. Knowing about a planned eviction and foreclosure at the scene of a fire may be important information for a prosecutor or jury to consider in a criminal trial, but it adds nothing to the scientific analysis of burn patterns. The patterns do not change when the investigator has such extraneous information in hand, Bieber argues, but the investigator is another story—he and his perceptions can be changed and unconsciously biased by that information.

When it was time for the district attorney's office to cross-examine Bieber, the prosecutor's goal was to show the judge that Bieber's ideas were extreme, far outside the norms most others in the arson investigation business endorsed or accepted. The twenty-year-veteran deputy district attorney given this task, Sean Carney, Los Angeles's most experienced arson prosecutor, started by asking Bieber how he conducted a fire investigation. The defense expert gave him the expected answer: He limited himself to the origin and cause determination, and avoided biasing and extraneous information. He said he might find, for example, that a fire's ignition source was an overheated extension cord that caused flammable materials in a nearby trash can to catch fire. The fire then spread to other fuels in the room, then throughout the house.

And then, Carney asked, you would classify that short circuit as either deliberate and incendiary, or accidental, right?

Wrong, replied Bieber. "Others can make that determination and classification."

Classification of a fire is typically the last step in a fire investigation and is different from the cause determination. There are currently four possible classifications: incendiary (arson), accidental, natural causes, or undetermined. But Bieber was saying he avoided making such a call in his cases.

Carney adopted a look of incredulity and asked, "What's the point of that?"

Because that conclusion, Bieber said, is not scientific. The lead detective in any criminal investigation, who is also looking at possible motives, the behavior of the homeowner, and other nonscientific information, can put all that together and decide between arson and accident, Bieber suggested. That way the origin and cause inquiry remains pure and unbiased, arrived at through the scientific method.

A verbal tug-of-war ensued, a tensely polite struggle in which each man sought to portray the other as unreasonable. Carney tried several different hypotheticals intended to show that Bieber's reasoning led to absurd limits on fire investigators. But Bieber remained adamant, soft-spoken on the stand—unlike his more forceful and salty personality outside the courtroom. The stalemate soon drew the judge in to ask his own questions. It would be the first of many times Judge Ryan would take the wheel away from one or another of the attorneys, because he was either curious or impatient, trying to cut to the chase in one question instead of the six queries the attorneys might ask.

"Wouldn't the cause necessarily require you to determine whether it was accidental, incendiary, or natural?" Ryan asked.

"No, sir. The cause is defined . . . as the identification of a physical ignition source. . . . Not whether the circumstances were intentional or not." The first part was a scientific finding, he said. The rest was outside the realm of science.

When the judge expressed continued puzzlement, Bieber added, "It's kind of like saying to a fingerprint examiner, 'Why aren't you figuring out whether the finger was placed there intentionally or accidentally?' Well, because it is outside the domain of a fingerprint examination."

The judge nodded. The nuances were clear now, he said: The origin and cause investigation looks at the fire scene only and seeks to explain what happened to start and spread a fire. The classification looks at the totality of circumstances, scientific and non-scientific, and draws a conclusion.

This was intolerable to Carney because if the judge accepted Bieber's view that his was the best possible way of investigating a fire fairly, it meant that Jo Ann Parks had come that much closer to freedom. The Parks team wanted the judge to view the lead arson investigator in the original trial as having gone too far, mingling science with gumshoe detective work, inviting bias and violating the scientific method along the way. So Carney tried another hypothetical: What if you investigate a fire and find clear proof it was caused by a short circuit in a malfunctioning electrical appliance. "Wouldn't it follow that that would be an accident?"

Bieber would not concede. "Yes, it would, but the conclusion that it was an accidental cause would not be a scientific, technical, or engineering process. It would be the application of common sense to the totality of the circumstances. That's not the role of a forensic examiner."

"But that's commonly done in the fire investigation industry?" a frustrated Carney responded.

"Yes, sir. Just to be clear, it is common for fire investigators to take that additional step and classify the cause of the fire," Bieber said in a tone that made it clear he believed that most fire investigators were wrong to do so. "The person who is impacted by bias is unaware of it."

It was downhill from there. Carney could not shake or rattle Bieber, even when he launched a line of questioning that suggested the National Fire Protection Association had failed to employ the scientific method when it insisted fire investigators use the scientific method. Bieber just shook his head and said he was confused by the notion that asking investigators to follow the scientific method could be unscientific. Judge Ryan started reading paperwork, looking heavy-lidded.

Carney next asked if Bieber would change his mind about the quality of the original investigation if he knew Ron Ablott had been aware of the then-new NFPA guidelines in 1992 debunking arson myths and requiring the scientific method.

The trick question didn't fool Bieber, who knew Ablott had testified that though he had not read the guidelines, he believed no investigator worth his salt would fully embrace them. Bieber said it wasn't just a matter of awareness of the guidelines, but acceptance. And very few fire investigators on the law-enforcement side were accepting back then, Bieber added.

Finally Carney turned from hypotheticals to specific details from the Parks case. What if you found what looked like an attempt to deceive fire investigators? What if those sabotaged wires were planted there not to actually start a fire, but staged to lead investigators into believing a short circuit accidentally started the fire?

"Couldn't that be evidence," Carney asked, "for an investigator to infer that a fire was incendiary?"

Again, Bieber refused to give Carney what he wanted. Finding meaning in a bundle of wires that did *not* start the fire would require nonscientific conclusions—or cognitive bias, he said. "That misleading evidence does not provide any information as to what the true ignition source was," Bieber explained. He'd still have to find the true origin and cause of the fire. The wires wouldn't help him do that.

This line of questioning from Carney was illuminating, however. First, it signaled that the prosecution—probably through one of its own experts who would testify later—had come up with an entirely new theory of the case. At trial, fire investigators and the prosecutor insisted that Jo Ann Parks had assembled a crude incendiary device—the bundle of wires and drapery and small cuts in the insulation—to start a fire. When it failed to ignite, they said she must have then set the fire by hand with a match or lighter. But now Carney was suggesting a scenario in which the cut wires had been staged merely as a ploy to fool investigators into declaring the fire an accident.

It's an interesting new theory that implies Jo Ann Parks was some kind of criminal mastermind. But it brings with it an unintended implication as well: that Ablott's original investigation had been even more flawed, deceived, and off base than the innocence project had claimed.

Near the end of his testimony, Carney did get Bieber to admit one thing: Even a biased investigator, or one using outdated science, could still reach the correct conclusion about the origin and cause of the fire. Bias doesn't automatically make the investigator wrong in the Parks case, or any other, Bieber agreed.

"It's a lot like throwing darts when you're blindfolded," he told the judge. "Occasionally you might still hit the bull's-eye. But that's not the way to throw darts."

. . .

Out in the hallway, Cohen expressed cautious optimism about Bieber's impact on the case.

"No way do I feel, 'Oh good, we've got this,'" she said. "But it was a good appetizer to set the foundation for what's to come."

The prosecution team came away seeming to feel much the same about the opening witnesses, though with a bit of unease about the judge mixed in. "No one in the business takes Bieber seriously," Nordskog said with confidence.

But then the arson detective frowned, wondering: What if the judge finds the cognitive bias argument persuasive? Judge Ryan seemed interested in the idea and took over the questioning at one point, the arson detective mused, engaging in the age-old courthouse practice of trying to read a judge's mind based on anything from eye blinks to yawns to how many times the person on the bench interrupts one side versus the other. So far the judge spent way more time interrupting the district attorney's side.

"It worries me," Nordskog said.

Meanwhile, the expert witness, released from the bonds of courtroom decorum, said that the prosecutor's line of questioning suggested that the government was living in denial about investigators' ability to figure out what happened inside the Parks apartment during that fire.

"It's not that we've got better at doing that," he said. "It's that we know better today how badly we suck at it. Except these guys don't seem to know that. . . . In 1992, we didn't have the capacity to determine where the fucking fire started in a room that burns for ten minutes. We don't have that capacity today. We used tarot cards then. We use bigger tarot cards now. We use tarot cards on our iPhones. But they're still just tarot cards."

17

Unhinged

Habeas hearings are not for the faint of heart. Or the easily bored. The pace, at least in Los Angeles Superior Court, is analogous to LA traffic at rush hour: slow, frustrating, and subject to epic delays.

The main problem is that, notwithstanding their high stakes, habeas proceedings are low priority in the justice system. This seems especially true within the insanely busy tower of crime that is the main criminal courts building in downtown Los Angeles. The Clara Shortridge Foltz Criminal Justice Center is a twenty-one-story, sixty-one-courtroom factory for dispensing justice in twenty thousand felony cases a year, named after the first woman allowed to practice law in California. This is where the annual crime-of-the-century trials play out in LA, from O. J. to Phil Spector to Michael Jackson's doctor to Hollywood Madam Heidi Fleiss to the Night Stalker, in courtrooms equipped with the most uncomfortable, spinal curvature–inducing wooden benches ever devised. Less prominent trials with their speedy-trial mandate flow through here many times a day, along with massive amounts of potential jurors—ten thousand a month, jamming the meager bank of elevators. Change of plea hearings, sentencings, and time-consuming hearings for continuances and status checks come in a daily avalanche.

Habeas proceedings, whose only constituency consists of convicted criminals, have no speedy-trial requirements and are generally viewed by the bean counters who keep the place more or less running as the criminal justice equivalent of a nuisance suit. There is only one judge and one courtroom set aside to hear all the complex habeas cases, as well as other unusual post-conviction matters. These other matters include an endless series of legally mandated resentencing hearings for convicts imprisoned under California's harsh, 1990s-era Three Strikes repeat offender law, famous for its life sentences for such minor crimes as stealing a slice of pizza. Judge Ryan draws them all, but he also has to share a courtroom with another judge. What this amounts to for Jo Ann Parks and her case's cast of characters is two days of court time a month. Judge Ryan starts no earlier than ten thirty in the morning due to sharing his courtroom with the daily calendaring judge, recesses at noon for the courthouse standard ninety-minute lunch break, then goes to four thirty P.M. before calling it a day. With the inevitable breaks and delays, innocence lawyers, prosecutors, and witnesses are lucky to get eight hours of court time a month to battle over Parks's fate.

This is how a hearing that could have been finished in ten consecutive full days in court instead began in October 2017 and continued through August 2018.

Raquel Cohen spent the time in between poring over transcripts and reports, alternately consoling a sobbing Jo Ann Parks as she languished at county jail and tamping down her swings into exuberant hope and unrealistic expectations of a speedy release. As the next hearings approached, Cohen became obsessed with the lengthy report from the prosecution's leading expert witness, a retired ATF agent with a storied career leading a National Response Team that swoops in to major bombings and fire disasters.

Brian Hoback's report on the Parks case had to be turned over to Cohen well in advance of his testimony, and she soon covered it with sticky notes, most of which contained the initialism *WTF?* She griped about having to create a clean copy for courtroom use.

Hoback, it turned out, was the source of the new theory in the case that the sabotaged wires were not intended to start a fire, but were Parks's way of creating the appearance of an accidental fire. Hoback's report carefully constructs an alternate take on Ron Ablott and his work, a portrait that is diametrically opposed to Cohen's harsh criticism of the retired investigator. The former ATF expert asserted that Ablott and his colleagues were careful, meticulous, unbiased, and, far from embracing the old myths of arson, conducted a thoroughly modern investigation that would pass muster today. In fact, Ablott might not have gone far enough, according to Hoback, who believed Parks probably had started a third fire in Ronnie Jr.'s bedroom as well as the girls' room and the living room.

Assuming an almost defiant stance, Hoback seemed to be saying that despite revelations of junk science used to lock up the innocent in other cases nationwide, there had been no real revolution in fire science, and therefore no need to re-evaluate the outcome in the Parks case. Ron Ablott had been brilliant, as Hoback saw it, and Jo Ann Parks was right where she belonged.

It was this denial of a fire science revolution that most galled Cohen, because it was so unexpected and so contrary to what she believed had become mainstream thought. Then she began worrying that someone of Hoback's stature might convince the judge that this position is valid. So she began searching desperately for some bit of evidence that this was more posturing than sincere belief from the prosecution experts, perhaps some sort of admission that they, too, had previously acknowledged a revolution had taken place. As the next hearing date neared, Cohen thought she might have found it, though doubts continually nagged at her.

At the courthouse, tensions grew and once-collegial communications between the two sides became fraught. When the hearing resumed a month after Bieber's testimony and both sides had gathered in the hallway outside Ryan's courtroom, Cohen found herself sitting on a bench close to Hoback. She had just stowed her cellphone after talking with her daughter, who was home sick from school and ended the conversation by pleading, "I want you to come here and hug me, Mommy." Hitching a smile on her face, she turned to Hoback and joked, "You don't mind if I sit next to you, do you?"

The normally affable Hoback blushed to the top of his balding head, then said in his soft Memphis accent, "Actually, I do." And he got up and moved to a different seat.

Civility took a few hits inside the courtroom, too, as the second expert for Parks took the stand.

Veteran fire investigator David Smith of Bisbee, Arizona, with his rumpled khaki jacket and air of vague irritation at being there, had come late to the witness list. He was the stand-in for John Lentini, having been one of the co-authors of the 2012 Arson Review Committee report that provided much of the original basis for the court to grant Parks a habeas hearing in the first place. The report hadn't aged well—it had some dated material in it about high carbon monoxide levels in fire victims proving flashover had occurred (an indicator that was debunked after the report was written), and it asserted that there was a back hallway in the Parks house that didn't exist.

At first, Smith defended the report's finding under friendly questions from innocence project second-in-command Alex Simpson, and wrote off those errors as having no impact on the report's conclusions. In anticipation of Hoback's coming testimony, Smith, who has been investigating fires since the 1970s, said there definitely had been a revolution in fire investigation since the Parks case. Ablott's claims that he could read burn patterns easily because there was no flashover proved that his work in the case did not reflect the new thinking, Smith said. Ablott simply could not have made the same conclusions in the Parks case if he had acknowledged that flashover occurred, Smith testified. And Ablott's failure to consider the Parks television as a potential fire starter meant he lost the ability to credibly determine that the fire had been arson, according to Smith.

"It would be absolutely improper to classify this as an incendiary fire if we have accidental ignition sources that have not been properly eliminated," Smith told the judge.

Later he and Judge Ryan had an exchange that unnerved the prosecution team. Smith, asked about the cognitive bias issues Bieber had detailed, asserted that walking into the fire scene and immediately seizing on "that jumble of wires" as an incendiary device suggested to him the original investigators entered with a predetermined finding of arson in mind. At that point, Ryan had interrupted the lawyers to ask his own questions.

"Are you suggesting that it's because of the bias you are describing that the investigator goes in, sees the cut wire, and has an Aha! moment?"

"I do," Smith responded, "if you mean the investigator has the idea that it's an arson to begin with, then this fits in that Aha! moment."

"It fits the narrative that the investigator already has in his or her head?"

"That's right, Your Honor. . . . You have that in your mind . . . then you are going to attach everything you see that fits that preconceived idea . . . and discard the other stuff because it doesn't fit."

With a chuckle and an unmistakable drawl of sarcasm, Ryan sat back in his chair and said, "What a surprise!"

This seeming affirmation of a key innocence project claim had the two prosecutors exchanging worried looks. Members of the prosecution team of lawyers and experts would fret among themselves for months after that Ryan might be leaning in favor of Parks.

Lead prosecutor Erika Jerez seized the opportunity to try to reverse their fortunes by hammering Smith on errors in the report. The expert soon began to sound ill-prepared and querulous, answering questions with questions of his own. He appeared unfamiliar with the report he had signed as a co-author, and misstated some of the findings. Cohen scribbled furiously on a notepad as she watched helplessly, feeling any advantage they had gained with Bieber's testimony slipping away. Then Jerez sprung a trap on Smith, surprising him with evidence that much of the arson report he said he'd co-authored was a direct copy of another, earlier report prepared by a fire investigation company called Kodiak.

Apparently others on the Arson Review Committee had reviewed Kodiak's work on the case and then adopted the company's conclusions and findings along with their own as drafts of the report were passed around among the committee members. All were working on the case for free at that point, using whatever resources they could cobble together, but Kodiak was not named as one of the final report authors. Jerez's implication was clear: There was something shady about the report that was central to the habeas hearing being granted in the first place.

Smith stammered that he knew Kodiak by reputation but had not known one of its investigators wrote parts of the Parks report. He said he had provided his own input in the form of comments, saying that these group efforts often had many contributors, but that each co-author had to review his colleagues' findings and the evidence supporting them before signing off. After several rounds of comments and edits, a final version of the report was adopted.

Despite the explanation, the prosecutor had scored a point. But when Jerez kept pressing Smith to admit this process had been improper, Ryan grew impatient, then interrupted.

"I just want to say, for the record, it's highly unlikely you will get a Perry Mason moment out of this witness," Ryan said, naming the fictional lawyer who has become a mocking cliché in the nonfictional legal community for always and improbably getting malefactors to admit their guilt on the witness stand. "There is no jury present. . . . Save the attitude for argument."

Ryan had previously expressed occasional irritation at Jerez, contributing to the prosecution team's worry that they were losing ground with the judge, but she did not take the judge's hint about abandoning this line of testimony and moving on to the next topic. Instead she put up a slide on the courtroom monitor showing a side-by-side comparison of the Kodiak report and the final report filed in the Parks case. Ryan again interrupted, asking Smith if this origin of the first draft of the report mattered to him, or if he simply had adopted the Kodiak findings as he did with his named co-authors' findings. Smith did take the hint: No, it didn't matter, he said, and yes, he did adopt the conclusions.

Jerez was livid. "It's plagiarism, Your Honor!"

Judge Ryan shrugged. "Which is not a crime. If he adopts the conclusions, they become his. . . . I think it's fair for you to confront him with it. But I don't think it's a Perry Mason moment."

Later, during a discussion of possible motives for Parks to set fire to her house, Jerez brought up a newly discovered taped police interview with one of Parks's half sisters, presumably made years after the fire. On the tape, the sister recalled Parks talking about what had happened, and saying that when she heard Ronnie Jr. screaming for help during the fire, he called out to his grandmother instead of her. Parks allegedly told her sister that made her angry.

"Is that not potential evidence of motive to commit a fire?" Jerez asked Smith.

Smith looked genuinely puzzled. "We are indicating the fire is already going?"

Jerez shook her head. "The statement didn't specifically state one way or the other. The statement was during the fire . . ."

Ryan interrupted. "That would mean the fire was already going unless *during* means something different to you than the rest of the people in the community."

Jerez said, "With all due respect, Your Honor . . ."

Ryan broke in again. His manner had changed. His normally droopy hound's eyes were narrowed. "Don't ever start a sentence with 'all due respect,' " he said, "because everyone knows what you really mean is, 'Look, you moron.' "

The horrified prosecutor sputtered that she meant no such thing, then tried to salvage the point by asking again if that statement showed Jo Ann Parks had expressed a motive to kill, at least according to her estranged sister's recollection.

"Of course not," Smith answered. "The fire is already going, and something makes her mad, so that's why she set the fire before it made her mad?"

Jerez surrendered a few moments later and ended the cross-examination. Then the prosecution team hurried from the courtroom to the elevator bank. Ed Nordskog said he worried that they may have just lost their case and that Jo Ann Parks was going to walk.

Raquel Cohen did not see it that way. She thought much of David Smith's testimony had been shaky and vague. She worried he had come across at times as both condescending and unprepared. Only the prosecution's ability to irritate the judge had saved the day.

Her co-counsel Alex Simpson was more upbeat. In a long and complex hearing, he said, the overall impressions and basic takeaways are critical. Smith would end up spending three days on the witness stand. What would the judge remember of all that? Simpson suggested that the judge would most likely recall that the prosecution had focused overmuch on who wrote a report, but had not disproved its or Smith's fundamental conclusions: that flashover had occurred and had been ignored by the original investigation, and that those same investigators entered the fire scene with preconceived notions.

Cohen still looked grim as the defense team of lawyers, interns, and Parks's surrogate family lined up at the elevators. "I hope you're right," she said, then dialed home to see how the kids were doing.

At the end of January 2018, four months after the habeas hearing began, the last witness for Jo Ann Parks arrived from Kentucky on a mission to shake things up. He'd either win the case outright,

Raquel Cohen figured, or they might as well just pack up and leave. The fireworks between judge and prosecutor notwithstanding, Cohen felt if the innocence project case had ended after David Smith's appearance, the outcome would be too close to call.

Paul Bieber's bias testimony was interesting enough—but even he had to admit that a biased investigator, the blindfolded dart player, could still hit the mark. And Smith had adequately explained what he believed were the Parks investigation's shortcomings and fatal errors, but he had also been halting, forgetful, and hostile. When the prosecution experts' turn came next to testify, they could fight the evidence so far to a tie, Cohen feared. And then the prosecution would argue that there was no justification for overturning the trial verdict because all we have here are a bunch of fire experts agreeing to disagree, just as happened at the original trial in 1993, because that's what experts do.

That take on the case was the very definition of a tie, Cohen knew, and ties always favor the status quo rather than upsetting the apple cart.

Now Dr. Greg Gorbett would take the stand, with the promise of bringing something new to the courtroom—a visual analysis of the fire no one else had done, which he assured Cohen would turn those impenetrable photos of sooty, charred burn patterns into an easy-to-grasp graphic that would prove the case against Parks was scientifically indefensible.

"Absolutely," he assured Cohen during their pre-hearing discussions. "There's no question."

Gorbett, a fire science expert and a professor at Eastern Kentucky University, directs the nation's first and only undergraduate degree program in fire investigation. Unlike controversial figures such as John Lentini, the affable Gorbett appears to get along with all factions in fire investigation circles. In addition to university teaching, he researches the behavior of fire and fire investigators, works on wrongful convictions, investigates fire scenes as a consultant, and conducts seminars and burn exercise sessions aimed at helping credentialed fire investigators deal with flashover and build scientifically sound cases.

Alone among the many experts who have examined and opined on the burning of the Parks home, Gorbett decided to make sense of the complexities of the fire at 6928 ½ Sherman Way by creating a heat and flame vector analysis. That may sound like a complex and esoteric scientific process, Gorbett says, but that's just the name: Visually it is a simple way of diagramming a fire's burn patterns, making a large amount of confusing data and disturbing pictures understandable at a glance—and revealing fire behavior that might otherwise be missed.

Gorbett, in essence, produced a road map of that 1989 fire in Bell—which, if accepted by the court as accurate, would be the map to freedom for Jo Ann Parks, depicting a house fire with a closet door likely open, no evidence of a second fire, and no scientifically sound way to conclude a crime even occurred.

The map was shockingly simple in concept. Scrutinizing all the photos of the fire scene, Gorbett studied one room at a time, examining each surface in that room: wall, door, ceiling, floor, furniture, even bodies. The house was burned so extensively that each surface had multiple burn patterns and damage on it. Looking at a wall, an area nearest the entryway into the room might be the most damaged, because that's where the fire entered from an adjacent room. The point farthest from the door likely would have the least damage on that wall. Gorbett then would draw a vector (the fancy science word for an arrow) pointing from the area of greatest damage toward the least damage. Now the path of fire along that particular area of the wall is clearly revealed. Then he repeats that process for every surface in every room. What is revealed is the path fire and heat took, and that, in turn, allows some determination to be made about where the fire originated. This is a method that can help overcome the problem Steve Carman's burn-cell exercises revealed.

In a simple fire, one without flashover or full-room involvement, or one that is extinguished quickly after the onset of flashover, the vector road map is often simple and the area of origin well defined. Most fire investigators do this analysis in their heads, if they do it at all. But in complicated fire scenes, such as the Parks fire, the road map is incredibly complex and impossible to keep clear without a physical chart. Yet very few fire investigators use this method. No one in 1989 did it in the Parks case, and no expert other than Gorbett did it for the latest hearing.

"It should be, but it's not universally done," Gorbett testified. "This is a complex problem we are trying to solve. . . . I think some people thought that it takes [too much] time."

Another problem with doing this analysis in your head, Gorbett added, is that there often is too much data to remember, and there is the risk that cognitive bias would trick an investigator into remembering only the vectors that supported his or her theory, and none of the conflicting data. He suggested that was part of the problem with the Parks case; Ablott had testified that his method was to poke charred areas with a penknife and keep the measurements in his head. Gorbett found this doubly problematic because the penknife method is known to be highly inaccurate and because no one could remember all the measurements needed in the Parks fire without recording them in some way.

So Gorbett used his map to take Judge Ryan for a ride through the Parks house from the flame's point of view, starting with arrows superimposed on photos of the blackened, ruined interior of the house, and ending with a simple floor plan with red arrows showing the movement of heat and flame.

He showed Ryan how the fire spread from the living room and kitchen-dining area into the girls' bedroom, but how lower down, damage near the girls' door showed heat or flame moving from inside the bedroom back into the kitchen. It was that second pattern that helped convince Ablott that a second fire had been started in the girls' bedroom, which, if true, would powerfully support the case for arson.

At the trial, the defense tried to explain away a possible second fire near RoAnn's bed as the result of flaming debris or tiles falling from the ceiling that started a secondary fire after the rest of the house was already aflame. But Gorbett and his map showed a simpler explanation: The tiny garage conversion had abnormally large windows, big enough for a mansion. There were two such big windows in the girls' bedroom. When they broke, the influx of air from outside plunged down into the room, while hot smoke and flame vented up and out, creating swirling, chaotic, and conflicting flows of air, heat, and flame in the room.

"Those two very large windows . . . when they fail, they are going to turn the fire back around," Gorbett explained. That swirling phenomenon is a ventilation effect that is now known and predictable, and Gorbett explained how it could have created patterns in the room, on the bed, and on RoAnn's body that the prosecution falsely claimed could only have occurred because a separate fire was set in that bedroom.

Gorbett explained that fire scientists and investigators did not fully understand this phenomenon in 1989. The full impact of ventilation and flashover on fire scenes and origin and cause investigations was not made clear until a seminal research paper was published on the topic in 2008. Gorbett told the judge he knew

Ablott mistook ventilation effects for a second point of origin because his vector map showed far too little damage for a separate fire to have started in that room.

Ronnie Jr.'s bedroom had similar conflicting patterns, with fire moving in from the living room and out from the bedroom door when the three huge windows in the room failed. Not only did this massive amount of ventilation from all the windows stoke the fire to flashover in most rooms of the house, Gorbett concluded, but the burn patterns and damage caused by the ventilation effectively masked the true area of origin of the fire.

When all the areas of damage and airflows were mapped out, Gorbett found, it was impossible to narrow down the area of origin for the fire through a scientific analysis. It could have started anywhere in the living room, the kitchen, or in the area around Ronnie's closet and produced exactly the same burn patterns and vectors his map revealed. What Ablott saw as an area of origin in the living room was a pattern generated by massive ventilation through the shattered living room windows, he said. There is no way to determine if the fire began there, or if it spread there from another location.

"So our area of origin has to go more broad. It can't go more narrow when we have all these complications. . . . The more narrow you go, the more likely you are going to be wrong. To say we can find multiple origins in that is just scientifically not defensible."

In short, Gorbett's analysis meant Ablott's determination of the area of origin under the living room windows cannot be justified. Had there been proof that the television or electrical wires had started the blaze, that would have made narrowing the origin area possible. But the wires were disproved as an ignition source, and the TV was not properly analyzed. And no other possibilities elsewhere in the house were checked because Ablott incorrectly narrowed the area of origin to be searched.

Prosecutor Jerez asked Gorbett to consider Hoback's theory that the "sabotaged" wires were put in place to mislead investigators into declaring the fire an accident, and she wondered whether that information could be used to narrow the origin area.

No, Gorbett said. He had been unimpressed by the government's ideas about the wires—in 1989, as well as 2018. Damaged electrical wires are found all the time in fire scenes and under windows, he said. When the original theory that tampered wires started the fire was disproved, he said, investigators should have expanded their area of origin and searched for other ignition sources. Instead, they leapt right to concluding Parks must have set the fire by hand as the only possibility.

As for Hoback's new theory about staging the cords in order to trick investigators, Gorbett accused the government of spinning one theory after another in order to "have it both ways." First Parks is too incompetent an arsonist to construct a working incendiary device, he said, then she's so brilliant she's plotting to trick investigators into an erroneous conclusion that the fire was accidental.

"It didn't make sense to me at all how you can instantly flip something to make it still seem suspicious," he complained.

As for whether the findings of other points of origin in either bedroom by Ablott and Hoback could be justified scientifically, Gorbett said, "Absolutely not. We just don't have the science to do that."

Jerez tried to blunt the impact of Gorbett's testimony by asserting that a field investigator who visits a fire scene in person always has the advantage over experts who come late to the case and only have photos to work with. Wasn't Ablott in the best position to make the call?

Gorbett could have pointed out that this "home-court" advantage was not inevitable but instead a deliberate tactic by the government, which had prevented anyone else from investigating the scene by destroying evidence and letting the house be torn down before any charges were filed. Instead, he denied there was any advantage at all, saying photographs, particularly flash photography, can reveal details that are missed during a visual inspection at the scene.

"And if a photograph does not capture the entire scene?" Jerez asked, sensing an opening.

But Gorbett turned that back on her, too, saying if there were missing images then the field investigator did a poor job. Every significant image and bit of data that has a bearing on the case should be documented.

"So long as it's done correctly, then you should be able to do it sitting behind a computer without actually going to the scene."

Jerez switched to another line of attack, asserting his analysis was just another opinion among many. "Wouldn't you say . . . fire pattern analysis is somewhat subjective?"

"That's the problem. It's really not," he said. "It shouldn't be subjective at all. . . . Part of the problem right now in the profession is that people still think that they can do that. . . . There should never be a discrepancy between two experts saying this is charred and this is not charred. . . . We should see the same stuff."

Next the prosecutor tried to shake Gorbett's contention that the understanding of flashover and the impact of ventilation had only become clear to mainstream fire investigators in recent years. Jerez cited several older journal articles dating back to the 1980s that mentioned the idea. Didn't this mean the science hadn't really changed after all since the Parks fire and, therefore, there was no reason to grant her a new trial?

Gorbett shook his head. A few obscure journal articles no one but a few engineers read did not mean these ideas were accepted or understood by the fire investigation community, he said. No one was taking the true impact of ventilation into account in their investigations at the time of the Parks fire, he added. "It was definitely on the fringe."

More important, he said, it was obvious from his work on the Parks case that Ablott lacked the knowledge of the true impact of changing ventilation on interpretation of fire patterns.

"There is a difference between knowing the data and being able to properly analyze the data. . . . That's where they were missing the boat in the Parks case. . . . If they could not recognize that [flashover and] full-room involvement occurred, they could not recognize the impact ventilation has."

Gorbett testified that in the years following the Parks fire, there had been mainstream acceptance of a list of eight indicators that flashover occurred in a fire. Not all of the indicators have to be present to conclude there was flashover, but the more there are, the more confident the conclusion can be. These indicators are straightforward and not subjective, and most of them were present in the Parks apartment:

—Witnesses seeing flames extending out of openings.
—Hot gas layer descending to the floor.
—Window breakage.
—Floor to ceiling charring/thermal damage.
—All ignitable fuels in the compartment exhibit burn damage.
—Widespread burning at floor level.

— Charring under doors.
— Absence of a line of demarcation (a line separating two fire effects, such as a horizontal line on a wall that marks how far down the hot gas layer in a room extended).

When Gorbett described this list as a relatively recent creation, developed long after the Parks fire, Jerez went on the attack again. She accused him of cribbing this list from a 1986 video played for jurors in the original Parks trial—which, she said, meant it was neither new to the case nor new science.

A puzzled Gorbett said no, the list came from a 2010 ATF training video and was, in fact, based on new science about fire behavior developed twenty years after the Parks fire.

Before Jerez could challenge that, an exasperated Judge Ryan shook his head and told the prosecutor he recalled the films and that she had gotten it wrong. "It was a different video."

Finally, Jerez bewildered Gorbett by asking him to consider a hypothetical in which a second fire was set in the girls' bedroom, and if that would convince him the house fire was arson.

"I think the entire gist of my testimony is that you are unable to do that," Gorbett said, reminding her that he had specifically found no evidence that would justify such a finding. "The science does not allow that."

When Jerez persisted, Judge Ryan, who had already warned the prosecutor a third time about trying to be Perry Mason and a second time for starting a sentence with "all due respect," got exasperated. "Isn't that what this whole hearing is about? That sort of begs the question. He just testified science doesn't provide it. You are asking him to assume something contrary to physics. Is that what your question is, to assume something contrary to the evidence?"

Jerez said it was the government's position that science *does* support such a finding.

"That's lovely," the judge said, putting a firm stop to any more questions on this topic. "But we haven't heard that evidence yet."

Some of Gorbett's most dramatic testimony did not come directly out of his mapping analysis, but focused instead on his observations of the closet door in Ronnie Jr.'s room. As at the original trial, the prosecution in the habeas case was relying on the barricading of the little boy during the fire as its most powerful evidence of Parks's criminal intent, and one that prosecutors considered fairly bulletproof, in that it could not be written off as a flashover error.

Gorbett, however, again came up with some new observations, once again faulting the prosecution for ignoring clear evidence that should have led them to a different and less incriminating conclusion about that closet.

First he found burn patterns moving across the bedroom wall and across the closet. If the door was closed, that diagonal pattern—the line of demarcation—should have continued unbroken across the front of the door. It did not. But a picture of the open door showed that line continued across the inner side of the closet door, suggesting it was open during the fire.

Next he observed severe charring on the inside stile of the door on the hinge side, which should have been protected if the closet had been closed. A picture of the door in the closed position shows severe charring along the edge of the door where it fits into the closet doorjamb. That area should have been protected had the door been closed. The carpet that a closed door would be over should have been protected from fire, but it was not, photographs showed.

Most dramatically, he took on the government's analysis of the door hinges as showing mirror-image fire damage that proved the door had to be shut during the fire. The hinges were supposed to be the government's most powerful evidence that the closet door was closed, since the eyewitness accounts by police and prosecutors had been deemed unreliable in the first trial.

Gorbett said the government's analysis was dead wrong.

What the prosecution expert was seeing on those hinges was not mirroring, but the heat transfer marks of the screws that hold the hinge plates to the door. The screws are mounted in wood and as the wood burns, the screws heat up and cause damage to the hinge plate where the screw heads are seated.

"We have twenty burn rooms at EKU [Eastern Kentucky University] with hinges. Every single one of those has that same mirror image, and it's not because the doors were closed. It's the heat transmission."

The hinges in the Parks case, he concluded, tell us nothing. This was new evidence, based on data Gorbett collected during live burn exercises at his university. If the judge accepted it as accurate, and the government failed to rebut it, the proof that Ronnie had been blocked inside the closet no longer held water.

Gorbett also dismissed the prosecution's one other piece of evidence that the door was shut: the government's assertion that because Ronnie's hair was not burned off, the door could not have been open during the fire.

Gorbett described an equally probable alternative that incriminated no one: He said the boy had clothing piled on top of him in the closet, as photos clearly showed. The material either fell, or the boy burrowed. In any case, it was sufficient to provide protection to his hair and much of his body even with the door open. Gorbett pointed out that the older girl, RoAnn, also had hair that had not burned entirely simply because one side of her head was lying on the mattress.

He concluded it was impossible to say if the door was open or closed with any scientific certainty, which meant the government's theory on the closet was unprovable and unscientific.

"There is too much evidence that is inconsistent with this door being closed," he said, adding that this is one of many times the prosecution adopted a level of certainty that science and data could not justify.

Finally, he dismissed as physically impossible the prosecution's theory about a wicker hamper barricading the closet door. Ablott's theory, adopted by the current prosecution experts, was that with the closet closed, the bottom of the door showed very little burn damage. The reason for that, according to the prosecution, was that the hamper barricade protected the lower part of the door from the flames. Gorbett found that ridiculous, as had Robert Lowe twenty-six years earlier.

"It was a wicker basket that combusts quickly, putting off a lot of heat. . . . It would in fact cause damage to the closet door." Burning objects, in short, do not protect other surfaces from heat and flames. They cause them to burn, he said—and to exhibit burn damage.

He concluded his testimony by seeking to provide the proof that the innocence project had promised the judge in its pleadings and arguments: that the case against Jo Ann Parks was built on a web of false evidence and biased expert certainty in opinions unsupported by science.

"The area of origin is basically the center east portion of the entire house," Gorbett said. "That is the best scientifically we can do. That is from fire patterns, fire dynamics, and witness statements. Because of that, we cannot determine multiple fires.

"It could be a single natural outgrowth of a single fire that has all these different effects that people are interpreting incorrectly. We cannot establish multiple fires. Because of that, the only proper listing for the cause of the fire is 'Undetermined.'"

Gorbett looked at the judge as he spoke. His testimony, if persuasive, meant the finding that the fire was set deliberately could not be justified. If the judge bought Gorbett's analysis, it meant the burden under the law of habeas corpus had been met. If his views won out over the prosecution's, it meant there was no proof a crime had been committed.

With that, the lawyers for Jo Ann Parks rested their case.

18

What Revolution?

After months of being berated and worn down by a judge they perceived as hostile to their cause, the prosecution team launched its side of the case with its surprising strategy: the claim that there had been no scientific revolution in fire investigation, and there was therefore no reason to overturn the verdict in Jo Ann Parks's case.

Even Judge Ryan seemed taken aback when Deputy DA Jerez launched her opening statement with this bold contention. He expected all her other points: that the prosecution experts would confirm that the fire was deliberately set, that there were multiple areas of origin, that a child had been barricaded in the closet, that there was a tampered electrical cord, and that all possible accidental causes of the fire were satisfactorily eliminated. In short, the original investigation got it right in every essential way. Those parts the judge saw coming.

But then Jerez delivered her bombshell: "You will see from the testimony of respondent's experts that the science fundamentally has not changed. Petitioner has failed in her burden to prove that there are significant changes in any of the science fundamentally underlying her conviction."

To the judge, it was as if she was saying the past three months of testimony had not taken place.

"You are essentially telling me," he asked, "that the science that was used at the time of the investigation is still the current science?"

Jerez said that was exactly what she was saying.

This was bold for many reasons, not the least of which is the fact that Cohen had provided the court a list of other arson cases in which judges had ruled the opposite. Jerez was asking Judge Ryan to ignore such cases as the conviction of Han Tak Lee. Lee had been imprisoned for murdering his daughter in an arson fire in Pennsylvania in July 1989, just three months after the Parks fire. He served twenty-four years before he was exonerated and released a year before Parks filed her habeas petition. The judge who freed him wrote an opinion that began with an extraordinary account of the very scientific revolution Jerez claimed had not occurred:

> "Slow and painful has been man's progress from magic to law."
>
> This proverb, inscribed at the University of Pennsylvania Law School on the statue of Hsieh-Chai, a mythological Chinese beast who was endowed with the faculty of discerning the guilty, is a fitting metaphor for both the progress of the law and the history of this case. . . . Sometimes, with the benefit of insight gained over time, we learn that what was once regarded as truth is myth, and what was once accepted as science is superstition.
>
> So it is in this case.

> In 1990, Han Tak Lee was convicted of arson and murder in connection with the death of his daughter, Ji Yun Lee . . . upon what was at the time undisputed scientific evidence concerning the source and origin of this fire.
>
> Today, with the benefit of extraordinary progress in human knowledge regarding fire science over the past two decades it is now uncontested that this fire science evidence . . . is invalid, and that much of what was presented to Lee's jury as science is now conceded to be little more than superstition.

Initially, Ryan's seeming impatience with the prosecution continued as Jerez began presenting her case. The judge forced her to cut her opening presentation to a fraction of what she intended to present, berating her for injecting closing arguments into her opening statement, which is supposed to simply preview the evidence she intends to present.

"You're killing me with these details," he chastised. "This is not a jury trial, and this is all argumentative. Just tell me what your witnesses will testify to."

Such an interruption and curtailing of an attorney's opening statement in midstream is never a good sign. It flustered Jerez, who had to scramble to skip over dozens of slides she had wanted to show the judge, while the rest of her team sat grim-faced, staring down at their files or their hands or exchanging looks—anything but watching their colleague's discomfort.

But then Jerez finished and Brian Hoback took the stand. The tone changed almost immediately. With his soft, slow Memphis drawl and tendency to blush bright red, the former ATF investigator's lack of experience as a witness and "yes, ma'am" and "no, ma'am" answers charmed the judge and many others in the courtroom. For the first time, the prosecution team saw a receptive audience in Judge Ryan as Hoback settled in. There were fewer interruptions from the bench. Ryan joked with Hoback. The prosecution team sensed it, and so did Cohen and her innocence project team.

Suddenly, after Gorbett's seeming triumph, it was anybody's game again.

As Jerez had promised, Hoback asserted that there had been no revolution in the arson investigation field. Knowledge had expanded, of course. Techniques had improved. Old myths had been discarded. He even conceded that the original investigation could have been better documented and photographed. But in the end, nothing consequential had changed in the science of fire investigation, and in his view, Ron Ablott and his colleagues had done everything right. The man who had spoken of *NFPA 921* with contempt and never read it, and who had investigated the Parks fire scene as if flashover had not occurred had, in Hoback's view, followed modern principles to the letter.

"They did not fall into the traps, as some had of that time, of equating old myths as proof of something criminal," Hoback concluded.

In his report on the case, Hoback only mentioned once that he disagreed with Ablott's finding that there had been no flashover in the Parks fire, but he asserted that it didn't matter and had no effect on the validity of Ablott's conclusions. This position left Cohen beside herself, for it went to the heart of her case, as well as contradicting the widely hailed work of John Lentini dating back to the Lime Street fire.

Whereas Gorbett and Cohen's other experts had been adamant that failure to account for flashover rendered Ablott's findings about the fire's origin and cause worthless, Hoback insisted that the fact that flashover occurred simply meant that you had to "be more careful" and "think twice" when charting the progress of a fire. He insisted Ablott had done exactly that in the original investigation, and his own careful analysis confirmed each and every one of Ablott's reasons for determining that this was a case of arson and murder.

He took pains to explain that, far from suffering from bias, Ablott had taken a deliberate approach to the Parks case, visiting the scene multiple times and withholding final judgment for months. In Hoback's view, sending the wiring to an electrical engineering expert and learning that the supposedly sabotaged cord was not the cause of the fire did not highlight Ablott's investigative mistakes, but his willingness to revise his thinking.

But as he explained the reasoning behind his endorsement of Ablott's investigation, weaknesses in Hoback's analysis emerged.

In creating a timeline for the fire that supported his belief that Parks had ample time to start a separate fire in the girls' bedroom, he did not mention the testimony of Tuxedo Man, who saw indicators of flashover elsewhere in the house long before Hoback's scenario allowed.

In rejecting as untruthful Officer Bruce's information about the lack of fire in the girls' bedroom when he arrived at the scene, Hoback did not account for the police interview of neighbor Lloyd Powell, who had corroborated most of Bruce's account. And in insisting the closet door was closed, Hoback appeared not to consider Ablott's reluctant testimony under cross-examination in the original trial that the door was partially open.

Hoback never mentioned this oddity buried in the mounds of transcripts from the original trial, though it contradicts the position that the prosecution has maintained across three decades:

that the closet door was shut with the hamper pressed against it during the fire. Ablott in later years has even recalled that the hamper left behind telltale patterns on the surface from contact with the door. Hoback adopted Ablott's version of events, but no such thing is apparent in the photos. And though it was ignored and forgotten over time, the transcripts show that Ablott admitted during Parks's original trial that the protection patterns in the carpet proved that if the hamper was there, then there was a gap rather than direct contact with the closet door—a gap of as great as three inches between them.

Which begs a question: Could that hamper truly have been a barricade? Or could a slim preschooler squeeze through that space, especially if he leaned his weight against the door and the hamper rocked back? Hoback never addressed this possibility.

Hoback's insistence that the closet door in Ronnie's bedroom was closed and barricaded was also based on his analysis of the door hinges—a type of analysis he had never done before the Parks case. Hoback testified that he followed instructions for analyzing hinges published in an authoritative text, *Scientific Protocols for Fire Investigation,* authored by John Lentini. Lentini later reviewed Hoback's work on the hinges and reached the same conclusion Gorbett did: Hoback was wrong, there was no mirroring present, and the hinges were worthless as evidence.

Hoback said his hinge analysis and belief that the closet door was closed during the fire was bolstered by eyewitnesses. But this support is a reference to the testimony of Dirk Wegner, the first firefighter to enter the house, and the recollections of the first policeman to arrive, Bell police reserve officer Timothy McGee. Hoback seemed unaware that these witnesses had contradicted themselves and each other in their testimony, and that the original trial prosecutor had finally stated in open court that their testimony had no credibility—an admission that Jerez had even quoted in her response to Cohen's habeas petition. Hoback was relying on information that had been repudiated in the first trial. There were no witnesses who could reliably recall whether the door was open or shut during the fire.

As for the sabotaged wiring—what in the original trial was termed the "failed incendiary device"—Hoback, like the rest of the prosecution team, described it as an electrical extension cord that had been cut or sawed, then wrapped in drapery. Hoback went on to explain his theory of the significance of this discovery, contradicting Ablott with his own new idea:

"The fire setter wanted the fire investigators to believe that this fire was an accidental fire. Thus, placing the 'cut' and 'sawed' electrical cords within drapery material and placing those cords that are wrapped in the material underneath the boxes in the living room near the north wall. Once the electrical cords were found, then the theoretically lazy fire investigator assumes it was an electrical fire, seeing the melted cords underneath the boxes which were pinched and caused a fire. That scenario has been seen before in reference to this case. It was at Mrs. Parks's house fire approximately one year prior to this fire."

In his earlier testimony, Gorbett derided this idea as a kind of "have it both ways" flip-flop unsupported by evidence, but the problem with this testimony goes deeper. For years—decades, really—the prosecution had consistently pushed a misleading description of this "device." Once again, buried in the transcripts from the original trial, there is a description of what was really found at the fire scene. Ablott admitted that the cuts in the wires he found so suspicious—and that he originally believed had caused a deliberate short circuit that started the fire—were on a length of an extension cord with no drapery wrapped around it, which makes it hard to imagine this as "a device." Another small section of the wire dubbed "the octopus" really was wrapped in a bit of drapery, according to evidence photos and testimony—but not the cut parts.

For all the possible shortcomings in his analysis, Hoback nevertheless remained one of the more impressive witnesses to testify. He stayed calm and unwavering when questioned by the innocence project lawyers. Although he had no new science or technique behind him, as Gorbett had with his vector analysis, Hoback's genteel, steady, reasonable manner held the judge's attention. He had been nervous about being cross-examined—Hoback had not testified in more than a decade before taking the stand in the Parks case—but nothing could shake him from his opinion that Parks was a killer.

"An analysis of an investigation should be to find the truth," Hoback concluded in his written report, which he quoted in his testimony. "This author believes the investigators in 1989 through the 1993 trial did indeed find the truth."

The prosecution's other experts, fire science specialist Jamie Lord and Los Angeles County Sheriff's arson investigator Ed Nordskog, backed up Hobart's testimony, agreeing that there was ample evidence that the fire had been deliberately set.

Lord, a flashover expert, surprised the courtroom by saying that he agreed with almost all of defense expert Greg Gorbett's findings. He disagreed with just four vectors on Gorbett's fire map, only one of which he deemed significant. But by altering that one arrow, Lord revealed what he said was a pattern that provided strong support for the theory that a second, separate fire had been set in the girls' room.

In his testimony, Nordskog parted company with Hoback on the cut wiring, arguing that it had, in fact, been constructed to start a fire, but failed because its builder didn't know what she was doing. He continued to describe a "device" that consisted of cuts in a wire wrapped in drapery, despite the absence of any testimony or photographs to prove that such a thing was found, and Ablott's clear, if buried, testimony that he found no such thing. Nordskog later explained that the wrapping was not what convinced him that the cords had been used to try to set a fire. He found the deliberate cut marks and placement of the cords to be the definitive evidence of sabotage.

Nordskog also described in detail his analysis of burn patterns on the children's bodies. With gruesome pictures of the small corpses at the fire scene and in the morgue displayed on courtroom screens, he pointed out how the relative lack of severe burning on Ronnie's body suggested the closet door had to be shut. Then he turned to the multidirectional burn patterns on RoAnn's body, which he said provided clear evidence of a second fire set in the room and spreading outward. He criticized the innocence project's experts for not taking this into consideration.

Gorbett, however, had previously testified that he had looked at the patterns on the bodies and he found that they no more proved a second fire had been set in the room than any of the other burn patterns found and photographed in that room. He said the same swirling, multidirectional air and heat currents caused by the massive windows breaking in the room created both the conflicting patterns on the bed and walls, and on RoAnn's body as well. It was the same ventilation-controlled phenomenon at work—missed by Ablott, and now missed by Nordskog as well, according to Gorbett.

When asked why he had not included an analysis of burn patterns on the bodies in his fire map presentation, Gorbett had shaken his head in disgust. He said he didn't feel the need to parade upsetting images of dead children to illustrate a point that could be made just as effectively with comparable burn patterns on the bed and walls.

Indeed, Parks had been covering her face with her hands and appeared to be sobbing quietly throughout this portion of Nordskog's testimony, until Judge Ryan glanced over, held up his hand to quiet the witness, and asked Cohen if her client would rather sit out the rest of this testimony. Parks looked up and nodded and mouthed the word *yes,* and the bailiff cuffed her and took her to the lockup.

"I should have caught that before," the judge said. "It didn't occur to me."

Nordskog was unfazed, as he's convinced that Parks is a manipulative child killer who fits the profile of a serial arsonist, and that such emotional displays cannot be taken at face value. He went on to testify that he found it highly suspicious and unnatural that a child RoAnn's age would not get up and try to flee the fire at some point. He had previously opined in his report that the girls had been drugged, notwithstanding negative autopsy results for drugging.

"They're old enough to flee," he told Judge Ryan. "If they're conscious."

Lord and Nordskog both insisted, as Hoback did, that there had been no major changes in fire science that could undermine Ablott's investigation or Parks's conviction. Some myths were exposed, particularly ones that led investigators to mistakenly conclude that ignitable liquids such as gasoline had been used, but the prosecution witnesses said none of those old myths applied to the Parks investigation. As far as the Parks fire was concerned, there had been no fire science revolution, they agreed, just a gradual evolution that didn't require changing a single finding in the case.

At the end of the prosecution's presentation, however, Alex Simpson asked Nordskog, "Would you agree that the fire scientists . . . made investigators such as yourself realize that a lot of what arson investigators believed and were taught was absolutely wrong?"

Simpson got the answer he and Cohen had hoped they'd get. Nordskog said, "To say 'a lot' is an exaggeration."

At the conclusion of the case, Cohen would file with the judge a copy of a 2016 article from the *Los Angeles Times* quoting Nordskog on this very topic: "The arson industry was turned on its head twenty-five years ago when fire scientists got involved and realized a lot of what arson investigators believed and were taught was absolutely wrong, scientifically not correct," Nordskog had told columnist Patt Morrison less than two years earlier. "And the scientists have come a long way in fixing that part of the industry."

Nordskog was the final witness. And with his exit from the courtroom, only the final arguments remained. These would be a last attempt by each side to convince the judge that something monstrous happened in this case—a pair of alternate realities rather than nuanced differences.

"There is no new scientific research that applies to this case that undermines this conviction," prosecutor Jerez assured the judge. "This is fatal to the false evidence claim."

"Every day we ask jurors to put aside their gut feelings and to pay attention to the evidence," Cohen countered. "But the investigators did not do that in this case. This investigation was riddled with bias. And this conviction was based on unsupported evidence, bias, and nonscientific investigation."

With that, the case went to the judge. He would wade through the documents and testimony searching for firm footing amid the ambiguous evidence and opposing expert testimony. He would have to decide if false information and cognitive bias led to Jo Ann

Parks's conviction, or if the original investigation held up nearly thirty years later.

Had the prosecution raised enough doubt about the innocence project's claims, turning the proceeding into a case of dueling experts with no side clearly ahead on points? If so, the conviction would stand.

Or had the innocence project team succeeded in showing that no unbiased fire investigation could possibly tell where or how the fire started, or whether a child had been trapped inside a closet? If so, then the judge would not only have to release Parks. He would also have to find that there was insufficient evidence that any crime had been committed at all.

Judge Ryan smiled as each side rested, thanked the attorneys for an interesting presentation, and gaveled the proceedings to a close. He offered not a single clue as to which way he might rule, other than saying that they had given him a great deal to think about.

As the testimony moved toward wrapping up in May 2018, Jo Ann Parks had become convinced that the judge would order her set free in time for her to read her essay at the talent show. It had become her dream. She told her friends to stop depositing money in her commissary account, and asked them to bring some clothes to the jail for when she was released.

It fell to Raquel Cohen to try to roll back those expectations. Yes, she said, the testimony would end in early May, but then there would be oral arguments and briefs to file, and then the judge could take months to rule if he wanted to. Yes, it was possible he could rule from the bench then and there. Possible, but unlikely.

She also had to remind her client once again that all Judge

Ryan could do, if they won, was erase her conviction and grant a new trial. Then he might set bail. But he also might not allow her release while awaiting trial. The district attorney could, and probably would, appeal Ryan's order if he overturned the conviction. The appeals process that ensues from that would add more years to her confinement. She had to steel herself.

Her fantasy of reading her essay at the Los Angeles Athletic Club—along with the dreams of freedom with which she ended that essay after twenty-seven years in prison—faded for the time being.

"I'll wait," she told her lawyer. "I'm good at that."

OUTSIDE

My thoughts about the outside is the smell of fresh air. Seeing large green trees and the smell of different flowers in the air. Seeing all the buildings and signs, some old ones, some new. Watch all the different colors and styles of cars as they pass by. To feel the air against my face. My hair blowing in the wind.

Going to the beach for my first time hearing the crashing of the waves, the seagulls' squawk, the smell of the ocean's water and the salt in the air. The feel of sand between my toes. It is going to be a surreal experience.

The first time going into a store to shop for clothing. Seeing and feeling all the different materials, colors, and designs. Choosing and trying on to find a style that is comfortable for me to wear. Walking out with my bags in my hands, the feeling of excitement and joy.

Going to the grocery store, walking up and down the aisles and looking at all the different products, labels, and choices I have to make. Walking side by side with other customers and with a fleeting thought, "No one knows where I have been. How long I have been locked up. Or that I was ever in prison." To them I am just another person sharing the same experience they are of walking up and down the aisles shopping.

I arrive at home. I feel the warmth of Rosie the dog and the softness of her fur. Her licks and kiss and the excitement of me being home. I roll around with her on the floor and play for a few minutes. I then walk through the house taking in everything around me. The furniture to the pictures hanging on the walls, the color of the rooms and the style of the furniture. I go to my room and fall on my bed, feeling the softness of a real bed. I go to the bathroom and check out the tub and shower and look at myself in a real mirror for the first time. I acknowledge that I made it, I am free, I thank God.

I unpack and settle in. I then go to the kitchen and start to help prepare dinner. I am excited to live my life and to see everything I can do and accomplish in my life.

Epilogue: The Curse of Uncertainty

After the closing arguments, Raquel Cohen climbed into her car for the 120-mile trip from downtown Los Angeles to San Diego. Rush hour traffic would make that a four-hour drive at least, time enough to stew for a while, then wind down from the tension of wrapping up such a high-stakes case.

Ryan Cohen had come along to watch his wife's closing and to provide moral support. He drove as the two attorneys began their standard ritual of critiquing the day in court, with Raquel obsessively fretting over small details she neglected to mention to the judge.

"I say this in the most positive way possible," her husband finally said. "You vomited so much information that you just can't beat yourself up about some random detail. You nailed it."

Just then her cellphone rang. Denise, Jo Ann Parks's girlfriend, was calling from Hawaii and wanted the latest news. "Jo Ann's pretty upset," Cohen began, "but she usually is after a court hearing. So nothing to worry about there."

She explained what could happen next: Judge Ryan could rule

against Parks, which would mean the California Innocence Project would appeal that ruling. Or Parks could get a win from the judge and face a retrial within sixty days if the prosecution decided to refile.

"But the district attorney will have a lot of problems retrying," Cohen told Denise. " A lot of their experts from the original trial are dead or unavailable."

The lawyer declined to predict what the judge would do, but told her, "We gave it the best shot ever. I feel very good about it. And I think the DA had a very weak argument."

Mildly cheered by this news, Denise hung up after Cohen agreed to send word as soon as the case was decided. "I will be checking my mail daily," she promised. "Obsessively."

If a retrial did take place, Cohen wanted to make new scientific evidence the heart of her case: She wanted to hire an expert to recreate the fire. He said he could do it, reconstructing the converted garage, right down to its furnishings. Then they would burn it using the prosecution's theory of how the fire occurred and spread: an origin point in the living room and a second fire set in the girls' bedroom. If, as she expected, the experiment proved that the fire could not have happened the way prosecutors claimed, it would be powerful evidence of innocence. Or, at least, evidence that the prosecutions' assumptions and expert opinions were wrong.

"The only problem is," Cohen said, "it will cost $100,000 to do it."

The innocence project has no budget for such a costly experiment. Yet Cohen said they would find a way. "It really could mean the difference between prison and freedom. . . . It would show that this absolute certainty all the prosecution experts have about their opinions in Jo Ann's case is completely unjustified."

. . .

Whatever Judge Ryan rules, the case of the *People v. Parks* will not end when he renders his decision. Nor will the larger questions of science, law, and bias it raises. One side or the other will appeal. And the battle to find some measure of certainty, some way to pierce the ambiguity about what really happened in Bell, California, on April 9, 1989, will continue.

The justice system despises ambiguity and demands certainty—especially in a case in which three small children die. When meeting that demand is not possible in a particular case, a pretense of certainty is often accepted instead. That pretense has been laid bare in the 2,250 and growing slam-dunk cases that, years later, have fallen apart, often from bad forensics or cognitive bias. The certainty with which a Han Tak Lee or a Kristine Bunch were locked away makes the eventual exoneration of that prototypical "monster" dad and mom all the more chilling. "Slow and painful has been man's progress from magic to law" is, indeed, a signature principle for the age. We know we're supposed to want the progress and the rationality of law, but we all too often settle for the magic.

The question is where Jo Ann Parks fits into that spectrum. Hers is a case overflowing with ambiguity, with its murky evidence, conflicting testimony, and a defendant whose behavior and credibility will always raise questions. Then add to the mix the combination of art and science, guesswork and assumptions that characterizes many fire investigations, rendering them uniquely vulnerable to the mind-bending effects of cognitive bias. Confusion about this issue of bias is systemic. The prosecutor at the center of the Parks case—a case with the potential to make or change the law should an appellate court grab hold of it—asks with complete sincerity, "Isn't fire pattern interpretation subjective?"

And the expert answers, “No, that’s the problem. It shouldn’t be. And yet it is.”

A tangle of plugs and extension cords becomes an incendiary device in the eyes of investigators who express unwavering certainty in their views. A closet door, carelessly thrown away by government officials so no one else can examine it, is said definitely to have been shut and barricaded, another subjective opinion rendered without hesitation or doubt. Indecipherable marks on door hinges become clear evidence of murder—a definitive opinion in a capital case from an “expert” whose total experience examining hinges includes only this case. Not only is his error rate in making such an analysis unknown, he also offered no scientific evidence that hinge analysis in any arson case has any scientific validity. Yet these experts profess certainty.

As the original fire investigator on the Parks case put it, “If I am wrong, then everything I have ever been taught and those people that have been taught before me, would all be wrong.” The stakes simply do not get higher than that. The justice system craves certainty, and it seems someone is always ready to step up and provide it with a bite mark or a fingerprint or a fire pattern or a door hinge, if not with science and law, then with magic.

Is that what happened in the Parks case? Perhaps. Perhaps not. But the inability to answer that question with any confidence may be the real problem.

It wasn’t supposed to be this way. Forensic sciences were developed across the past century and a half to bring certainty to the justice system, so that instead of relying solely on fallible human memory, instead of needing an eyewitness or a felon caught red-handed to solve a crime, justice could be done with microscopes and measurements and hard data. Judges eagerly admitted all sorts of new and untested forensic sciences into their courtrooms, with expert witnesses, the men and women with lab coats, taking on new prominence. The prosecution of Jo Ann Parks is the logical outcome of this trend, certainty built on the evidence of ash and char and the ability of trained experts to read burn patterns like an ordinary person reads words on a page. It has taken decades for the justice system to acknowledge the existence of the flaws in many forensic practices—the bite-mark comparisons, hair and fiber matching, and burn pattern analyses that seemed so convincing and certain, yet lacked scientific rigor, have led to wrongful convictions.

The justice system is still grappling—rather poorly—with how to respond to this new reality. There is no systemic review of potential forensic errors under way or even contemplated—just the case-by-case battles that occur when the California Innocence Project or some like-minded individual or group plucks a case from obscurity and champions an individual convict's cause.

Then there is what Ed Nordskog calls the holy war: pitting traditional police detective work against the scientific method. This argument, in turn, is really about the larger war within all forensic disciplines over cognitive bias.

Nordskog finds the whole bias discussion insulting, little more than a gimmick deployed by those in the exoneration "business." What they see as bias he sees as a good detective following leads, using his or her instincts and knowledge of human behavior to inform an investigation. Detectives, this view holds, have to move beyond the bounds of a scientific inquiry in order to find the larger truth—the messy truth of people in extreme circumstances. It is possible to have that information, Nordskog believes, and still conduct a fair and thorough crime scene investigation. In fact, he sees it as an essential combination. Science has its place, Nordskog says, but it's the detective who makes the case.

Raquel Cohen, on the other hand, has come to see cognitive bias not as a niche idea, but as something that is deeply rooted in the justice system, in politics, in all our institutions. It animates many of the conflicts, hate, and intolerance tearing the country apart: "People see what they expect to see," she says. "And they are blind to it."

Every prosecution expert in the Parks habeas case, she believes, has been influenced by unconscious cognitive bias. She argues that this has led them to select only the facts from the old trial record that confirm their views while ignoring contrary information, including reliance on police and firefighter testimony that even the original prosecutor on the case deemed not credible. "Once you start looking for it, you start to see cognitive bias everywhere," Cohen says. "It is pervasive."

Paul Bieber's solution is to keep forensic examiners in the blind. Let them focus on the science and stay ignorant of the criminal case information, avoiding exposure to potentially biasing information, such as allegations of poor parenting, drugging, and profit motives against Jo Ann Parks. Did this in fact bias the Parks fire scene investigation? It's impossible to say with certainty. It's just as impossible to rule out, says Bieber. Yet making forensic analysis independent of law enforcement, to avoid the cognitive bias that linkage can cause, is not even on the table for discussion.

In fact, there isn't even a table anymore. Spurred on by a National Academy of Sciences report on problems with forensics, a presidential commission convened during the Obama administration to find solutions to forensic failures and how to make the various forensic science disciplines stronger. The initiative was canceled by the Trump administration. Forensic reform—or, at least, exposure of forensic failures—is now back to a case-by-case basis. Jo Ann Parks is just the latest in line. More will follow.

. . .

Should the judge rule in her favor, Jo Ann Parks has modest plans for the future. She will stay with the family of her old fire expert. Mary Ross has become her confidante and supporter, and there is a room waiting for her at the Ross family's home in San Juan Capistrano, California. There she can readjust to the outside, to a world she left when no one had smartphones or browsed the Web, before DVDs or Netflix or Amazon, when the Disney cartoon *Aladdin* was the most popular film in the United States and O. J. Simpson was known only as a football star, actor, and pitchman for Hertz rental cars. In time, she may move to Hawaii to be with her paroled girlfriend. Beyond that, it is hard for her to plan. Painful, really, she says. "Because who knows if any of it will come true?"

Her mother is dead, her ex-husband is dead, her children are dead, her siblings have nothing to do with her. She has no money, no resources; she is no one's constituency. She has been the outcast since her rape and the birth, foster placement, and death of her first child, David, was "handled" by the Mormon church. Her own mother sent her off to foster care, and then fate brought her to that Laundromat and Ron Parks. She has no idea, she says, how normal people live. Prison is now her norm.

She says she is filled with regrets about things she wished she had done differently, choices she made or didn't make. She wishes she had been strong enough to leave Ron. She wishes sometimes that she had died in that fire, trying to save her babies. She is still haunted by the words her husband uttered in court, that their kids were like spilt milk to him. She is haunted by the thought that the police looked at her and her life and were disgusted by what they saw, disgusted by the monster they perceived in her skin. "Do you know," she once asked, "what it's like to be called a monster?"

The question that always comes up about Jo Ann Parks is the most obvious: Do you believe she is innocent? That question won't be answered in these pages. Or anywhere else. It is not answerable. There is no DNA test or alibi witness or scientific method that can deliver that answer, that certainty.

The more answerable yet ambiguous questions, the ones that have legal weight, are whether there was ever sufficient evidence to convict her, and whether there is sufficient evidence left standing to justify keeping Jo Ann Parks in prison until she dies.

There is that tangle of wires with a few small cuts in the insulation and some charred material from old drapes that could have been wrapped by an arsonist—or by a child, or through sheer messiness, or by accident. There is a closet door no one can be certain was open or closed, or whether the child inside was hiding on his own or barricaded by his mom. There is a hamper that is supposed to have burned against a door without leaving evidence of burning against a door. There is a child who played with matches and who was known to rise late at night to turn on the old TV. There is a mother who saved herself instead of trying to save her kids, then lied about it. There is a mother who didn't grieve or cry the way some people thought she should. Is all this enough to imprison a woman for life? Is there even enough evidence to say with any degree of certainty that a crime was committed at all?

Before her trial, Parks could have sought a deal to testify against her husband in return for her freedom or a reduced sentence, but she didn't. When facing death, she again could have accused her husband to save her own skin, but she didn't. She could have blamed her son for setting the fire, but she didn't, except for that one blurted comment to her neighbor while the apartment blazed. She could have bought insurance before the fire, but she didn't. She could have died trying to save her kids, but she didn't.

Is all of this evidence of guilt or innocence or cowardice or simply human fallibility?

She sits behind bars now, waiting. She waits not for proof of innocence or surety of guilt, but for the realization that ambiguity is not evidence. She waits for a judge who must decide what to do about that. There will be a ruling. There will be appeals. There will be slow and gradual reforms to forensics and fire science, most likely because courts will force these reforms, though they likely will not go as far as some might wish.

As she says, Jo Ann Parks is good at waiting.

A resolution of sorts arrived late Friday, November 2, 2018: Judge William Ryan denied the petition for a new trial. In a ruling that read more like a punt than a firm rejection, the judge decided little had changed in thirty years. Then, as now, he said, it all boiled down to a muddle of dueling experts, and he was not about to pick one scientist over another. Yes, there was false evidence about flashover at the original trial, but he found this insufficient to free Jo Ann Parks.

"The world of fire science and fire investigation is a complex area," he wrote, "rife with differing opinions and contentious debates that continue to this day."

Raquel Cohen told her devasted client to take heart; that years of appeals and waiting were inevitable no matter how Ryan ruled. Instead of reserving it for a new trial, she said the re-creation of the fire would become the centerpiece of her appeal—if she could raise the $100,000 needed to stage a re-creation. The case is not about dueling experts, Cohen insists, but about experts who claim scientific certainty where none exists.

"That isn't an opinion," she says. "It's a lie. And I'm going to prove it."

Sources

Note: Copies of original reports, interviews, and other key documents referenced in *Burned* may be found at www.EdwardHumes.com/burned.

Chapter 1: April 9, 1989

From the testimony of Bill and Shirley Robison in the preliminary hearing (April 15 and April 20, 1992) and the jury trial (August 6, 1992–February 26, 1993) in the *People of the State of California v. Jo Ann Parks,* Los Angeles County Superior Court Case No. VA009503; from the author's interview with Shirley Robison; and from the report dated April 9, 1989, by Bell Police Department officer Frank Espejo.

Chapter 2: 1,100 Degrees

The explanation of the stages of a house fire leading to flashover is based on publications and videos from the US Fire Administration, the National Fire Protection Association, the Bureau of Alcohol, Tobacco, Firearms and Explosives, fire expert Greg Gorbett, and testimony in the Parks trial and habeas hearing. The times noted in this description are hypothetical and can vary; in some situations, flashover can occur more quickly or take longer.

Information regarding the Parkses' landlords is drawn from court records and from the article "Slum Citations Mount in 4 Cities Against Landlords; Tenants Say Owners Refuse to Repair Shoddy Living Conditions," by James M. Gomez, *Los Angeles Times,* April 20, 1989.

Chapter 3: Firefighting

From the testimony of David Haney (misidentified as David Laney) in the Parks preliminary hearing, as well as preliminary hearing and trial testimony from Bob and Shirley Robison, Bell police officer Pete Cacheiro, Bell reserve officer Timothy McGee, and Los Angeles County firefighter Dirk Wegner.

Additional information came from the April 9, 1989, Bell Police Department incident report by Officer Jeff Bruce; the author's interview with Bruce; and defense fire expert Robert Lowe's notes on and analysis of Bruce's actions and his own conversation with and testimony about Bruce.

Lowe's report dated March 8, 2006, on his investigation of the Parks case, provided a detailed timeline of events before, during, and after the fire.

The Los Angeles County Sheriff's Department supplementary report dated September 11, 1992, by homicide detectives Jacqueline Franco and Patrick Robinson detailing their interview with Parks's neighbor Lloyd Richard Powell; and the February 6, 1992, sheriff's report filed by Franco and Detective Frank Salerno on their interview with David Haney (Tuxedo Man) provided details about the fire and the timing and sequence of events, much of which was overlooked later in the case.

Note: The role of Officer Bruce has been a point of controversy and debate from the beginning of the investigation of the Parks fire. Bruce exaggerated his heroics that day in describing his entry into the girls' bedroom prior to the room flashing over. He later admitted as much but maintained the rest of his official report was accurate. Notably that report was written immediately after the fire.

Bruce's version of events—the timing of the window breaking and the fact that there was little or no fire in the room until after he broke the window—is more favorable to Jo Ann Parks's defense than to the prosecution.

Officer McGee's version of events—that the back windows were all intact until they all blew out at once—fits the prosecution's theory of the case better. McGee, a reserve officer, wrote no report and did not provide a detailed description of events until two years after the fire. McGee was incorrect in several of his other recollections about the fire, which is normal for anyone asked to recall events years after the fact.

At Parks's trial and ever since, police and prosecutors have asserted that McGee's account is the accurate one and that nothing Bruce reported is credible. But they ignore a police interview with the Parkses' neighbor Lloyd Powell, who recalled watching an officer banging on a window with what appeared to be a baton, and finally breaking the window. Smoke and flames then shot out.

Chapters 4–5: Statements–Victims

The events occurring at the police station were described in the April 9, 1989, report by Bell Police Department officer Frank Espejo detailing his interview with Jo Ann Parks; the preliminary hearing and trial testimony of Espejo and Shirley Robison; author's interview with Paul Garman; Los Angeles County Sheriff's Department supplementary report dated November 29, 1991, by Detectives Franco and Salerno, on their March 29, 1991, interview with Paul Garman; the testimony of Ronald Parks; a handwritten statement by Ronald Parks entitled "Statement: Night of Fire"; and a handwritten statement by Jo Ann Parks.

Events at the house were described in detail in the testimony of the first responders, in particular Dirk Wegner; and in LA County fire investigator William Franklin's testimony and investigation report.

The phone call from Kathy Dodge was detailed in the Bell Police Department report dated April 12, 1989, by Sergeant William Talbott.

Chapter 6: Arson Expert

Kathy Dodge's allegations are described in detail in the original Talbott report; a transcript of an August 20, 1989, interview conducted by Jacqueline Franco and Michael Lee, Los Angeles County Sheriff's Department homicide detectives; a transcript of a June 7, 1991, interview with sheriff's detectives Franco and Salerno; and transcripts of the Parks trial in which the judge, prosecutor, and defense attorney discuss Dodge outside the presence of the jury.

Fire investigation information is derived from the author's interviews with retired sheriff's arson investigator Ron Ablott and sheriff's arson investigator Ed Nordskog; preliminary hearing and trial testimony of Ablott and William Franklin; the 2006 Lowe report; fire expert reports filed in the habeas proceedings authored by the Arson Review Committee (John Lentini, David Smith, and Michael McKenzie), Brian Hoback, and Thomas May; and the testimony in habeas proceedings of Smith, Hoback, Paul Bieber, and Greg Gorbett.

Information about the Parkses' activities between the time of the fire and Jo Ann Parks's arrest is drawn from the author's interviews with Jo Ann Parks and Mary Ross; Parks's autobiographical statement, "Her Story"; and correspondence between Ron Parks and Robert Lowe.

Chapter 7: Three Days in October 1991

From the author's interview with John Lentini; "The Oakland Experience," by John J. Lentini, David M. Smith, and Dr. Richard W. Henderson, *Fire Technology* (vol. 28, no. 3) August 1992; "The Lime Street Fire: Another Perspective," account by John J. Lentini, *Fire and Arson Investigator*, vol. 43. no. 1, September 1992; and "Badly Burned: Long-Held Beliefs about Arson Science Have Been Debunked After Decades of Misuse and Scores of Wrongful Convictions," by Mark Hansen, *ABA Journal*, December 2015.

Arrest information based on the Los Angeles County Sheriff's Department arrest report of Jo Ann Parks, and the author's interview with Parks.

Chapter 8: The Pit

From the author's interviews of the staff at the California Innocence Project, including Raquel Cohen, Alissa Bjerkhoel, Justin Brooks, Alex Simpson, and Michael Semanchic.

Details on cases, crimes, and exonerations in this chapter are drawn from individual court pleadings and rulings, and from the National Registry of Exonerations, a joint project of the University of California, Irvine; Newkirk Center for Science & Society; the University of Michigan Law School; and Michigan State University College of Law.

Chapter 9: Growing Up Jo Ann

From author's interview with Jo Ann Parks; "Her Story," by Jo Ann Parks; "Life with Ron," by Jo Ann Parks; author's interviews with Mary Ross, David Corrigan, and Carey Corrigan; 2006 report by Robert Lowe; and Los Angeles County Sheriff's Department investigative reports and search warrants for records related to the birth, foster care, and death of Jo Ann Parks's son David.

Homicide detectives initially sought to link David's death to foul play by Parks rather than sudden infant death syndrome, under the theory that she was a serial killer with a compulsion to kill her own children. The investigation, however, exonerated her of any involvement with David's death. He was in a foster home sixty miles away from Parks at the time of his death.

Chapter 10: They Told Me I Couldn't

Much of the information for this chapter is drawn from author interviews with Raquel and Ryan Cohen and Alissa Bjerkhoel, along with California

Innocence Project case summaries and court records for Jason Rivera and Luis Vargas.

Chapter 11: It's All Gonna Come Out in the End

Jo Ann Parks is the primary source for information on her and Ron's background and life together, supplemented by letters and written statements from Ron Parks and interviews from friends and relatives by investigators.

Information on the 1988 Lynwood fire is from the non-fire incident report of the Lynwood Fire Department dated April 26, 1988 (documenting Jo Ann Parks's complaints of electrical problems and the fire department's verification of faulty wiring at the house and a code violation); Los Angeles County Sheriff's Department fire report dated April 27, 1988, on the fire at the Parkses' Lynwood rental house (with additional information on the April 26 examination of electrical problems at the house); the supplementary fire investigation report dated June 28, 1988, by Ron Ablott; the deposition of Jo Ann Parks dated August 21, 1990, taken in the lawsuit the Parks family filed against their former landlords in Lynwood, *Parks v. Segueira,* Los Angeles County Municipal Court Case No. 89C02092; and the Los Angeles County Sheriff's Department homicide investigation supplementary report dated April 10, 1991, by Detectives Franco and Salerno on their interviews with Lynwood Fire Department fire prevention officer Jerome Samuel and other fire personnel.

The Parkses asserted that they made nothing from the lawsuit filed in the Lynwood fire. Prosecutors have suggested they made $30,000 through fire-related lawsuits, but this is based on testimony from Ron Parks that they were offered that sum at one point; elsewhere in the testimony, Parks says the lawsuits were dropped. Other than this testimony, prosecutors and police cite no evidence that the Parkses received any sort of monetary settlement in connection with either house fire. They did, however, receive about $30,000 in donations made after news coverage of the fatal fire.

Police reports and transcripts of interviews with Kathy Dodge are the primary sources of information about her interactions with Jo Ann Parks and her family, along with the case notes and opinion filed in the habeas proceedings by Ed Nordskog, and "Long Trail Led to Arrest of Mother in Children's Deaths," by David Ferrell, *Los Angeles Times,* December 1, 1991.

Chapter 12: Everything Which Is Not Law

Author's interviews with Raquel Cohen, retired Deputy District Attorney Dinko Bozanich, Mario Trujillo, and Justin Brooks.

Scalia's errant error rate calculation came in *Kansas v. Marsh,* 548 US 163, 182 (concurring opinion of Justice Scalia) (2006). The more scientific calculation can be found in "Rate of False Conviction of Criminal Defendants Who Are Sentenced to Death," by Samuel R. Gross, Barbara O'Brien, Chen Hu, and Edward H. Kennedy, *Proceedings of the National Academy of Sciences* (PNAS), May 20, 2014.

There were 2,253 known exonerations in the United States between 1989 and July 2018 for major crimes. This number does not include cases in which new trials were granted to inmates due to wrongful convictions who then negotiated a plea to lesser charges in exchange for immediate release, rather than face years of appeals and a new trial. Exoneration data and details are from the National Registry of Exonerations, http://www.law.umich.edu/special/exoneration/Pages/about.aspx and from "First DNA Exoneration: Gary Dotson," article published online by the Bluhm Legal Clinic, Center for Wrongful Convictions, Pritzker School of Law, Northwestern University http://www.law.northwestern.edu/legalclinic/wrongfulconvictions/exonerations/il/gary-dotson.html.

Fire scene investigation information is from the author's interview with Ron Ablott and the testimony of Ablott and William Franklin in *People v. Parks.* The original investigators in the case identified one major area of origin for the fire as below the living room windows because of the extremely large V-pattern in that location. However, testimony from defense experts decades later in the habeas hearing suggested that large V-pattern was caused by ventilation—the massive influx of fresh air that occurred when the living room windows shattered from heat and flames. The size of the V-pattern therefore could not be used as evidence of area of origin, especially because there was no evidence of an ignition source in that area once the wires were shown not to have started the blaze.

Negative corpus was commonly used in arson investigation for many decades and was considered proper methodology at the time of the Parks fire. However, beginning in 2011, the most authoritative guidelines for fire investigation, *NFPA 921* (published by the National Fire Protection Association) took a strong stance against the use of negative corpus as "unscientific."

The following language is taken from the 2014 edition of *NFPA 921* section 19.6.5:

> The process of determining the ignition source for a fire, by eliminating all ignition sources found, known, or believed to have been present in the area of origin, and then claiming such methodology is proof of an ignition source for which there is no supporting evidence of its existence, is referred to by some investigators as *negative corpus* . . . [Negative corpus] is not consistent with the scientific method, is inappropriate, and should not be used because it generates untestable hypotheses, and may result in incorrect determinations of the ignition source and first fuel ignited.

On the position of the closet door, Bozanich told jurors they could not believe Wegner's or McGee's testimonies. In habeas pleadings, Deputy DA Erika Jerez reaffirmed this point in her formal response:

> The prosecutor conceded during closing argument that the only two prosecution witnesses who testified to seeing the door closed were wrong, because although it had been closed during the fire, it had been opened by the first responders before Ronnie was discovered.
>
> As stated by DDA Bozanich, the People did not "rely on the testimony of either Wegner or McGee that the closet door was closed to establish that the closet door was closed at the time of the fire. . . . [One] could hypothesize with both of them that that's how it was when they first saw it. But a long time later when they were finally asked some questions about it," their memories of when they saw it closed versus open merged together. Rather, the People relied on the condition of the door hinges and the condition of the boy's body to show that the closet door was closed during the fire.

Chapter 13: "If I Am Wrong, Then Everything I Have Ever Been Taught . . . Would All Be Wrong"

Much of this chapter is based on Parks trial transcripts. Additional information about Robert Lowe was provided by his daughter Mary Ross.

Chapter 14: Sherlock Was Wrong

For perspectives on flaws in forensic science, including fingerprinting, the most comprehensive sources are "Strengthening Forensic Science in the

United States: A Path Forward," National Research Council, August 2009, and "Forensic Science in Criminal Courts: Ensuring Scientific Validity of Feature-Comparison Methods," President's Council of Advisors on Science and Technology (PCAST), September 2016.

The PCAST report had this to say about the current state and needed reforms for fingerprint matching:

> The method was long hailed as infallible, despite the lack of appropriate empirical studies to assess its error rate. In response to criticism on this point in the 2009 National Research Council report, those working in the field of latent fingerprint analysis recognized the need to perform empirical studies to assess foundational validity and measure reliability and have made progress in doing so. Much credit goes to the FBI Laboratory, which has led the way in performing black-box studies to assess validity and estimate reliability, as well as so-called "white-box" studies to understand the factors that affect examiners' decisions. PCAST applauds the FBI Laboratory's efforts. There are also nascent efforts to begin to move the field from a purely subjective method toward an objective method—although there is still a considerable way to go to achieve this important goal.
>
> PCAST finds that latent fingerprint analysis is a foundationally valid subjective methodology—albeit with a false positive rate that is substantial and is likely to be higher than expected by many jurors based on longstanding claims about the infallibility of fingerprint analysis. The false-positive rate could be as high as 1 error in 306 cases based on the FBI study and 1 error in 18 cases based on a study by another crime laboratory. In reporting results of latent-fingerprint examination, it is important to state the false-positive rates based on properly designed validation studies.
>
> With respect to validity as applied, there are, however, a number of open issues, notably:
>
> *Confirmation bias.* Work by FBI scientists has shown that examiners often alter the features that they initially mark in a latent print based on comparison with an apparently matching exemplar. Such circular reasoning introduces a serious risk of confirmation bias. Examiners should be required to complete

and document their analysis of a latent fingerprint *before* looking at any known fingerprint and should separately document any additional data used during their comparison and evaluation.

Contextual bias. Work by academic scholars has shown that examiners' judgments can be influenced by irrelevant information about the facts of a case. Efforts should be made to ensure that examiners are not exposed to potentially biasing information.

Proficiency testing. Proficiency testing is essential for assessing an examiner's capability and performance in making accurate judgments. As discussed elsewhere in this report, proficiency testing needs to be improved by making it more rigorous, by incorporating it systematically within the flow of casework, and by disclosing tests for evaluation by the scientific community.

Scientific validity as applied, then, requires that an expert: (1) has undergone relevant proficiency testing to test his or her accuracy and reports the results of the proficiency testing; (2) discloses whether he or she documented the features in the latent print in writing before comparing it to the known print; (3) provides a written analysis explaining the selection and comparison of the features; (4) discloses whether, when performing the examination, he or she was aware of any other facts of the case that might influence the conclusion; and (5) verifies that the latent print in the case at hand is similar in quality to the range of latent prints considered in the foundational studies.

Concerning the path forward, continuing efforts are needed to improve the state of latent-print analysis—and these efforts will pay clear dividends for the criminal justice system. One direction is to continue to improve latent print analysis as a subjective method. There is a need for additional empirical studies to estimate error rates for latent prints of varying quality and completeness, using well-defined measures.

A second—and more important—direction is to convert latent-print analysis from a subjective method to an objective method. The past decade has seen extraordinary advances in automated image analysis based on machine learning and other

> approaches—leading to dramatic improvements in such tasks as face recognition and the interpretation of medical images. This progress holds promise of making fully automated latent fingerprint analysis possible in the near future. There have already been initial steps in this direction, both in academia and industry.

The PCAST report was scathing on the lack of rigor for bite-mark evidence:

> Available scientific evidence strongly suggests that examiners not only cannot identify the source of a bitemark with reasonable accuracy, they cannot even consistently agree on whether an injury *is* a human bitemark. For these reasons, PCAST finds that bitemark analysis is far from meeting the scientific standards for foundational validity.
>
> We note that some practitioners have expressed concern that the exclusion of bitemarks in court could hamper efforts to convict defendants in some cases. If so, the correct solution, from a scientific perspective, would not be to admit expert testimony based on invalid and unreliable methods but rather to attempt to develop scientifically valid methods. But, PCAST considers the prospects of developing bitemark analysis into a scientifically valid method to be low. We advise against devoting significant resources to such efforts.

The description of the ATF burn-cell training exercises and the difficulty fire investigators had in identifying the correct area of origin after flashover came from the author's interviews with John Lentini and Steve Carman, and from "Improving the Understanding of Post-Flashover Fire Behavior," by Steve Carman, *Proceedings of the 3rd International Symposium on Fire Investigation Science and Technology*, 2008.

Information on the Kristine Bunch case and stereotypes in the prosecution of female defendants was based on court records in the Bunch case and "Death, But Is It Murder? The Role of Stereotypes and Cultural Perceptions in the Wrongful Convictions of Women," by Andrea L. Lewis and Sara L. Sommervold, *Albany Law Review*, vol. 78.3, Spring 2015.

Chapter 16: The Bias Man

Sources in this chapter include interviews and testimony of Paul Bieber and Ed Nordskog.

Information on the Souliotes case is based on information from "Anatomy of a Wrongful Arson Conviction: Sentinel Event Analysis in Fire Investigation," by Paul Bieber, 2014, and habeas ruling in the case of George Souliotes, dated April 26, 2012.

Chapter 18: What Revolution?

Two witnesses testified to finding an extension cord in the living room that had cuts in the insulation in one section and drapery wrapped around another section. This became the basis for prosecution expert witnesses asserting for decades something subtly, but vitally, different: that Jo Ann Parks created an incendiary device consisting of cuts in wiring covered over by drapery material.

However, a careful reading of the testimony shows that one of the two witnesses, LA County fire investigator William Franklin, despite initially describing what sounded like a crude incendiary device, did not actually discover (or photograph) cuts in a cord covered over by drapery. Instead, he recalled that someone else, possibly LA Sheriff's detective Ron Ablott, found it while Franklin was preoccupied with his own tasks working nearby in the living room.

Then Ablott's testimony about those same events reveals what Franklin missed. Ablott said he did indeed find an extension cord that had some drapery wrapped around a portion of it. But there were no cuts in the cord at that point. Ablott followed the cord along the floor beneath the windows in the living room, and found a section of wiring that was badly burned with the plastic insulation gone or completely consumed by fire, along with a smaller section that was well preserved because it had been underneath a small plastic crate or basket with clothes inside it. Most of the crate had been burned away, leaving just a plastic mesh bottom stuck to the carpeting. When he pulled up the partially melted bottom of the crate, he found a section of the wire that had four small cuts in the insulation—but no drapery.

Over the years, this information from two witnesses has been distorted into cut wires wrapped in drapery to form an incendiary device.

Here is an excerpt of Franklin's testimony, under cross-examination, starting at transcript page 2829, with sections showing Franklin did not actually see the key moment of "discovery" in boldface:

Q: Where was the cut in the wire?
A: I can't answer that. I did not pick that piece of wiring to do that. I was doing something else and I forget whether it was Ablott or [his partner] Love started playing with it and came up, untwisted it and said, hey, you know, look.

Q: Untwisted it?
A: Well, unwrapped the burned fabric from around it.

Q: Was the burned fabric actually around it?
A: Well, I saw it was . . . it was . . . it was adhered to it, okay? He had peeled it away from the wiring.

Q: Let me see if I have it straight. The cut area that you are talking about, this was something that you saw then?
A: I saw it there, yes, sir.

Q: And it was a bare wire?
A: It was a wire—two wires and a cord appearing to be a service cord, a larger type of service cord. Under that area it had most of the insulation still in place. . . . Again, I was not the one who picked it up and manipulated it.

Q: You have, I believe, testified that the cut wire was wrapped in something?
A: Yes, sir.

Q: That you saw with your own eyes?
A: Yes, sir.

Q: Tell us about that.
A: It had a fabric on it appearing to have the same weave and backing as would a set of drapes.

Q: That was actually on the wire?
A: Adhered to it, yes, sir.

Q: Well, how did he take it off, with a knife?
A: I believe he just unwrapped it with his hands.

Q. This was a piece of a kind of drapery material? Was it kind of melted into the wire?
A: It was adhered to it, yes, sir.

Q: What do you mean by "adhered"?
A: It had melted and adhered to the wiring and the wiring insulation.

Q: Some drapery material adhered to the insulation and Detective Ablott, in your presence, got that off the insulation somehow?
A: Either Detective Ablott or Love, and I am not sure which one.

Q: And they peeled it off with their hands?
A: I am sure they did, yes, sir.

Q: And then what happened to the piece of drapery material?
A: I believe the preponderance stayed here and to the wire. They would just kind of very carefully peel it back.

Q: And where they peeled it back you were able to see a cut in the wire?
A: Yes, sir.

Q: That's the only cut that you observed there?
A: That segment of wire, yes, sir.

Q: How long was it?
A: Very short.

[skipping several questions]

Q: And that cut had been earlier wrapped with some of this material that looked like a drape?
A: Yes, sir.

Q: And you saw him remove that in your presence from that wire?
A: Remove it, no, sir.

Q: How did you know it had been wrapped?
A: I saw what appeared to be a wrap. How exactly, how he manipulated it to expose the wiring, I cannot say. . . . I believe the first

time I saw the wire the material was adhered to it, and then the wiring now is exposed with the insulation exposed where I can see the knife cuts.

Q: So you can see knife cuts, but at the same time on the opposite side of the wire you can see some of what looked like drapery material or adhering to—is that a fair statement?
A: Yes, sir.

Q: Now the material that he peeled back, was that still adhering or was part of it taken off and discarded or something?
A: Being I wasn't present or wasn't observing him when he peeled it, there may have been more that he peeled off and fallen, but I can't answer. All I saw was the part that was still adhered when I looked at it.

Q: Now that process of doing that, that's not recorded in your photography, is it?
A: No, sir, it is not.

Next, here is Ron Ablott's testimony, beginning on page 2938 of the trial transcript, about finding the cuts in the extension cord, and how it did not involve peeling back any drapery material, but peeling the bottom of a plastic crate from the carpet it had melted and stuck to. Key sections about these two separate discoveries are in boldface.

Q: In that area of origin, did you see anything which you felt was suspicious?
A: Yes, I did.

Q: What?
A: While overhauling, which is a term we use which means we are digging out or actually removing the ash from the fire in layers, getting down to the floor in the area so you have an idea what it looks like prior to the fire, I found that there was an electrical cord that extended from the outlet next to the front door on the west wall of the living room. This outlet was on that same wall. It came from the outlet and ran down the north wall right next to it to an area where the V-pattern

was and then continued up. In this same wire assembly, there was a multi-plug outlet attached which went off due south someplace into some broken wires.

Q: Meaning they were probably connected up to something?
A: Yes.

[skipping several questions]

Q: Was there something more about this cord that was suspicious that you have already described?
A: Yes.

Q: What?
A: **As I began to follow it back to the outlet, I noticed that part of the electric cord had been wrapped with some type of material or material had been draped over it and then containers placed on it. This material had burned or melted onto the wire itself and appeared to be some type of rubber-backed drapery material.**

Q: What's so unusual about something like this around the wire?
A: Well, the problem with that is that the wire itself, when electricity goes through it, generates heat. When you insulate that wire, you are asking that heat to build up and possibly start a fire.

Q: What was there about the insulation of this cord, if anything, that drew your attention?
A: **As I followed this back, I then ran into an area which, when I removed the clothes, there was what appeared to be a probably 12-, maybe 14-inch lavender or possibly purple or blue bottom of a plastic clothes basket which was melted onto the carpet. Upon removing that, I found a complete section of the wire which had the insulation intact, but there was a portion of the wire where the insulation had been cut away from the wire itself and exposed the bare wires.**

Q: What's so unusual about that?
A: Well, going back to my training and the things I had learned, modification of an appliance, and this cord would be a modification, is somewhat of a strong indicator that an arson may have—

Q: You used the word "appliance." Are you including a cord within the definition of appliance?
A: Yes, I am.

Q. So that—did this cord look like it had been—was the subject of wear that the insulation was gone?
A: No, sir. It actually had been cut and cut away. . . . The only reason this particular insulation was found was that this plastic basket, which had clothes in it, had protected that portion of the cord from the fire. The cord on either side of the basket had the insulation either melted or burned off. This section was not damaged, and that was the only reason I found it.

[skipping questions]

A: This is part of the electrical wire that we seized from the living room area along the north wall. . . . It had this rubber backed drapery material which was melted around part of the bare cord melted around it, and this is the part that ran from the wall towards the basket.

Q: So that this wire was not the one that had the cuts on it?
A: No, sir.

[Skipping questions. Ablott is asked to explain the "octopus" section of the extension cord where other cords are plugged into it.]

A: This cord had part of the rubber insulation cut away from it, and had been done in such a manner that the insulation had been removed from the wire itself. . . . **There is material wrapped around the wire, prior to the cut,** and this material is burned and melted on to the wire.

[skipping ahead]

Q: This part right here, isn't that what you are talking about where there is some copper shining through the insulation?
A: Yes, it is, sir.

Q: Now, there is no burning there, is there, or melting of the insulation at that particular spot?
A: No, there's not.

Q: And there's no sign of carpet having been melted into it at that particular spot, is there, where this particular wire is bared?
A: No, sir.

Q: There is no other wire touching that particular wire at that point, is there, to cause a short or arcing?
A: No, sir.

Q: There is no drapery material wound around it, or caught up in it at that particular point, is there?
A: No, sir.

Q: And this point where this wire is bared, is that what was underneath some kind of a clothes hamper, or something, in your opinion when you found it?
A: It was underneath a round base of like a clothes basket, or a trash basket–type thing. It's round plastic.

Q: But it was underneath some item?
A: Right. And that was melted onto the carpet.

Q: Yeah, but it was not melted onto the wire here, was it?
A: No, sir.

At a preliminary hearing before the trial, Ablott was even more clear that the cuts were not wrapped in any drapery material:

A: The wiring was exposed due to the fact that the rubber coated insulation had been cut away from the wire itself, exposing the metal multi-strand cord or wire.

Q: With regard to that wire, the exposed area of wire, what, if any, contact did that have with this material?

A: **It was actually past that area which had been wrapped in the cord by a few inches.**

The confusion about the cuts and the drapery appears to stem from an ambiguous statement Ablott made on page 2953 of the transcript, in which he explains why he seized the wires.

A: The electrical wire which ran from the outlet on the west wall and ran along the north wall which had been either wrapped or folded into the drapery material which had containers placed on top of it and then continued under the laundry basket, and I am talking a small laundry basket which was either purple or blue, and then ended, which also had the octopus on it. **That was the wire I did seize because of the cuts in the insulation and the drapery material which had been wrapped around it.**

Q. Now, at that point, by taking that material into custody, was that synonymous with saying that at least from your standpoint that this explained that area of origin as the cause of the fire?
A: Yes. It appeared to be the obvious thing that started the fire. . . . That the insulation had been stripped away to cause a direct short and then the circuit was purposely overloaded to heat up the wire, cause it to short and start the fire.

His subsequent testimony made clear that what he was saying was that he seized the wire because one part of it had cuts in the insulation—a deliberate and suspicious "modification" of the wire, in his opinion—and that other parts of the wire had been wrapped in material to cause the wire to overheat. But this quote was taken out of context and, because of its phrasing, used to suggest that the cuts in the wiring were covered over with drapery material. Nordskog relies on this interpretation in his report filed in the habeas proceeding:

> Det. Ron Ablott, the most experienced and educated investigator at the scene, testified that the wire "had been either wrapped or folded into the drapery material which had containers placed on top of it . . . that was the wire I did seize

because of the cuts in the insulation and the drapery material which had been wrapped around it." He testified later that it was "electrical sabotage." He was the first person to recognize the item for what it was, a crudely constructed attempt at an incendiary arrangement or device. Ablott has a unique perspective that no other investigator in this case has. He was a former homicide detective, and at the time of this fire he had been a bomb and arson investigator on over 1,000 cases. He was the person best equipped to recognize this item for what it was.

Acknowledgments

A work of nonfiction isn't just about storytelling. It's also an exercise in patience and generosity—not by the author, but by those who inhabit the story and are willing to share their knowledge, insights, and expertise. I'm not sure why they put up with inordinate numbers of questions in otherwise very busy lives, but a very large number of kind folks did just that, and their goodwill and willingness to share their stories made *Burned* possible.

In particular I wish to thank:

The staff and volunteers of the California Innocence Project, including Raquel Cohen, Alissa Bjerkhoel, Mike Semanchik, Alex Simpson, Audrey McGinn, Katherine Bonaguidi, and the project's director, Justin Brooks; Ed Nordskog of the Los Angeles County Sheriff's Department Arson/Explosives Detail; Los Angeles County Deputy District Attorney Erika Jerez; Paul Bieber; Greg Gorbett; retired Deputy District Attorney Dinko Bozanich; and Jo Ann Parks, for allowing access without conditions; and Mary Ross, whose hospitality and help were invaluable and most appreciated.

I also wish to thank my editor at Dutton, Stephen Morrow, for his support and good ear and, as always, the wonderful team at Writers House, A Literary Agency, where my incomparable agent and friend, Susan Ginsburg, and Stacy Testa have long done their best to keep me in line.

Index

Ablott, Ronald R. *See also* Incendiary device theory and television evidence
Bell home fire investigation by, 43–48, 127–28, 137–41
biographical information, 136–37
closet barricade theory of, 46–47, 147–50, 159–60, 247–50, 256–57
Cohen on evidence by, 129–30
Gorbett's testimony on work of, 240–50
Hoback's testimony on work of, 231
Lynwood home fire investigated by, 113–15, 140
methodology used by, 141–42
NFPA 921 (National Fire Protection Association) and, 58–59, 199, 226
prosecution in Parks case based on opinions of, 150–52
retirement of, 176
Smith's testimony on work of, 233
testimony of, at Parks 1992 trial, 154–63, 166, 180
American Academy of Forensic Sciences, 194
"Animal magnetism," 218–19
Armstrong, William, 144
Arson. *See also* Burn patterns; Evidence; Fire science
arrest of Parks for, 59–61
crazed glass and, 53–54, 57, 199
dogs for arson investigations, 213
forensic science controversies about, 198–203
initial investigation of Jo Ann and Ron Parks, 43–50
Lime Street fire (1990) and, 55–57
NFPA 921 (National Fire Protection Association) recommendations on, 57–59, 199, 226
Oakland firestorm (1991) and, 51–55
Arson/Explosives Detail (Los Angeles County Sheriff's Department), 43–50
Arson Review Committee report (Los Angeles County Fire Department, 2012), 73–74, 232–38
Asphyxiation, 12

Backdraft, 161–63
"Bad mother" archetype, 75, 202–3
Banks, Brian, 135
Barilla, Raquel. *See* Cohen, Raquel

INDEX

Bell, James, 13
Bell (city), early history of, 13–14
Bell Police Department
  Bruce and, 20–24, 30, 46, 172, 255
  Cacheiro and, 18, 170–71
  Dodge's allegation of arson to, 43, 44, 47–49, 137
  Espejo and, 27–31, 39
  Parks children's deaths revealed to parents by, 35–42
  Talbott and, 137–41
Bendectin, 192–93
Beyler, Craig, 200
Bieber, Paul, 214, 215, 217, 221–28, 270
Bishop, Bob, 137
Bite-mark evidence, 188–90
Bjerkhoel, Alissa
  California Innocence Project job of, 70
  Long case and, 104–5
  Parks case and, 101, 103
  Rivera case and, 92–95, 104
Black holes, 53–54
Blind investigation process, 217–21, 270
Bozanich, Dinko. *See also* Trial of Jo Ann Parks (1992)
  on flashover, 146
  on Parks's character and credibility, 160–63
  on Parks trial, 153–54
  summation by, at Parks trial (1992), 150–52, 170
Brady, John Leo, 98
Brady materials, 98, 131
Brooks, Justin
  California Innocence Project inception and, 130, 133–36
  on Parks case, 174, 179–80
Brown, Jerry, 135, 205
Bruce, Jeff, 20–24, 30, 46, 172, 255
Bunch, Kristine, 200–203
Burden of proof, 73
Bureau of Alcohol, Tobacco, Firearms and Explosives, 198–200, 240, 246
Burn patterns
  Ablott's investigation of Parkses' Bell home, 43–48, 127–28, 137–47
  Carman on burn-cell exercises, 198–200, 240
  forensic science controversies about, 157, 198–203 (*See also* Habeas hearing for Parks)
  heat and flame vector analysis of, 237–47
  investigation of Parkses' Lynwood home fire, 113–15, 140
  pour patterns, defined, 55
  temperature and timing of, 11
  V-patterns, defined, 55–56

Cacheiro, Pete, 18, 170–71
California Innocence Project, 65–76. *See also* Cohen, Raquel; Habeas corpus petitions; Habeas hearing for Parks
  California Western School of Law, 65, 89, 135
  case load of, 65–67
  Cohen's review of Parks case, 61, 67–77
  founding of, 130, 133–36
  funding of, 94, 266–67
  Long case and, 104–5
  nature of work, 68, 87–88, 100–101, 125–28
  Richards case and, 95–96, 189–90
  Rivera case, 89–95, 104
  Vargas case and, 95, 97
  XONR8 abbreviation of, 104
California (state)
  "California 12," 135
  death penalty in, 60, 163–65
  expert witnesses used in, 70
  governor's pardoning in, 135, 205
  Three Strikes repeat offender law, 230
  volume of habeas corpus petitions submitted to, 125
  on withholding evidence, 98

INDEX

California Western School of Law, 65, 89, 135. *See also* California Innocence Project
Canen, Lana, 185
Canine alerts, 213
Carbon monoxide, 10, 12
Cardozo School of Law, 133
Carman, Steve, 198–200, 240
Carney, Sean, 223–27
Center on Wrongful Convictions, Northwestern University, 201
Century Regional Detention Facility (Los Angeles County), 206–7
Chanot, François, 219
Chowchilla (women's penitentiary), 87, 206
Christian Scientists, 35–42, 49, 109, 116
Church of Jesus Christ of Latter-day Saints (Mormon Church), 77, 79, 81, 83–84, 271
Clara Shortridge Foltz Criminal Justice Center, 229
Closet barricade theory
  Ablott on, 46–47, 147–50, 159–60, 247–50, 256–57
  clothes hamper position and, 46, 149–51, 159, 160, 249, 256, 272
  door hinges and, 148, 248, 256
  events of fire and Ronnie Jr.'s death, 29–34, 72
Cognitive bias, 213–28
  Ablott's investigation and, 137–47
  Bieber on Parks case, 214, 215, 217, 221–28, 238
  blind investigations as solution to, 217–21, 270
  Cohen on, 137–41, 178–80
  defined, 138, 186
  investigative bias and, 213–17
  Nordskog on, 178–80, 217, 228, 237
  uncertainty and, 269–73
Cohen, August, 87
Cohen, Raquel, 87–106. *See also* California Innocence Project; Habeas hearing for Parks
  biographical information, 87–89, 94, 99–100, 103–4
  on cognitive bias, 137–41, 178–80
  Long case and, 104–5
  Parks case researched by, 61, 67–77, 96–106
  Richards case and, 95–96, 189–90
  Rivera case and, 89–95, 104
  Vargas case and, 95, 97
Cohen, Ryan, 87, 100, 103–4, 265–66
Cole, Simon, 184–85, 187, 193
Conan Doyle, Sir Arthur, 188
Convictions, error rate of, 131–32
Corrigan, Carey, 79–80
Corrigan, David, 79–80
Cough medicine accusation
  Dodge on, 49, 105, 110, 124, 164–65, 168, 215
  Nordskog on, 177
Cowans, Stephan, 185
Crazed glass, 53–54, 57, 199
CSI (TV show), 131

Dactylography, 184
Darigold ice cream packing plant, 28, 29, 39, 79, 111
Daubert v. Merrell Down Pharmaceuticals, 192–93
Daubert test, 192–94
David (Jo Ann Parks's first child), 48, 82–83, 118
Death penalty (California), 60, 163–65
Defense. *See* Trial of Jo Ann Parks (1992)
Department of Justice (US), 139, 196
Dissociative disorder, 84–85
DNA testing
  credibility of, 188
  early use of, in criminal cases, 89, 132–33
  faulty eyewitness identification disputed by, 220–21
  Vargas case and, 95

Dodge, Kathy
accusation about arson by, 43, 44, 47–49, 137
accusation about cough medicine by, 49, 105, 110, 124, 164–65, 168, 215
argument between Jo Ann Parks and, 117–20, 123–24
as potential trial witness, 163–65, 168–70
Dogs, for arson investigations, 213
Dotson, Gary, 132–33
Double-blind investigation process, 219–21

Eastern Kentucky University, 238, 248. *See also* Gorbett, Greg
Error rate of convictions, 131–32
Espejo, Frank, 27–31, 39
Evidence. *See also* Burn patterns; Closet barricade theory; Firefighting; Fire science; Flashover; Incendiary device theory and television evidence
bite-mark evidence, 188–90
Cohen's review of, for Parks case, 97–99
Daubert test and, 192–94
DNA testing for, 89, 95, 132–33, 188, 220–21
fingerprint analysis, 183–88, 190–92
flashover as, 196–203 (*See also* Flashover)
National Registry of Exonerations on forensic analysis of, 187, 194–96
suspicion of matches used by Jo Ann Parks, 127, 158
suspicion of matches used by Ronnie Parks Jr., 5, 29–31, 35, 116, 149, 272
uncertainty of forensic analysis, 265–73
windows as, 20, 115, 237–47
Expectation bias. *See* Cognitive bias

Failed incendiary device. *See* Incendiary device theory and television evidence
FBI
crime statistics on arson, 199
on Madrid commuter train bombings, 139, 185–88
Plaza case, 193–94
Federal Law Enforcement Training Center, 196–200
Fingerprint analysis, 183–88, 190–92
Fire Department. *See* Los Angeles County Fire Department
Firefighting. *See also* Los Angeles County Fire Department
attempts to rescue Parks children, 14–25
breathing apparatus needed for, 10
carbon monoxide, 10, 12
flammable items and, 7, 9–10
"nozzleman" position, 23
overhaul procedure, 44–45, 142, 159–60
oxygen as fuel for fire, 10–11
primary search, 31
smoke and smoke detectors, 10–11, 12, 41, 100, 113, 122, 143
Fire science, 51–63. *See also* Burn patterns; Flashover
backdraft, 161–63
black holes, 53–54
crazed glass and, 53–54, 57, 199
dispute about changing approaches to (*See* Habeas hearing for Parks)
heat and flame vector analysis, 237–47
house fires, causes of, 7–12
importance of burn patterns to, 55–56 (*See also* Burn patterns)
Lee case and, 252–53
Lime Street fire (1990) and, 55–57
negative corpus, 127, 145
NFPA 921 (National Fire Protection Association) recommendations on, 57–59, 199, 226

Oakland firestorm (1991) and, 51–55
point of origin, 40, 46
V-patterns, 55–56
Flashover. *See also* Habeas hearing for Parks; Second fire theory
controversy of, 157, 196–203, 237–47, 254–55, 258
defined, 11–12, 23
indicators of, 245–46
Lime Street fire recreation of, 56–57
Parkses' Bell home fire events and, 73–74, 145–50
Parkses' Lynwood home fire events and, 115
Forensic analysis, 183–203. *See also* DNA testing; Fire science; Incendiary device theory and television evidence
bite-mark evidence, 188–90
Cohen's review of, for Parks case, 97–99
Daubert test and, 192–94
fingerprint analysis, 183–88, 190–92
of flashover, 196–203 (*See also* Flashover)
National Registry of Exonerations on, 187, 194–96
uncertainty of, 265–73
Forensic Science Commission (Texas), 200
Franklin, Benjamin, 218
Franklin, William. *See also* Los Angeles County Fire Department
overhaul of fire scene and, 44–45, 137–41, 155
search for Ronnie Jr. by, 32–33, 44–45
French Academy of Sciences, 218–19
Fuzell, Lester "Fuzzy," Sr., 137, 155

Galton, Sir Francis, 191, 192
"Gambler's Fallacy," 140–41
Garman, Paul, 35–42, 49, 109, 116
Gessler, Charles, 154–63, 166, 171–72. See also Trial of Jo Ann Parks (1992)
Gideon rights, 131
Glass, crazing of, 53–54, 57, 199
Gorbett, Greg
on flashover and ventilation (visual analysis of fire), 237–47
habeas hearing and prosecution's case, 254, 256–59
on incendiary device theory, 247–50
Guillotin, Joseph, 218

Habeas corpus petitions
defined, 68
Hamilton and Jefferson on, 93
for Parks case, 93, 125–30, 152, 172–80, 214, 250
for Rivera case, 93–94
volume of, 125
Habeas hearing for Parks, 229–50, 251–64
appeals process, 263
Bieber's testimony, 214, 215, 217, 221–28, 238
Gorbett's testimony, 237–50, 254, 256–59
Hoback's testimony, 231–32, 233, 243, 253–58, 260
Jerez's prosecution of, 251, 253–58, 260–62
judge's ruling, 262–63, 265–73
Lord's testimony, 258, 260
Nordskog's testimony, 258–61
Parks's views on her habeas hearing, 208–9
Smith on Arson Review Committee report, 232–38
time devoted to, 230–31
venue for, 229–30
Hamilton, Alexander, 125
Hand, Learned, 131–32

Haney, David "Tuxedo Man"
events of fire and, 14–18, 21, 24
search for Ronnie Parks by, 32
witness account of, 46, 255
Hanline, Michael, 135
Hiller, Clarence, 183–85, 191
Hinges, mirroring of, 148, 248, 256
Hoback, Brian, 231–32, 233, 243, 253–58, 260

Incendiary device theory and television evidence
cognitive bias issues of, 137–47, 215, 217, 221–28
Gorbett on, 247–50
Hoback on "sabotaged" wires, 231–32, 233, 243, 257
Nordskog on, 177, 179–80
"octopus" of cords, 137–38, 258
Parks fire investigation and, 48, 71–73, 116, 121–23, 126–28, 143, 145
Parks trial (1992) and, 154–60, 163, 178
India, fingerprinting practice in, 191–92
Innocence projects. *See also* California Innocence Project
Center on Wrongful Convictions, Northwestern University, 201
Northern California Innocence Project, 221–23
reverse detective work by, 92–93
"Inside" (Parks), 209–11

Jefferson, Thomas, 125
Jennings, Thomas, 184–85, 191
Jerez, Erika. *See also* Habeas hearing for Parks
early discussions with California Innocence Project, 174–75
Gorbett testimony and, 243–44
Hoback testimony and, 253–58
Smith testimony and, 234–37, 246–47
on state of fire science, 251, 261
Justice Department (US), 139, 196

Kodiak, 234–35

Lake St. Charles Retirement Community, 59–60
Laughing gas, 219
Lee, Han Tak, 252–53
Lentini, John
on Lime Street fire (1990), 55–57, 145
reputation of, 157, 199
Scientific Protocols for Fire Investigation, 256
Lewis, Andrea L., 202
Lime Street fire (1990), 55–57, 145
Lineup identification, 221
Long, Kimberly, 104–5
Lord, Jamie, 258, 260
Lorraine (Jo Ann Parks's mother)
daughter's childhood and, 77–78, 81–84, 86
daughter's incarceration and, 207
Ron Parks and, 109–10, 120
Los Angeles County Century Regional Detention Facility, 206–7
Los Angeles County Fire Department
Arson Review Committee report (2012), 73–74, 232–38
California Innocence Project and, 67–70, 73
NFPA 921 (National Fire Protection Association) and, 58–59, 199, 226
Parks house fire investigation by, 40–42, 137–41
Parks house fire response by, 14–25
search for Ronnie Parks by, 31–34
Los Angeles County Sheriff's Department. *See also* Ablott, Ronald R.
arrest of Parks by, 59–61

Arson/Explosives Detail, 175–80 (*See also* Nordskog, Edward)
Arson/Explosives Detail investigation, 43–50
Los Angeles County Superior Court, 96–97. *See also* Habeas hearing for Parks; Ryan, William; Trial of Jo Ann Parks (1992)
Los Angeles County District Attorney's Office. *See* Jerez, Erika; Trial of Jo Ann Parks (1992)
Los Angeles Police Department, 221
Los Angeles Times, on arson industry, 261
Louis XVI (king of France), 218–19
Lowe, Bob
advocacy of Parks following 1992 trial, 172–75
California Innocence Project and reopened Parks case, 67–70, 73
testimony at Parks trial (1992), 154–63, 166
Luna, Albert, 91–95
Luna, Dominic, 90–95
Lynwood home fire (Parks family)
Bell home fire prosecution on, 151
Dodge on, 124
events of and Ablott's investigation, 111–15
Nordskog on, 176

Madrid commuter train bombings (2004), 139, 185–88
Maniac Latin Disciples gang, 134–35
Marx, Walter Edgar, 188
Maryland, Brady case in, 98
Matches
Jo Ann Parks and accusations about use of, 127, 158
Ronnie Parks Jr.'s behavior with, 5, 29–31, 35, 116, 149, 272
Mayfield, Brandon, 139, 185
McGee, Timothy, 19–24, 256
Mesmer, Franz, 218–19
Miranda rights, 131
Mirroring, 148, 248, 256
Mormon Church (Church of Jesus Christ of Latter-day Saints), 77, 79, 81, 83–84, 271
Morrison, Patt, 261
Mulero, Marilyn, 134–36

National Academy of Sciences, 187, 270
National District Attorneys Association, 58, 196
National Fire Protection Association
on canine alerts, 213
NFPA 921 (1992), 57–59, 199, 226
on scientific method, 226
National Registry of Exonerations, 187, 194–96
Navarette, Manuel Martin, 90–95
Negative corpus, 127, 145
Neufeld, Peter, 133
New York City, house fire (2017) in, 8
NFPA 921 (National Fire Protection Association), 57–59, 199, 226
Nitrous oxide, 219
Nordskog, Edward, 175–80, 217, 228, 237, 258–61, 269
Northern California Innocence Project, 221–23
Northwestern University, 201
"No Walk," 154
"Nozzleman" position, 23

Oakland firestorm (1991), 51–55
Obama, Barack, 270
"Outside" (Parks), 263–64

Parks, Jessica "Jessie" (daughter). *See also* Second fire theory
attempts for rescue of, 14–25
autopsy of, 49
discovery of body of, 25, 99, 164–65
Lynwood home fire and, 113
Parks, Jo Ann. *See also* California Innocence Project; Habeas hearing for Parks; Trial of Jo Ann Parks (1992)

Parks, Jo Ann *(cont.)*
actions during Bell home fire events, 3–6, 9, 38, 120–24
arrest of, 59–61
biographical information, 77–85
California habeas corpus petition for, 93, 125–30, 152, 172–80, 214, 250
characterization of, 3–6, 18, 37–38, 79–80, 84–85, 127–28, 160–63
children's deaths revealed to, 35–42
Cohen's research of case, 61, 67–77, 96–106
cough medicine accusation against, 49, 105, 110, 124, 164–65, 168, 215
donations to, 47
Fontana home of, 116–20, 124
"Inside/Outside" (essay), 209–11, 263–64
investigation of (*See* Ablott, Ronald R.)
Lynwood home fire and, 111–15, 124, 140, 151, 176
marriage to Ron by, 85–86, 107–11, 156
move to Bell by family of, 14
as part of "California 12," 135
portrayal as "bad mother," 75, 202–3
prosecution of, 102–4
statement to police by, 27–31
teenage rape and pregnancy of, 48, 83, 118
television interview of, 41, 47
views of, 205–9
Parks, Norma (Ron's first wife), 109, 110
Parks, Ro Ann (daughter). *See also* Second fire theory
attempts at rescue of, 14–25
autopsy of, 49
birth of, 102
discovery of body of, 25, 99, 164–65
Parks, Ron, Jr. (son of Ron and Norma Parks), 110
Parks, Ron (husband), 107–24
Bell home fire events, 120–24
children's deaths revealed to, 35–42
divorce from Jo Ann and death of, 208
Dodge on statements about "getting rich" by, 118, 123–24
donations to, 47
electrician training and related work of, 46, 47, 107
Fontana home of, 116–20, 124
as hostile witness at wife's trial, 165–68, 171–72
ice cream packing plant job of, 28, 29, 39, 79, 111
investigation of, 59, 71–72
lawsuits against landlords by, 167
Lynwood home fire and, 111–15, 124, 140
marriage to Jo Ann by, 85–86, 107–11, 156
marriage to Norma by, 109, 110
reaction to children's deaths by, 37–38, 41–42, 47, 162–63, 167, 208, 271
television interview of, 41, 47
Parks, Ronnie, Jr. (son of Ron and Jo Ann Parks). See also Closet barricade theory
attempts at rescue of, 14–25
autopsy of, 49
behavior by, 5, 29–31, 35, 116, 122, 149, 272
discovery of body of, 31–34
Gorbett on flashover and ventilation in bedroom of, 242
mother's comments about calls for help by, 236
question about playing with matches, 5, 29–31, 35, 116, 149, 272

INDEX

Parole boards, 94
People of the State of California v. Jo Ann Parks, 68, 136, 267. *See also* Trial of Jo Ann Parks (1992)
People v. Rivera, 93, 99
Plaza, Llera, 193–94
Police department, Bell (California). *See* Bell Police Department
Police Department, Los Angeles, 221
Pollak, Louis, 193–94
Pour patterns, 55
Powell, Lloyd Richard, 21, 255
President's Council of Advisors of Sciences, 187
Primary search, 31
Prosecution. *See* Trial of Jo Ann Parks (1992)

Repeat offender law (California), 230
Resistance heating, 40
Reuben, Shelley, 215–16
Reverse detective work, by innocence projects, 92–93
Richards, Bill, 95–96, 189–90
Rivera, Jason, 89–95, 104
Rivera, Jennifer, 90
Robison, Bob, 3–6, 14–18, 29, 162
Robison, Shirley
  characterization of Jo Ann Parks by, 80, 160–63
  events of fire and, 3–6, 15–18
  at police station with Jo Ann Parks, 28–31, 37
Ross, Mary, 173, 207, 271
Ryan, William. *See also* Habeas hearing for Parks
  court schedule of, 96, 230
  Vargas case and, 97

Samuel, Jerome, 113
Scalia, Antonin, 68–69, 132
Scheck, Barry, 133
Scientific Protocols for Fire Investigation (Lentini), 256
Second fire theory
  Ablott's investigation and theory about, 127, 141, 145
  Cohen's demonstration plans for, 266
  cough medicine theory about, 177
  flammable liquid theory about, 143
  Gorbett's visual analysis and dispute of, 239–42, 246, 259–60
  lack of motive and, 49
Shelton, Donald, 194
Sheriff's Department. *See* Los Angeles County Sheriff's Department
Simpson, Alex, 190, 233, 237. *See also* Habeas hearing for Parks
"Six-pack" lineup identification, 221
Smith, David, 232–38
Smoke
  danger of, 10–11
  smoke detectors, importance of, 12
  smoke detectors and Parkses' use/lack of use, 41, 100, 113, 122, 143
Sommervold, Sara L., 202
Souliotes, George, 221–23
Sperber, Norman "Skip," 189–90

Takach, Steve, 143, 146
Talbott, William, 137–41. *See also* Bell Police Department
Teardrop Rapist, 95
Television as evidence. *See* Incendiary device theory and television evidence
Temperature, in fires, 11
Texas Forensic Science Commission, 200
Three Strikes repeat offender law (California), 230
Trial of Jo Ann Parks (1992), 153–80. *See also* Closet barricade theory; Cough medicine accusation; Incendiary device theory and television evidence; Second fire theory
  California Innocence Project's habeas petition and, 93, 125–30, 152, 172–80, 214, 250

Trial of Jo Ann Parks *(cont.)*
Dodge as potential witness, 163–65, 168–70
on "incendiary device" (faulty wiring), 126–28, 137–47, 163, 178
jury of, 128, 154, 170–72
Lowe's advocacy of Parks following, 172–75
Parks's views on, 207–8
People of the State of California v. Jo Ann Parks, 68, 136, 267
prosecutor's summation in, 150–52, 170
prosecutor's views on, 153–54
Ron Parks as hostile witness, 165–68, 171–72
testimony by arson experts during, 154–63, 166, 180
Trujillo, Mario, 128
Trump, Donald, 270
"Tuxedo Man." *See* Haney, David "Tuxedo Man"

University of California, Irvine, 184–85, 187
US Supreme Court, on Brady materials, 98

Vargas, Luis, 95, 97
Voice, The (television show), 219
V-patterns, 55–56

Wegner, Dirk, 23–24, 32–34, 147
Willingham, Cameron Todd, 69, 200
Windows
Gorbett on flashover and ventilation, 237–47
Parkses' Lynwood home fire and, 115
Ron and Jo Ann Parks on, 20

About the Author

Edward Humes is a Pulitzer Prize–winning journalist and author whose fourteen previous books include *Garbology*, *Mississippi Mud*, and the PEN Award–winning *No Matter How Loud I Shout.* He splits his time between Seattle and Southern California.